Conversion of Tropical Moist Forests

WITHDRAWN

A report prepared by Norman Myers for the Committee on Research Priorities in Tropical Biology of the National Research Council

NATIONAL ACADEMY OF SCIENCES
Washington, D.C.   1980

NOTICE: The project that is the subject of this report was approved by the Governing Board of the National Research Council, whose members are drawn from the Councils of the National Academy of Sciences, the National Academy of Engineering, and the Institute of Medicine. The members of the Committee responsible for the report were chosen for their special competences and with regard for appropriate balance.

This report has been reviewed by a group other than the authors according to procedures approved by a Report Review Committee consisting of members of the National Academy of Sciences, the National Academy of Engineering, and the Institute of Medicine.

The work of the Committee on Research Priorities in Tropical Biology was supported by Contract NSF-C310, Task Order No. 374 with the National Science Foundation; Dr. Myers' survey was supported under Subcontract ALS-20-78-265.

COVER PHOTOGRAPH: Courtesy of the National Science Foundation

Library of Congress Cataloging in Publication Data

Myers, Norman.
  Conversion of tropical moist forests.

  Bibliography: p.
    1. Deforestation—Tropics. 2. Rain forest ecology. 3. Man—Influence on nature—Tropics. 4. Forest surveys—Tropics. 5. Forests and forestry—Tropics.
  I. National Research Council. Committee on Research Priorities in Tropical Biology.
  II. Title. SD418.3.T76M9   333.7′5′0913   80-12477
  ISBN 0-309-02945-7

Available from:

Office of Publications, National Academy of Sciences
2101 Constitution Avenue, N.W., Washington, D.C. 20418

Printed in the United States of America

COMMITTEE ON RESEARCH PRIORITIES IN TROPICAL BIOLOGY

iii

Preface

The tropical moist forest biome is biologically the richest and least well known portion of the earth's surface. In this biome are to be found several million kinds of organisms of which no more than a half-million have even been given a Latin name. Many of the known and unknown species of organisms in the tropics offer significant potential for utilization by man, and all are of intrinsic scientific interest. A number of tropical plants, including rubber and oil palm, have been brought into wide-scale cultivation within the past century. Many more should be investigated as to their useful properties.

Because of the exceptional scientific interest of tropical moist forests, the National Research Council in 1977 appointed a Committee on Research Priorities in Tropical Biology, charged with investigating which biological questions can be answered only in the tropics, or can be answered better or more efficiently there than elsewhere. It is well known that the tropical moist forest contains baseline conditions for many biological phenomena and that these baseline conditions are not yet all well understood. Not only is the extrapolation of assumptions derived from studies of temperate ecosystems undesirable, but major differences between different areas of the tropics are becoming apparent. These latter greatly increase the difficulty of reaching scientific generalities or of applying the results of particular studies to development for human purposes. Consequently, many development schemes now being pursued in the tropics are very unlikely to succeed on a long-term basis.

It is widely recognized that tropical forests are being converted rapidly, and on a wide scale, to alternative patterns of land use. This situation lends urgency to the kinds of biological priorities that the Committee seeks to formulate, and made it seem desirable to commission a review of the state and rate of such conversion. In part, this review is a response to what we perceive as a growing worldwide concern with the impact of tropical forest destruction on human welfare. The report is based on the results of a survey conducted by Norman Myers between July 1978 and April 1979. During this period, Dr. Myers collected, collated, and evaluated such documentary evidence as he could obtain concerning different forms and degrees of conversion. His findings are summarized in this volume, which the Committee, with but one abstention, moved to make readily available, such that they may be taken into account in formulating scientific priorities for tropical research and also in the search for patterns of development that can be sustained for human welfare.

PETER H. RAVEN, *Chairman*
NRC Committee on Research Priorities in Tropical Biology

Contents

1 Methods

This survey is an attempt to review widespread conversion patterns in a biome whose climatic range is reputed to cover 16 million km² and whose present forest cover of different types is variously estimated to cover 9–11 million km². An effort has been made to assess the respective impacts of at least four major forms of conversion, paying particular attention to a key question of assessment—reliability of information—as well as a host of additional factors. To accomplish as much as possible of these various objectives, the survey has adopted several approaches.

PREVIOUS SURVEYS

As a starting point, previous surveys, notably two surveys of the mid-1970s, were used as a basis from which to build. Replicating these previous surveys was not the intent (though an attempt was made, where appropriate, to up-date them), but rather assessing and evaluating the findings of previous surveys, and presenting a synoptic overview of information available as of early 1979—plus a review of gaps in our knowledge.

Reports of the two surveys in question have been published by Persson (1974) and Sommer (1976). Each of these surveys has been conducted in whole or in part under the auspices of the Food and Agriculture Organization of the United Nations (FAO). FAO, as an agency of the United Nations, depends on reports submitted by Member States

1

for much of its information. While government organizations represent the principal, and often the sole, sources of information, this approach can sometimes be subject to basic constraints. It is dependent on the quantity and quality of information that governments wish to make available, and it effectively precludes FAO from applying the rigorous appraisal that should be an integral part of an objective survey (if governmental contributions are too closely scrutinized, they tend not to be furnished at all). This is not to say of course that the FAO investigators in question have not done a competent job with the information supplied to them. But all too often they have had to accept the information mostly at face value.

The problems that these constraints present are well summarized by Sommer (1976), when he describes how he and his colleagues were confronted with "a voluminous mass of confusing reports, yielding very few facts." He indicates some of the major inadequacies characterizing the documentation examined. The required information was not always available for the countries concerned, and not all countries forwarded their information to FAO headquarters; available information often proved to be obsolete, irrelevant, or of doubtful validity; definitions used in country appraisals varied considerably, and it proved very difficult to synthesize them; forest inventory data often referred only to selected areas, and were less than representative of whole countries; repeated surveys were very rare, making assessments of ongoing changes problematic; and the same sets of figures were repeatedly used in statements and reports with little concern for their origin and accuracy. Sommer summarizes his experience by stating:

Therefore, a global appraisal of tropical moist forests undertaken at this time can only base its research on the material available—a mass of incomplete data and a number of assumptions. It will yield rather rough results. This applies in particular to this study, which does not produce any clear answers. The outcome of our research consists in estimates of a varying degree of reliability—their exactitude should not be overvalued.

At present, an accurate appraisal of the climax and actual areas of the moist tropical forest at the global level, based on the information available at FAO headquarters is not yet possible.

In conclusion, Sommer stresses that precision could not be the main characteristic of his report, due to the paucity of reliable data.

Yet Sommer still believed—justifiably so, in this author's view—that his survey was worthwhile insofar as it provided an overview estimate, albeit rough, of some of the conversion forces affecting tropical moist forests (TMF). Sommer ventured to offer preliminary figures for remaining forest cover and for biome-wide conversion rates, in order that governments, international agencies, and other institutions become aware of the speed with which TMF appear to be regressing. He proposed that forest cover amounted in the mid-1970s to 9,350,000 km² (58.5 percent of the TMF climatic climax area, and 54.5 percent of statistically reported official forestland area), and that the regression rate was 110,000 km² per year (or 1.2 percent of presumed forest cover).

Persson (1975) reported similar difficulties and reservations in the course of his own efforts to prepare a biome-wide assessment. His overall results differ somewhat from Sommer's, though his statistical summary does not diverge markedly. More significantly, Persson comments that 6 percent of his final data for forest resources in the tropics can be considered accurate within 10 percent, 15 percent within 20 percent, 25 percent within 40 percent, and 55 percent of less than 40 percent accuracy. This means that much less than half of Persson's summary results are accurate within limits that many statisticians consider all but minimal for meaningful conclusions to be drawn. Despite this severe reservation, it is the view of many observers that Persson, like Sommer, performed a valuable service in enabling governments and agencies to realize the nature and scale of the challenge confronting them if they wish to maintain substantial sectors of the TMF biome into the next century.

However, certain qualifications must be attached to those parts of these survey reports that have received most attention, notably the figures for biome-wide regression rates. This applies particularly to Sommer's calculation to the effect that 110,000 km² of TMF are disappearing each year. The figure derives from an analysis of only 13 of some 60 countries that Sommer examined, comprising only 18 percent of the biome's forest cover. Sommer acknowledges the extreme limitations of his "heroic extrapolation," but regrettably his reservation has rarely been mentioned by those many persons (notably representatives of the popular media) who have proclaimed that the biome is declining by an average of 20 ha per minute—a flat assertion that violates the substance and spirit of Sommer's survey report. Plainly, the statement should be amended to read: "So far as can be ascertained, on the basis of very limited assessments and with an extremely meager data base of highly variable reliability for most of the biome, TMF appear to be declining at a significant rate that could be put, for want of any better assessment, at somewhere in the region of 20 ha a minute—though the actual rate could turn out to be much different."

A further reservation attaches to Sommer's conclusion that a large part of the TMF cover has already been eliminated. He cites figures of 37 percent regression for Latin America, 41.6 percent for southern and Southeast Asia, and 51.6 percent for Africa, with an average of 41.6 percent for the biome. He bases his calculations solely on climatic parameters to determine the extent of "TMF climax area," *viz.*, 16 million km², without taking account of factors such as edaphic and topographic variations that could considerably reduce the theoretical climax area. At best, Sommer's figures for regression rates can be construed as a very rough indication of what may have maximally occurred in certain parts of the biome. Nevertheless, Sommer's conclusions have been frequently cited to the effect that the biome has certainly been grossly reduced already, with over one-third of Amazonia's forests eliminated, and so on.

In early 1979, FAO released the findings of a further survey (Lanly and Clement, 1979), focused primarily on tropical forest resources with respect to the timber trade; it proposes that logged-over forest can be considered to still constitute forest in the usual sense, *i.e.*, the study does not differentiate between primary and secondary forest (nor does it take account of the pronounced tendency for logging tracts to be used by forest farmers who thereby penetrate deep into the heart of forest territories that have hitherto been closed to them, effectively eliminating large areas of forest). This study proposed in addition that, within the perspective indicated, the loss between 1975 and the year 2000 could average as little as 56,000 km² per year, or 11 ha per minute—by contrast with Sommer's figure of 20 ha per minute. Meantime, at the Eighth World Forestry Congress in Jakarta, Indonesia, October 1978, the Director-General of FAO, Edouard Saouma, stated that conversion of all forms was accounting for 40 ha per minute.

In view of this state of statistical uncertainty concerning the status of the TMF biome, FAO has tried to undertake a more detailed and systematic survey of TMF, utilizing the new mapping technologies made available through satellite imagery. In 1974, FAO formulated a Tropical Forest Cover Monitoring Project; and in late 1975, FAO began a 2-year pilot project to be conducted in four adjoining countries of West Africa, *viz.*, Togo, Benin, Nigeria, and Cameroon. Due to numerous delays, the results of this trial survey are yet to be made available.

BASIC CONSIDERATIONS FOR PRESENT SURVEY

To reiterate a central point, this survey comprises a broad-ranging investigation of an entire biome. Not only is the biome large and spread across three tropical regions, but it is much more differentiated than many observers suppose. It is divided among some 70 countries, of which almost 40 contain tracts of TMF that are appreciable in size or are significant for their ecological and biotic values, or are otherwise important for purposes of this survey.

As it happens, over four-fifths of the biome occurs in only nine countries—Bolivia, Brazil, Colombia, Peru, and Venezuela in Latin America; Indonesia and Malaysia in Southeast Asia; and Gabon and Zaire in Africa. This means that, were sound information available for the majority of these countries, the survey could yield a substantive assessment for the great bulk of the biome. (An outcome of this sort was in fact anticipated at the start of the survey.) Accordingly these nine countries received special attention during the survey. In fact, however, Brazil, containing at least one-third of the biome, declared it could not yet release its documented findings; Indonesia, with roughly one-tenth of the biome, still publishes a figure for its forest cover that is more than 20 years old, and that takes no account of the widespread logging, shifting cultivation, and transmigration programs that during the past two decades have affected large areas of undisturbed forest, possibly as much as one-third of its entire extent; and Zaire, also with roughly one-tenth of the biome, had virtually no statistical information whatever (Persson, who in 1975 and 1977 conducted the most substantive assessment available of Zaire's forests, states that his best estimate should be regarded as no more accurate than "within 40 percent either way").

In short, sound information, especially authoritative statistical information, is not easily obtained. Many organizations—governments, international agencies, research centers, academic institutions, and the like—offer documentary material that is little better than an estimate. True, when an estimate is carefully formulated, it is worth something; and when a few estimates for one country, each separately arrived at, point to the same conclusion, this represents a valid assessment of sorts. After all, information does not necessarily have to be quantitative to be worthwhile, and a number of qualitative contributions to this survey have been helpful. For example, if several reliable observers visit a tract of forest and state that it is much modified, this is certainly worth knowing, even if no observer can state how large the area is, and can give only a rough indication of how significant the modification is. In the main, however, much "information" is of doubtful value. While many TMF countries recognize the need for detailed statistical inventories, they also acknowledge that their data are generally crude and incomplete at best.

One aspect of tropical ecology that is central to an understanding of which forests are being cleared and why, and what can be anticipated in the future, concerns the relationship between the age of tropical soils and their fertility. Dense human populations and successfully sustained tropical agriculture have developed primarily on recent volcanic or alluvial soils. Many areas of the tropics, however, are underlain by ancient land masses where the soil has weathered very deeply and has lost most of its available nutrients through leaching.

These differences in soils strongly determine such phenomena as forest and agricultural productivity, whether permanent agriculture is readily practiced, and the length of time required for plots to recover from a period of cultivation in a shifting cultivation system. This study, however, will not examine differences in soil types, but does explicitly recognize their importance in the overall process of conversion of TMF.

RELIABILITY OF INFORMATION

This brings us to some key questions. How much of the information available is accurate? And how accurate? How can one differentiate? As indicated, there is sometimes no shortage of information; but if part of the information is plainly suspect, how is one to know that is is not entirely suspect?

To meet this difficult but central problem, the author adopted a strategy of critical appraisal that may be described as follows: Much information, while apparently plausible at face value, is quite likely to be little more than an educated estimate. Such information must be checked against its source, and preferably against other independent sources, before it can be accepted as fact. In short, any information about which one has doubts must be regarded as guilty until it can be proved innocent. Put another way, this approach means that many statistical assessments cannot be taken as precise accounts, though they may have value as indicators of a situation's general dimension. The author checked as much information as possible case by case. Because this exercise was so time consuming, much of the survey focused on establishing the authenticity of existing information rather than searching for new information. While it is not easy to test the validity of information, it is by no means an intractable challenge. For example, one can closely consult with the official, field researcher, statistician, or whoever served as source for a questionable piece of data. Within the restricted scope of this survey, the author was not able to deploy this tactic as widely as he wished. Nevertheless, he discussed the reliability of published forestry records with almost 300 persons from 26 countries (see below), including six of the nine countries that make up over four-fifths of the TMF biome. It is not difficult to identify adequately authoritative opinion, and to sift out grossly unreliable contributions, by applying certain dialectical techniques. The investigator can not only engage in detailed cross-examination, but can ask questions to which the answer is known, whereupon the response serves as a measure of the interviewee's reliability. The investigator can play the devil's advocate, in order to determine the degree of authenticity or conviction behind an interviewee's assertions. Various similar stratagems arise according to circumstances.

This critical approach is reflected in this report. The author attempted to reflect the range of reliability behind the statistical information presented, by qualifying statements with phrases such as "so far as can be ascertained . . . ," or "best-estimate judgments suggest that . . . ." In sum, the author tried on the one hand to avoid bogus accuracy, and on the other to describe semi-documented situations with an appropriate degree of precise imprecision.

Early in the survey, the author adopted a systematic grading of information through categorizing contributions as "authoritative" (reliable within 5 percent), "adequately reliable" (10 percent), "moderately worthwhile for certain restricted purposes" (20 percent), and "marginally acceptable in absence of anything better" (30 percent). This approach has proved far less widely applicable than had been hoped, due to lack of standardized criteria that could be utilized in a broad variety of situations. Nevertheless, it has helped to indicate the authenticity of information from a few countries, notably Malaysia, the Philippines, and Thailand (this has been noted in the country profiles in question—see Chapter 8). It has also served to demonstrate that much information, presented as ostensibly up-to-date and authoritative, does not withstand critical scrutiny. As a result, many quantitative assessments have been categorized as "educated estimates," "partially supported assessments," "little better than guesstimates," and so forth. This does not mean that the statements are to be rejected as irrelevant. The point is that information can be classified according to its validity: Information of limited worth can still serve a limited purpose provided its key constraints are clearly recognized.

MEANING OF "CONVERSION"

As mentioned, conversion can range from marginal modification to fundamental transformation. Modification can be construed as the result of human intervention whereby the physiognomy, structure, and dynamics of the original forest undergo change. In turn, this change can be slight, substantial, or severe. In its lightest form, *e.g.*, highly selective timber extraction, modification can merely entail some alteration in relative densities of tree populations and in the quantity of timber stocks; it need not necessarily cause a qualitative change in the species complement. A much more significant form of modification lies with shifting cultivation and other types of forest farming that induce secondary succession in the forest. In each of these instances, the original forest ecosystem maintains some continuity, provided there is no permanent loss of potential, *e.g.*, through soil impaction or erosion, or extinction of species. In these circumstances, it is at least theoretically possible that the primary forest can regenerate within a moderate length of time until it eventually resembles its former make-up.

Transformation, by contrast, amounts to a basically different category of conversion. In order to make way for permanent agriculture, plantations, or pasturelands, the forest is entirely eliminated, being replaced by a man-established ecosystem, or by inanimate structures such as highways, industrial installations, and urban settlements.

In between the extremes, all manner of variations are possible. Thus, "conversion" can mean a host of different things. It can imply floristic impoverishment, a diminution of standing biomass, a temporary disruption of successional processes, a gross disturbance of the species array (the change can be either quantitative or qualitative or both), and the basic shift entailed in alteration of primary forest to secondary forest—plus of course many other variations, together with gradients in between. Some changes may be of short duration, and the former state restored within just a few years; other changes are more profound, and may disturb the natural continuity for several decades; other changes may persist, for whatever reason, for still longer periods. In the course of some of these processes, there may be "threshold stages," at which, in a relatively short space of time, deep-seated and irreversible alterations may ensue. Moreover, these several categories of change can be imposed with different repercussions on different forest ecotypes, *e.g.*, rainforest and seasonal forest.

In this survey the author has tried to take account of these many meanings of conversion. Clearly, in a survey that has to account for many other variables, it has not been possible to classify these changes in accord with the conversion patterns occurring in individual countries. However, where possible the scale of differentiation outlined here has been recounted in the country profiles of Chapters 8–10.

LITERATURE ANALYSIS

Although there is a wealth of professional literature on TMF, most of it deals with ecology, taxonomy, and scientific aspects of similar sort. All too little deals with present status of the biome. A good number of writings deal with distribution of forest ecotypes in a general sense, but only a few with forest cover at country level. Moreover, such literature items as indicate the situation in individual countries tend to become quickly out of date. For this reason, the author has limited most of his citations from the literature to publications in the 1970s.

As for official documents, there are many "country reports" and related materials that have been presented at World Forestry Congresses, FAO Regional Forestry Commissions, Commonwealth Forestry Conferences, and other gatherings. In addition, there are many published proceedings of technical forestry meetings at national, regional, and global levels, organized by FAO, the U.N. Educational, Scientific, and Cultural Organization (UNESCO), the International Union of Forestry Research Organizations (IUFRO), and other bodies. There are also forestry studies by national and bilateral/multilateral agencies, such as resource surveys, land-use analyses, timber trend assessments, project reports, and some vegetation and forest maps. During the course of the survey, the author has perused some 800 items.

CORRESPONDENCE

Since the survey was primarily a "desk research" investigation, correspondence has played a large role. Several bulk mailings, totalling over 1,100 items, were dispatched, plus numerous follow-up inquiries.

Correspondence was fruitful, though not as much as had been hoped. The initial questionnaires, together with reminder letters, produced a 22 percent response rate, which is satisfactory for a survey of this type. Regrettably, the follow-up inquiries, requesting more substantive evidence, clarifications, *etc.*, produced only a 9 percent response rate—a poor return, presumably due to the fact that the information requested was not available or could not be conveniently supplied.

Moreover, the response pattern was patchy. Whereas 27 responses of one sort and another were received from the Philippines, 32 inquiries to Zaire failed to produce any response at all—which is more regrettable in view of Zaire's reputedly large amount of TMF cover.

In the main, correspondence seems to be a limited mode of inquiry for a survey of broad scope such as this. FAO comments that its attempt to revise its World Forest Inventory was abandoned in 1971, because of the meager response to its questionnaire which ". . . was sent to 56 countries and territories in 1970, but one year later, in spite of repeated reminders, only 20 replies had been received."

CONSULTATIONS AND DISCUSSIONS

As mentioned above, consultations and discussions played a major part in the survey. They were especially useful as a means to test the validity of government documents and other official publications. In addition, the author found that many individuals, not just government persons but many scientists, are reluctant to divulge their knowledge and opinions in writing, though they readily proffer information and views during the course of a personal interview. This is partly because, for institutional considerations, these individuals may not wish to have written remarks attributed to them, and partly because they believe they can transmit "gray-area accuracy" (to quote one of these contributors) better during the course of a face-to-face discussion than through correspondence with its black and white concision.

During the course of the survey, the author was able to visit the Eighth World Forestry Congress in Jakarta, Indonesia, in October 1978. During 2 weeks there, he held in-depth discussions with 146 individuals from 19 countries (primarily from Southeast Asia). Thereafter he spent 2 weeks traveling in Malaysia and Thailand. In February 1979, he spent almost one month in Brazil, Colombia, and Venezuela. In addition, he met with officials and scientists from several TMF countries of Africa. Altogether he held detailed consultations with 293 persons whom he believes are in a position to speak of TMF in their countries from a position of authentic experience if not authority.

In conclusion, the survey worked out differently from expected. Some of its modes of inquiry proved unusually productive, others yielded little. As this report reveals, the result is patchy to a degree. Certain countries contributed much information, others virtually none.

The survey certainly revealed no opportunity for speculation on overall figures for biome-wide conversion rates; and the same applies to the three main regions. Yet this may not be bad. After all, the scope for improved management measures for TMF lies with country governments in question, which exercise national sovereignty over the natural resources represented by their forests. The prospects for remaining forests in Indonesia or Papua New Guinea are little illuminated by what is happening elsewhere in Southeast Asia, and still less by what is happening in other regions of the biome.

2 Tropical Moist Forests

Despite the exceptional ecological and economic value of the tropical moist forest biome, and due to our lack of scientific knowledge, there is no standard and objective classification of "tropical moist forests" that can be applied uniformly from region to region across the biome. The problem is a difficult one because data from different countries are gathered by persons with different backgrounds using different systems, and it is not evident how these varied data can be readily converted to a single classification.

Bearing in mind the limited scope and scale of the National Research Council survey, a new approach in this field is not proposed. Rather, a summary classification from those existing is presented in order to arrive at a coherent basis for the overall investigation (Ashton, 1964, 1977; Baur, 1964; Beard, 1955; Brünig, 1977; Farnworth and Golley, 1974; Golley and Medina, 1975; Holdridge, 1967; Holdridge et al., 1971; Richards, 1952, 1973; UNESCO, 1974, 1978; Webb, 1977a, 1978; Whitmore, 1975). Accordingly, the definition of tropical moist forest (TMF) adopted for the purposes of this report is as follows: "evergreen or partly evergreen forests, in areas receiving not less than 100 mm of precipitation in any month for 2 out of 3 years, with mean annual temperature of 24+°C and essentially frost-free; in these forests some trees may be deciduous; the forests usually occur at altitudes below 1,300 m (though often in Amazonia up to 1,800 m and generally in

11

Southeast Asia up to only 750 m); and in mature examples of these forests, there are several more or less distinctive strata.''

True, this is a highly generalized approach, and does not take account of many significant subclassifications with their own intrinsic merits. However, the present survey has perforce had to deal with many other categorizations, notably with respect to multiple forms of human disruption of differing degrees of intensity. So, despite the deficiencies of the short definition proposed above, it has been adopted for purposes of the survey, in order to keep the overall approach tolerably straightforward. Clearly, there is a basic need for simplification while avoiding errors of oversimplification.

In accord with this definition, it is possible to recognize particular forest formations in different parts of the biome, e.g., in terms of structure and physiognomy. The definition can also take account of a number of further variations, such as ecological factors (edaphic formations and swamp forests), vegetational rhythms (evergreen and deciduous types), divergences of structure and physiognomy (dense and open forest), and evolutionary aspects (primary and secondary forest).

It is important to recognize as ramifications of the basic definition at least two salient characteristics of TMF—limited climatic seasonality and biotic diversity. These characteristics can be summarized as follows (though not all TMF feature all these characteristics—many areas feature only some of them, and certain areas only a few).

Limited Climatic Seasonality

There tends to be relatively limited seasonality, notably with respect to temperature fluctuation and precipitation. This applies especially along the climatic equator, which is governed by the annual movement of the tropical convergence zone with a front whose position corresponds to the zenithal position of the sun after a time lag.

Forest ecosystems appear to be hypersensitive to availability of moisture. This factor includes not only total amount of moisture, but its reliability and seasonal distribution. Moreover, a moisture regime may not be characterized solely by moisture made available through precipitation. The amount lost by evaporation and the transpiration of plants can also be significant (average water lost directly through evaporation from the canopy can be as much as 25 percent). Any month with over 100 mm of rain can be regarded as wet (precipitation exceeding evaporation), any month with less than 60 mm as dry (evaporation exceeding precipitation), and a month with 60–100 mm as moist (precipitation and evaporation more or less in balance [Whitmore, 1975, citing Mohr, 1933]).

In accord with precipitation patterns, there are fundamental variations of forest structure, phenology, and floristics. Of course, these variations can be further modified by orographic, edaphic, biotic, and humanly induced influences.

So important is seasonality that it is the main differentiating factor between rainforest and seasonal (monsoonal) forest, and between evergreen/semi-evergreen forest and semi-deciduous/deciduous forest (see "Rainforest" below).

Biotic Diversity

As indicated above, the TMF biome is, biologically and ecologically speaking, the most complex and diverse biome on earth. There is marked diversity of species, especially of trees, woody climbers, and epiphytes. This characteristic occurs notably in wetter areas with high atmospheric humidity. The complexity is dynamic, with an exceptional degree of biotic and physiobiotic interactions, and stable, able to maintain itself for long periods if not indefinitely. Since environmental conditions are relatively constant (while not necessarily uniform), a high level of dynamic stability can persist within a narrow amplitude of environmental fluctuations.

It is a mistake to suppose, however, that diversity and stability are interrelated in a simple and positive fashion. Indeed, recent theoretical and empirical research suggests that "communities with a rich array of species and complex web of interactions (the tropical rainforest being the paradigm) are likely to be more fragile than relatively simple and robust temperate ecosystems" (May, 1975). Similarly, "the reproductive mechanisms of TMF plant and animal species are more adapted to biological competition than to large-scale environmental disturbance" (UNESCO, 1978). Thus TMF ecosystems tend to be less resilient to change than temperate forest ecosystems.

The humid tropical environment permits the systems to persist in spite of their fragility because perturbations are relatively small and restricted to small areas. . . . Tropical forests are in a constant turmoil of phasic development . . . and they are stable only within a comparatively small domain of parameter space.

The dynamic relationship between complexity and stability is particularly significant insofar as it appears to depend on an important provision, *viz.,* external forces impinging on the system should not exceed certain threshold values, otherwise distinct and enduring changes may arise. Human intervention—which can be massive both in terms of immediate impact and long-run duration—can readily exceed the capacity of TMF regulatory processes to maintain the system.

One measure of this extraordinary richness is the large number of species that are believed to occur in the biome—a far greater abundance and variety of species, both in quantitative and qualitative senses, than are to be found in any other ecological zone. Extrapolation of figures from well-known groups of organisms suggests that there are usually twice as many species in the tropics as in temperate regions. If two-thirds of the tropical species occur in TMF, a reasonable extrapolation from known relationships, then the species of the TMF should amount to some 40–50 percent of the planet's stock of species—or somewhere between 2 and 5 million species altogether (Baker, 1970; Dobzhansky, 1970; Lowe-McConnell, 1969; Meggers *et al.*, 1973; Myers, 1976, 1979; Raup *et al.*, 1973; Raven, 1976; Raven *et al.*, 1971). In other words, nearly half of all species on earth are apparently contained in a biome that comprises only 6 percent of the globe's land surface. Probably no more than 300,000 of these species— no more than 15 percent and possibly much less—have even been given a Latin name, and most are totally unknown.

Many TMF species are unusually susceptible to extinction. Of all the biome's species, it is tentatively estimated that around 70–75 percent are arthropods, the great majority of them insects. Many of these species have highly specialized ecological requirements; many of them exist at low densities; and many of them are confined to localized distributions. These three attributes alone mean that these species are highly vulnerable to summary elimination when a tract of forest is subject to the more disruptive forms of conversion—a tract of forest does not have to be entirely cleared for a number of its resident species to become extinct.

Insofar as a number of recent surveys of conversion rates in the TMF biome are anywhere near correct (Persson, 1974, 1975, 1977; Sommer, 1976; and this report), it is not unrealistic to suppose that, within perhaps the next two decades, many thousands of species could disappear in TMF (it is even far from unlikely that at least many species are disappearing there each day right now) (Myers, 1979). Elimination of a substantial proportion of the planetary spectrum of species will mean a gross reduction of life's diversity on earth; and it will entail a permanent shift in the course of evolution, and an irreversible loss of economic opportunity as well.

PROBLEMS OF CONTRASTING TERMINOLOGY

Bearing in mind these two major attributes of TMF, we shall now consider two contrasting sets of terminology that have been widely (and loosely) applied to tropical forests: rainforest (*i.e.*, TMF) versus seasonal forest, and primary or climax forest versus secondary forest. Such consideration is necessary because these terms are important in relation to the regional surveys that follow, and their rather imprecise usage has contributed to the difficulty of comparing the sorts of forest that occur in tropical countries in different parts of the world.

Rainforest

The term "rainforest" is applied rather loosely to various types of TMF, and indeed, is essentially synonymous with TMF as defined at the start of this chapter. It was described by Schimper as long ago as 1903 as a forest that is "evergreen, hygrophilous in character, at least 30 m high, rich in thick-stemmed lianas, and in woody as well as herbaceous epiphytes." A more recent, and similar, description is that of Baur (1964), who terms it

a closed community of essentially but not exclusively broadleaved evergreen hygrophilous trees, usually with two or more layers of trees and shrubs and with dependent synusiae of other life forms such as vines and epiphytes. It includes the characteristic vegetation of the humid tropics, even where this has a somewhat seasonal climatic regime, as well as those of moist elevated areas of the tropics.

According to the life zone classification of Holdridge (1967), this description covers humid forest; very humid forest; rainforest in tropical lowland; premontane, low montane, and montane forest; and also pockets of dwarf forest. Translated into the classificatory system adopted by the International Union for Conservation of Nature and Natural Resources (IUCN) for its world conservation strategy (1979), the description covers lowland rainforest, montane (including submontane) rainforest, cloud forest, riverine forest, swamp and bog forest, and wetter forms of lowland seasonal forest.

The main factor determining the distribution of rainforest appears to be moisture. There must be plenty year-round except for the briefest dry spell: the critical factor is the seasonal distribution of rainfall as much as the total annual amount. Much of the lowland forest in tropical Latin America receives over 4,000 mm of annual precipitation—an amount that is rare in Asian TMF and virtually absent in Africa—indeed, 1,500 mm in Africa is often considered to be the lower limit of moist forest, whereas in Latin America this represents the midpoint for tropical dry forest. Not that moisture is the sole factor determining luxuriance and complexity of rainforest vegetation and the periodicity of its leaf-fall. Certain rather purist definitions of rainforest, such as that of Beard (1955), have suggested that rainforest is an entirely evergreen type of vegetation under optimal conditions of temperature and moisture. Such a definition excludes the formation from several areas of the moist tropics, *e.g.*, northeastern Australia where practically all moist forests are subject to seasonal lack of water but are not thereby classified as seasonal forests (Webb, 1977, 1978). Since seasonal drought in northeastern Australia is often correlated with evergreenness or deciduousness in accord with amounts of soil nutrients available and soil aeration among other ecological factors, it seems preferable to allow under the umbrella term "rainforest" less luxuriant and even marginally seasonal variations. Indeed, "evergreenness" is sometimes applied to Australian rainforest in which there may be up to 25 percent deciduous species.

Thus rainforest should be understood as a fully independent plant formation-type that can be subject to a variety of environmental determinants apart from moisture. Hence Baur's (1964) proposal to amend the classificatory term from "rain forest" to "rainforest"—and this latter spelling is accordingly adopted for purposes of the present report to designate the general formation-type of rainforest, comparable on a global scale with mixed deciduous forest of temperate regions, boreal forests, and so forth.

In all three main tropical regions, the structure and physiognomy of various kinds of rainforest are similar. By contrast the make-up of their species is entirely different, and they possess relatively few genera in common, though they feature some homogeneity at family level.

Rainforest formations differ markedly in structure and physiognomy as their elevation increases, and various types of montane rainforest can be recognized. Similarly, farther from the equator and closer to the latitudinal limits of rainforest, formations diverge until they must be classified as a distinctive type, *viz.*, semi-evergreen rainforest, characterized by a regular annual water stress lasting for at least a few weeks. Semi-evergreen rainforest thus forms a belt between evergreen rainforest and moist deciduous forest; it occurs patchily in Burma, India, Indochina, Sri Lanka, and Thailand. Still farther toward the fringes of the tropics, tropical rainforest gives way to a still drier variation, subtropical rainforest; examples occur in eastern Australia, southeastern China, and at the southern end of the coastal strip of rainforest in Brazil.

The most exceptional rainforest formation of all—at least, visually—is probably that of western Southeast Asia. In this zone, dipterocarps grow as lofty trees, the top of the canopy frequently reaching 45 and sometimes even 60 m above the ground. Moreover, the canopy does not consist of isolated emergents, as is usually the case for some of the rainforests of tropical Africa and Latin America. Instead, it comprises extensive groups of giant trees. These dipterocarp forests are among the richest biotic communities on earth. The relative homogeneity of their timber stocks also make them most attractive of all TMF to commercial loggers. Never so widespread as rainforest of tropical Latin America, they may well be all but eliminated before tropical Latin America loses even half of its rainforest cover. In tropical Africa, rainforest is a comparatively localized phenomenon, confined *sensu* Holdridge to small coastal enclaves. Moreover, by comparison with the other two regions, Africa's rainforest is a biotically exiguous formation (Meggers *et al.*, 1973).

Seasonal Forest

In general, seasonal forest replaces rainforest at the latter's latitudinal and climatic limits. Sometimes known as monsoon forest, it is a convenient term for those forest types that have developed in areas with a marked dry season, *i.e.*, where plant growth is seriously limited by water stress. It is discussed under various country sections extensively in the report because it intergrades so completely with TMF and is so important on a world scale, and because many systems of classification frequently include it in TMF.

To cite Schimper (1903) again, seasonal forest (which Schimper calls monsoon forest on p. 260 of his book) is a forest that is "more or less leafless during the dry season, especially towards its termination, tropophilous in character, usually less lofty than the rain-forest, rich in woody lianas, rich in herbaceous but poor in woody epiphytes." As such, it falls outside of the limits of TMF as defined above; but it is often discussed under the country treatments for the reasons just outlined. In the main, seasonal forests occur at elevations below 1,000 m, on well-drained lateritic soils. By contrast with rainforests, much light reaches the forest floor and undergrowth is dense. Seasonal forests are of less stature than rainforests; biomass is only about 70–80 t/ha,[1] as compared with 350–600 t for lowland evergreen rainforest and 230 t of upland evergreen rainforest. On top of all these characteristics, the main attribute of seasonal forests is that they are deciduous to a considerable degree, especially at the end of the dry season(s).

It is during a dry phase of the year that a seasonal forest's vegetation becomes inflammable. In the past, both lightning and man have caused fires in seasonal forests, to the extent that there is often a sharp differentiation between seasonal forest and rainforest (a factor that assists in TMF categorization). A further result of fire is that many seasonal forests have been degraded to open woodlands and savannah. Seen from the air during a dry season, a seasonal forest is often brown, whereas a rainforest tends to remain green at all times.

Seasonal forests of various sorts are widespread in Southeast Asia, notably in Burma, India, Indochina, Sri Lanka, and Thailand. They are also extensive in Africa, where rainforest is of limited extent. In Latin America, however, where wetter climates are more pervasive than in Africa and southern and Southeast Asia, seasonal forests are comparatively rare.

In those parts of southern and Southeast Asia where annual rainfall drops to 1,250 mm or less and the dry season lengthens to 6 months, seasonal forest tends to give way to dry dipterocarp forest, also known as savannah forest. This formation-type is typically found on dry, shallow soils with little humus. It is more open than deciduous monsoon forest, with more grass and bamboo undergrowth. Extensive tracts of this forest type are burned each year, a practice that has caused large areas to become grasslands with only scattered trees and groves along water courses. Biomass rarely exceeds 65 t/ha, and is often considerably less. Bamboo forest, which is often considered a separate forest type within the category of seasonal forest, sometimes occurs as a successional stage derived from fire; if allowed to mature, it usually develops into dry dipterocarp forest or deciduous monsoon forest, while in wetter localities it may eventually develop into evergreen forest.

Primary Forest and Climax Forest

Primary forest is forest that has been undisturbed for a long time, at least for decades and sometimes for centuries. Primary TMF is the richest and most complex expression of the biome. Primary forest is sometimes known as virgin forest, to distinguish it from disturbed, and

----

[1] t = metric tons throughout this report.

hence secondary, forest, but for reasons that will be discussed below, this is generally a less-than-accurate designation.

Primary forest often constitutes forest that has worked its way through successional stages of development as a young forest, and is now approaching or has attained a state of maturity, often considered to be a state of ultimate diversity and complexity. Such a formation has been termed by some workers, particularly in the past, a climax forest—one representing a vegetation type in dynamic equilibrium with the climate in which it occurs.

It has been important for this survey to differentiate wherever possible between primary forest and secondary forest, on the grounds that the former is much the more valuable in bio-ecological, scientific, and economic terms. This researcher has adopted the position that a primary forest can be sufficiently disturbed by even the lightest logging to eliminate its usefulness for certain kinds of scientific inquiry: When just a few trees are extracted, perhaps as few as five per hectare, the damage inflicted on the residual forest can cause significant disruption to the structure, physiognomy, and floristic composition of the forest community.

Secondary Forest

For reasons indicated above, the make-up of plant species in a secondary forest is fundamentally different from that in a primary forest. In addition, the structure and functioning of the community are different, and the ecosystem is less diverse. They do not remain that way. After a tropical primary forest has been cleared, and the plant life left to regrow, there is a rapid accumulation of new biomass until it peaks at roughly 15 years—after which only the nature of the plant life changes (Johnson, 1977). Through a process that occurs slowly or extremely slowly, pioneer species and low-ground vegetation disappear, their detritus providing nutrients for larger and longer-lived trees. Eventually the secondary forest develops steadily toward a formation akin to that of primary forest; and, in time, provided all the necessary complex of factors is available, primary forest will reestablish itself.

But secondary forests tend to persist for long periods. In areas of disturbed rainforest in northeastern Australia, 50 years' regeneration has produced forests that are floristically similar to nearby undisturbed forest, but that are still structurally dissimilar (Hopkins *et al.*, 1976). Around Angkor in Kampuchea (Cambodia), the forest of large areas that were reputedly cleared 600 years ago does not yet fully resemble surrounding patches of undisturbed primary forest. Indeed, it is thought that certain lowland rainforest ecosystems, after being grossly disrupted or destroyed, may need a successional process of as much as 1,000 years before a final-form primary forest ecosystem is reestablished (Opler *et al.*, 1977).

Generally speaking, it is human influence that causes secondary forests to appear in the contemporary TMF biome. But nonhuman factors can also lead to secondary forests. In parts of the western Pacific, notably in Melanesia, the Philippines, and parts of New Guinea, typhoons and other exceptional weather conditions can cause so-called catastrophic damage to primary forests. Thus forests in the region that have been little touched by man may not resemble what would be recognized as primary forests elsewhere. The storm forest of Kelantan in Malaya, which originated in November 1880, was still clearly recognizable as such in the late 1960s (Whitmore, 1975). During the course of this century, islands of Melanesia have been visited by cyclones on average once every 2.4 years; a cyclone that hit Santa Isabel Island in the Solomon Islands in 1972 destroyed around 330 km² of forest, a phenomenon from which the forest is not likely to make a full recovery for some 50–100 years.

Thus it can sometimes be an arbitrary exercise to draw distinction between primary and secondary forests. Nevertheless some kind of differentiation is necessary and valid. What is counted undisturbed or relatively undisturbed primary forest (including lightly logged forest), and what is called secondary (often a relatively impoverished forest— though the late stages of secondary succession can sometimes feature greater species diversity than primary forest)? The line of demarcation is not easy to establish. For example, in the state of Portuguesa in Venezuela, only 21 percent of former forest remained in 1825, but by 1950 the forest cover had expanded to 45 percent (Hamilton, 1976). After such a lengthy period of regeneration, is this forest to be considered secondary or primary? And if secondary, what degree of secondary? Similarly, in parts of *terra firme* forest that occupies some 95 percent of Amazonia's lowlands, there are archeological sites, notably along the TransAmazon Highway and at Jarí in Amapá, that provide evidence of formerly widespread and sometimes dense settlements of aboriginal groups (Smith, 1978). These former human habitations coincide with extensive forest formations that amount to secondary forest of variable size and development, certain of them being on the borderline (so far as we can ascertain) between secondary forest and primary forest. How shall these forest formations, extensive as they are, be classified by someone wishing to determine how much undisturbed, mature, primary, or climax forest remains in Amazonia?

Something of the same derivation may account for the islands of cerrado and grassland within the lowland forests, some of them ostensibly due in part to man-made fires.

Arguments along these lines arise with respect to certain of Central America's forests. It is known that the forests of what is now Guatemala, northern Honduras, and southwestern Mexico were widely felled at the time of the Maya civilization (D'Arcy, 1977; Nations and Nigh, 1978). The forests have since recovered to a form of primary forest. It is open to question, however, whether the new forests are restored forests, *i.e.*, much the same as before, or primary forests of a new and different type. No working definition of primary and secondary forests seems to be available to fit these circumstances: Certain forests in areas with a long history of human settlement, not only in Central America but also West Africa, are frequently accepted as primary, whereas, by comparison with primary forests of Borneo, they should perhaps be classified as "old secondary".

In point of fact, man's disruptive influence seems to have left its mark on many forests that are often thought to be virgin, and are thereby construed, albeit in a limited sense, to be primary forests. But in large parts of continental Southeast Asia there are probably few forests where human impact is slight or absent (Bethel and Turnbull, 1974; Lekagul and McNeely, 1977, 1978; Nuttonson, 1963; Spencer, 1966; Wharton, 1968; Williams, 1965). The monsoonal vegetation is readily burnt during the dry months. The result is that in Indochina

. . . only a small part of the forests, chiefly in inaccessible areas, is genuine virgin forest, although much of it is so dense that it gives the appearance of being so. Most of the forests have been exploited by man, who has extracted the most precious varieties from them or else they have been ravaged by "ray" (shifting cultivation) (Nuttonson, 1963).

With respect to the forests of what was formerly known as South Vietnam, the Dwyer Mission (1966, cited in Bethel and Turnbull, 1974) stated that "in the largest part of the forests, . . . shifting nomadic agriculture has gone on for centuries. . . . The forest is degraded . . . perhaps as much as two-thirds of South Vietnam's forests have suffered from this process." In summary review of South Vietnam, Bethel and Turnbull (1974) comment that " . . . there is little disagreement among competent observers that the forests have been heavily used by man for centuries, and they depart a great deal from the form and structure of the original virgin forest." In Thailand, swidden agriculturalists have been at work in the forests for hundreds of generations, with a result that many forests have been cleared at some time in recent history, many of them repeatedly; this applies not only to low alluvial plains with densely populated wet-rice areas, but to high altitudes in mountainous zones (Lekagul and McNeely, 1978; Wharton, 1968). The long-term effect of traditional cultures has been to extensively degrade drier primary forests, leaving some parts of them as open savannah woodlands, or even treeless grasslands; while in moister areas, human intrusion has replaced tall primary forest of complex structure with a lower, simpler secondary forest.

A similar tale can be told for the seasonal-forest zone of tropical Africa (Aubreville, 1947; Persson, 1975, 1977; Synnott, 1977). According to computations that depend largely on climatic data, the "moist forest climax area" of tropical Africa is more than twice as large as the actual area of present moist forests; while part of this discrepancy can be accounted for by edaphic factors, there is strong circumstantial evidence that human use of fire, to assist in both hunting and cultivation, has, during the course of millennia, eliminated large tracts of seasonal forest (Sommer, 1976). It is even thought that man has reduced extensive sectors of Africa's evergreen closed forests to degraded open woodlands.

These questions concerning human capacity to disturb TMF are all relevant to a survey that seeks to document man's present-day conversion of TMF. Which forest tracts have not already been converted, to greater or lesser degree, in the past? Which can be truly called undisturbed forests? How much modern disruption, as compared with man's previous activities, leads to significant bio-ecological impoverishment, and how fast can different sorts of forests recover from different sorts of intrusion? Has "primary forest" largely become a purist concept now? Or if it shortly becomes so, what new benchmark criteria can scientists postulate for forest tracts that most deserve protection for their exceptional values? These are questions which are presently difficult to formulate. There seems little doubt that answers will shortly be provided—whether by design or by default.

3 Role of Forest Farmers in Conversion of Tropical Moist Forests

By far the most important factor in conversion of tropical moist forests (TMF) appears to be the forest farmer. Of the various forms of forestland agriculture, the main ones are shifting cultivation of traditional style, smallholder agriculture of more recent style, and sundry types of squatter colonization. Shifting cultivation can likewise be categorized into variations in accord with local environmental factors in each of the three main TMF regions.

A characteristic common to all forms of forest farming is that the farmer clears a patch of forest of virtually all its trees, and then usually burns the wood (locally the larger logs may be sold). Hence a generic term for forest farming could be slash-and-burn cultivation—a term that is frequently though erroneously used in the limited sense of shifting cultivation.

Forest farming has been an established practice in TMF for millennia, almost entirely in the form of shifting cultivation as popularly understood. Indeed, shifting cultivation can be characterized as one of the major agricultural systems of the world. Widespread though it has been, shifting cultivation has not generally resulted in long-term elimination of forests. For example, Southeast Asia has featured shifting cultivation for at least 2,000 years, which indicates that the system is an essentially sound mode of utilizing forest environments within traditional patterns. Farmers would follow a locally migratory way of life by virtue of rotational agriculture: felling and burning a patch of forest, raising crops for 2 or 3 years until the soil lost its

23

fertility or until weeds encroached, then moving on to repeat the process in another patch of forest, eventually returning to the original location. This proved an agricultural strategy that allowed the cultivator to make sustainable use of the forest environment. As long as there were only a few cultivators per square kilometer, generally five or less (depending on local circumstances), and provided the patch of farmed forestland could be left fallow for at least 10 years in order to renew itself, the system worked. Indeed shifting cultivation has proved highly adaptive to a broad spectrum of conditions; when applied with an understanding of the forest's capabilities and limitations—an understanding that seems to have characterized shifting-cultivator communities of many different cultures—the system appears to have been a practical and successful way of utilizing land where poor soils, steep gradients, and heavy rainfall make conventional farming methods unproductive or impossible. (For further details, see Clarke, 1976; Conklin, 1963; Denevan, 1976, 1977, 1978; Greenland, 1975; Greenland and Herrera, 1977; Hauck, 1974; Kunstadter et al., 1978; Nations and Nigh, 1978; Sanchez, 1976; Watters, 1971.) Now, however, in many areas, the numbers of shifting cultivators have increased to a point where there are often 3 or more times as many people per square kilometer as formerly, with the result that they have less space for local migration. The upshot is that they tend to make intensive as well as extensive demands on forest environments, allowing local ecosystems insufficient time to recover. Soils then rapidly become exhausted, and especially in wetter areas, weeds encroach. After as few as two cycles, the cultivator is obliged to abandon the area altogether, and move on to start afresh in a new patch of primary forest, hence progressively disrupting undisturbed TMF. This 2,000-year-old phenomenon is rapidly disrupting very extensive tracts of hitherto undisturbed forest.

In addition, these traditional farmers are now being joined by large communities of subsistence peasants, who, due to lack of land elsewhere, are moving into forests where they adopt a slash-and-burn style of agriculture that leaves even less scope for forest regeneration. These recent arrivals, possessing little cultural adaptation to forest environments, tend to advance upon the natural forest in waves: They operate as ''pioneer fronts'' pushing ever deeper into forest tracts, leaving behind them a mosaic of degraded croplands and brush growth where there is no prospect of a natural forest reestablishing itself even in impoverished secondary form. In Peru, for example, the process has been graphically described in the following terms: ''The populations overflowing from the [Andes] mountains down to the Amazon plains do not settle there, but advance like a slow burning fire, concentrating along a narrow margin between the land they are destroying and are about to leave behind, and the forests lying ahead of them" (Dourojeanni, 1975).

All in all, these forest farmers have been estimated in the mid-1970s to total at least 140 million, occupying some 2 million km² (or over one-fifth) of the TMF biome (King and Chandler, 1978; Myers, 1979; Persson, 1975, 1977; Sommer, 1976; Schulte, in press). According to preliminary reckonings, they are believed to eliminate at least 100,000 km² of forest each year. The greatest loss occurs in Southeast Asia, where farmers clear a minimum of 85,000 km² each year (some of which are allowed to regenerate), adding to 1.2 million km² of formerly forested croplands in the region (Chandrasekharan, 1978; Kartawinata, 1975). Tropical Africa is believed to have lost 1 million km² of moist forest to these cultivators before the arrival of modern development patterns in the last quarter century; of Africa's present TMF expanse, as much as 400,000 km² may now be under this form of agriculture, with a current loss of forest estimated at 40,000 km² per year (Aubreville, 1947; Braun, 1974; Hauck, 1974; Persson, 1977; Sommer, 1976). A similar story applies in Latin America, though fewer details are available (Denevan, 1977; Watters, 1971).

How reliable are these estimates? Of all aspects of this survey, this may be the most difficult to evaluate. It is possible, however, to make a comparative assessment by approaching the problem from a different direction. There is reason to believe that the estimation of 140 million forest farmers represents a minimum number. At an average size of seven persons per family (a roughly acceptable figure for Central America, Colombia, Indonesia, the Philippines, and Thailand), this means there are some 20 million families. If each family clears one additional hectare each year, as seems to be minimal practice, the forest farmers are clearing some 200,000 km² of forest each year. True, many of these farmers exploit secondary forests; and in certain sectors of primary forest, *e.g.*, in Central Africa, population densities are still low enough to permit the forest to be used, while sustaining its quality and composition with prospect of eventual regeneration of primary vegetation. But so far as the author can determine, it is not unrealistic to suppose that forest farmers are converting at least 100,000 km² of primary forest to permanent cultivation each year.

In short, the factor of forest farming could well be accounting for over 1 percent of the TMF biome each year. When considered in conjunction with other factors—timber harvesting, planned agriculture, cattle raising, etc.—it becomes possible to credit that something approaching 200,000 km² of TMF, and possibly even more, are being converted each year. In turn, this throws light on the popular estimate of 20 ha disappearing per minute, equivalent to only 105,000 km² per year; the estimate offered by the Director-General of FAO, Edouard Saouma (at the Eighth World Forestry Congress, October 1978), of 40 ha per minute, equivalent to 210,000 km² per year; and the author's estimate advanced in an earlier assessment (Myers, 1979), based on far less detailed documentation and analysis, of 45 ha disappearing per minute, or almost 240,000 km² per year.

What impact are forest farmers likely to have on TMF within the foreseeable future? Here it is important to recall that population growth rates in many countries of the TMF biome are among the highest on earth. Certain countries (Table 1) already possess large populations in relation to available cultivable land—these generally being countries where the problem of forest farmers is most pronounced, *viz.*, Brazil, Colombia, Indonesia, Kenya, Madagascar, Malaysia (peninsular), Peru, the Philippines, Thailand, Uganda, Vietnam, and all countries of West Africa and of Middle America. Thus it is scarcely surprising that a number of countries are promoting transmigration and settlement programs for their TMF zones, *e.g.*, Brazil, Colombia, Indonesia, and Peru. Unless large-population countries proceed faster than hitherto with economic development that provides opportunities other than forest farming for landless people to make a living, it is possible that the numbers of forest farmers will grow at a rate faster than that of the overall populations. In other words, population growth in the countries in question is projected to produce an increase of 60-65 percent by the year 2000, but the number of forest farmers could double or increase even further.

Let us look at three countries to see how the prospect could work out in detail. Indonesia now contains over 140 million people, 82 percent of them rural; two-thirds of the total populace are concentrated in Java, where they are exerting unsustainable pressures on the island's life support systems, thus prompting the government to mount its transmigration program to shift millions of families to the outer islands. Despite an unusually successful birth control campaign, Indonesia's population is projected to reach 226 million by the year 2000—with all that could entail for the country's remaining forests. Because of the young profile of its population pyramid (meaning that an exceptionally large proportion of future parents have already been born), Indonesia may not achieve a stationary population until the year 2165, with a populace of 330 million. Similarly, Brazil, with a present total of 118.3 million (though only 40 percent rural), is projected to reach 205 million by the end of the century, and 353 million by the time it reaches a stationary population in the year 2070. Finally, the Ivory Coast, with a present population of rather over 7 million (80 percent rural), is projected to grow to 13.2–14.0 million by the end of the century, and to reach 41 million with a stationary population in the year 2135. Unless a substantial proportion of these expanding populations can eventually be concentrated in urban areas—probably only possible, with a basically acceptable level of living standards, through widespread modernization of their economies, especially via manufacturing—it is not difficult to visualize the impact that these huge throngs of agriculture-supported people are likely to have on remaining tracts of T M F unless their disruptive forms of farming can be modified.

A key suggestion thus arises. How can nonsustainable use of forest environments, as presently practiced by many forest farmers, be transformed into sustainable use? Alternatively stated, how can an extensive and wasteful pattern of agriculture be turned into an intensive and established form? There are various ways to step up the productivity of the forest farmer's croplands, and thereby reduce his incentive to move into fresh patches of forest every few years (Clarke, 1976; Dickenson, 1972; Greenland, 1975; Greenland and Herrera, 1977; Grigg, 1974; Janzen, 1973; Nations and Nigh, 1978, Ruthenberg, 1976; Sanchez, 1976; Seavoy, 1973). Research already indicates that shifting cultivation can be made much more intensive and efficient. Traditional farmers in West African forestlands usually achieve no more than 100 kg/ha of maize, whereas modern farmers in the same region produce many times as much (Pearson and Pryor, 1978). True, modern farming often requires a number of commercial inputs, such as fertilizer, pesticides, and high-yielding hybrid grain. But the fertilizer need could be partially met, although at much lower levels, through greater use of legumes by forest farmers; although if such crops are used as green manure, they yield no food and must be plowed under—an expensive process in a clearing in which the fertility of the soil is deteriorating and the weeds are increasing rapidly. Rice paddies are being enriched in south China by the cultivation of the water fern *Azolla* with its symbiotic blue-green algae, and this practice, although limited in the amount of nitrogen that can be provided, could well be useful elsewhere (Wittwer, 1978). In addition, a broad range of food crops can be grown, making more selective and integrated use of the forest environment. For example, Chinese farmers in western Borneo raise food grains, pepper, rubber, and a dozen sorts of vegetables, and intersperse them with fishponds and livestock grazing—a system that enables them to make permanent use of impoverished tropical soils, without need to move on every few years. The Lua of northern Thailand grow at least

TABLE 1 Population Data for TMF Countries

Region or Country	Population Estimate Mid-1979 (millions)	Rural Population (%)	Rate of Natural Increase (annual %)	No. Years to Double Population	Population Projection to Year 2000 (millions)	Per Capita GNP (US$)
Middle South Asia						
Bangladesh	87.1	91	2.9	24	155.1	90
India	660.9	79	1.9	36	1,010.5	150
Sri Lanka	14.5	78	1.8	38	19.9	200
Continental Southeast Asia						
Burma	32.9	78	2.4	29	52.7	140
Dem. Kampuchea (Cambodia)	8.9	88	2.6	27	13.7	n.a.
Laos	3.7	85	2.4	29	5.8	90
Thailand	46.2	87	2.3	30	75.9	410
Vietnam	50.1	78	2.3	30	77.8	170
Insular Southeast Asia						
Indonesia	140.9	82	2.0	35	210.5	300
Malaysia	13.3	73	2.5	28	20.1	930
Philippines	46.2	68	2.4	29	77.9	450
Papua New Guinea	3.1	87	2.9	24	5.1	480
SUBTOTAL	1,107.8	81.2 (Avg.)	2.4 (Avg.)	30 (Avg.)	1,725.0	—
Latin America						
Middle America	88.7				170.4	
Costa Rica	2.2	59	2.5	28	3.4	1,240
El Salvador	4.5	61	3.4	20	8.5	570
Guatemala	6.8	64	3.3	21	12.3	790

Honduras	3.1	69	3.5	20	6.2	450
Mexico	67.7	36	3.4	20	132.3	1,110
Nicaragua	2.5	51	3.4	20	4.8	830
Panama	1.9	50	2.3	30	2.9	1,220
Tropical South America	190.05				327.08	
Bolivia	5.2	66	2.8	25	8.9	540
Brazil	118.7	39	2.8	25	205.2	1,390
Colombia	26.1	40	2.2	32	42.3	710
Ecuador	8.0	58	3.1	22	15.1	770
French Guiana (mid-1978)	0.05	20	2.5	—	0.08	—
Guyana	0.8	60	2.0	35	1.2	560
Peru	17.3	38	2.8	25	29.5	830
Suriname	0.4	34	3.5	20	0.7	1,500
Venezuela	13.5	25	3.0	23	24.1	2,820
SUBTOTAL	278.8	48.1 (Avg.)	2.9 (Avg.)	24.4 (Avg.)	497.5	—
West Africa	99.1				194.0	
Ghana	11.3	69	3.1	22	21.2	380
Ivory Coast	7.7	68	2.9	24	14.0	710
Liberia	1.8	71	3.2	22	3.5	430
Nigeria	74.6	82	3.2	22	148.8	420
Sierra Leone	3.7	85	2.6	27	6.5	200
Central Africa	38.3				63.6	
Cameroon	8.3	71	2.3	30	13.1	340
Congo	1.5	60	2.6	27	2.5	500
Gabon	0.5	68	1.1	63	0.8	3,730
Zaire	28.0	70	2.8	25	47.2	130

Table 1 (continued)

Region or Country	Population Estimate Mid-1979 (millions)	Rural Population (%)	Rate of Natural Increase (annual %)	No. Years to Double Population	Population Projection to Year 2000 (millions)	Per Capita GNP (US$)
Eastern Africa					106.4	
Kenya	54.1	90	3.8	18	32.8	270
Madagascar	15.4	84	2.6	27	15.1	210
Tanzania	8.5	93	3.0	23	33.1	200
Uganda	17.0	93	3.0	23	25.4	260
	13.2					
SUBTOTAL	191.5	77.2 (Avg.)	2.8 (Avg.)	27.1 (Avg.)	364.0	—
Summary						
Southern and Southeast Asia	1,107.8	81.2 (Avg.)	2.4 (Avg.)	30	1,725.0	—
Tropical Latin America	278.8	48.1 (Avg.)	2.9 (Avg.)	24.4	497.5	—
Tropical Africa	191.5	77.2 (Avg.)	2.8 (Avg.)	27.1	364.0	—
GRAND TOTAL	1,578.1	68.8 (Avg.)	2.7 (Avg.)	27.2	2,586.5	—

NOTE: Certain regions have been omitted, e.g., the Caribbean and Melanesia, on the grounds that their TMF cover is insufficient to warrant their inclusion in this table. It should be noted that in certain instances, e.g., Brazil, the great majority of the population currently lives outside the TMF zone.

SOURCE: 1979 World Population Data Sheet, Population Reference Bureau, Inc., Washington, D.C., U.S.A.; UNESCO, 1978; World Bank Atlas, 1978.

120 different crops, including 75 food crops, 21 medicinal crops, 20 plants for ceremonial or decorative purposes, and 7 for weaving and dyes—thus achieving a partial mimicry of the diversity of natural forests (Kunstadter *et al.*, 1978). Similarly, Lancandón farmers in the forest of the state of Chiapas in southern Mexico grow as many as 80 varieties of food and raw material crops in a single hectare, and exploit the surrounding forest environment for up to 100 species of fruits and other wild foods, 20 varieties of fish, 6 types of turtles, 3 kinds of frogs, 2 types of snails, 2 species of crabs, 2 species of crocodiles, and 3 kinds of crayfish (Nations and Nigh, 1978).

In addition, there is now being developed a basically innovative strategy to provide alternatives for forest farmers: agroforestry. This approach persuades the peasant farmer to seek a livelihood off cleared forestlands, or at least to remain within secondary forest zones, by encouraging him to plant trees rather than cut them down. In practical terms, agroforestry depends on offering the cultivator incentives to establish a patch of fast-growing trees on his holding at the same time as he plants his food crops (Bene *et al.*, 1977; Budowski, 1977, 1978; Douglas and Hart, 1976; King, 1968; King and Chandler, 1978; Lugod, 1975; Pollisco, 1975; Valena, 1974; Wirakuswerah, 1979). By the time the cultivator is ready to move on, the newly planted trees will be about ready to close their canopy. The tree plantation itself is intercropped with food plants such as maize and bananas, and with coffee, tea, spices, fruit trees, and many other items. Trial projects now feature tall-growing timber or pulp trees, medium-height cash crops such as coffee, low-growing food crops such as manioc, and fish and giant snails in water channels. Thus food growing can be combined with reforestation of forest cover.

Field experience shows that agroforestry can be financially beneficial to both cultivators and foresters. In eastern Nigeria, a cultivator can earn $200–300 from the trees he plants, while the forestry sector finds that the plantation established through agroforestry costs only $200–300/ha compared with $800 through direct planting—the Forest Service has saved $5.7 million on 11,000 ha planted in this way (Van Nao, 1978). If the cultivators use these earnings to buy fertilizer and pesticides, they can then grow 4 times as much maize, cassava, yams, and other food crops (Grinnell, 1975). A more extended form of agroforestry is being attempted in Thailand, where cultivators are being encouraged to grow rubber. The Forest Industry Organization offers a farmer a plot of land on which to plant rubber and timber trees in conjunction with food crops. After 6 years, during which the Organization pays all expenses of raising the trees in return for the farmer's labor, the farmer starts to tap the rubber latex, paying the Organization 30 percent of the income. After 30 years, when the rubber trees are worn out, they become the property of the Organization, which converts them to timber. The entire exercise produces almost 2½ times as much net income for the Organization as would be the case if it established the plantations itself, while the farmer receives $880 per year in wages during the first 6 years, plus around $650 thereafter from rubber (Chaiyapechara, 1978).

Agroforestry can also be combined with private commercial enterprise; the Paper Industry Corporation of the Philippines embarked in 1974 on a program in conjunction with the World Bank to encourage farmers to rent patches of deforested land on the Corporation's 190,000 ha concession (Diaz, 1976; Draper, 1975; Keil, 1977; Tagudar, 1976; Valera, 1974). By late 1976, 3,849 farmers had planted 12,400 ha with almost 9 million trees, for eventual sale to the Corporation's pulpmills. By 1985, the Corporation expects to obtain about 40 percent of its 650,000 m³ of pulpwood per year from its agrofarmers.

Other commercial activities allow an entrepreneur to operate in conjunction with agrofarmers, not only through a combination of agriculture and forestry, but also involving grazing land, wildlife-rearing, bee-keeping, and the like. A start on projects of this sort has been made in Bangladesh, Burma, India, Indonesia, Papua New Guinea, the Philippines, and Thailand (Chandrasekharan, 1978). But the forest is disappearing rapidly under the onslaught of increasing numbers of forest farmers, and there is still little evidence of the effective dissemination of desirable practices such as those just described on an international, or in most cases, even a national scale.

4 Role of Timber Trade in Conversion of Tropical Moist Forests

A main reason why tropical moist forests (TMF) are increasingly exploited is that more people want more wood. This applies not only to the tropical countries in question, but to communities of the developed world that increasingly look to TMF to meet their consumption demands. (This review is based on Economic Commission for Europe, 1976; Food and Agriculture Organization of the United Nations, 1978; Myers, 1979; Pringle, 1976, 1977, 1978a,b.)

Estimates for the amount of wood cut worldwide in 1974 indicate that the total surpassed 2,500 million m³ (Table 2). Of this amount, some 47 percent was used as fuel, over four-fifths of it to meet the needs of the developing world; 43 percent was used as timber for construction needs, for panels, and for other "solid wood" purposes, two-thirds of it to meet the needs of the developed world; and 10 percent was manufactured into pulp products, seven-eighths for markets of the developed world. By the year 2000, aggregate wood use could approach 6,000 million m³, of which firewood could account for around one-third, solid wood for over one-half, and pulp products for at least one-sixth.

In short, consumption of wood is projected to increase by almost 135 percent during the last quarter of this century. This consumption trend will generate growing pressures to exploit those forests that have hitherto contributed relatively little to global timber needs, namely TMF. Although they contain about as much wood as their larger temperate counterparts, TMF now supply little more than one-tenth of total wood used worldwide as solid wood and as paper pulp.

33

TABLE 2   World Consumption of Wood: Present and Projected
Estimates

Type of Wood	1974		2000		Percentage Increase
	Million m³	%	Million m³	%	
Fuelwood	1,170	47	1,950	33	66
Poles, sawn wood, panel products	1,078	43	3,010	51	179
Wood pulp products	263	10	910	16	246
TOTAL	2,511	100	5,870	100	134

SOURCE: FAO, various papers.

CONTRIBUTION OF TROPICAL MOIST FORESTS TO INTERNATIONAL
TRADE IN HARDWOODS FOR SOLID-WOOD USE

During the last three decades, there has been a rapidly growing demand
on the part of developed nations for tropical timber, especially for
hardwoods, the kind of timber that makes up over 90 percent of TMF
(Table 3). Hardwood supplies many needs: housing construction; fin-
ished products such as furniture; and wood-based panels such as plywood, veneer, particleboard, and fiberboard. Of the world's hardwood
forests, the great bulk are located in the tropics. Hardwood forests of
temperate zones have been steadily depleted or are coming under
greater protection in order to meet environmental interests, and, as a
result, exploitation pressure is increasingly directed toward TMF.

After the economies of the developed world recovered from World
War II, they began to import tropical hardwood timber, some 4.2 million m³ in 1950 (Table 3). Within three decades, the volume has grown
by almost 1,500 percent, and it is projected to expand by more than half
as much again, to 95 million m³ by the year 2000. True, tropical regions
use a lot of hardwood timber themselves, but the amount has little more
than doubled since 1950, whereas the developed world's imports have
increased 15 times, and the total has recently surpassed consumption
by all tropical countries combined.

The largest single consumer of tropical hardwoods is Japan, now
accounting for over half of the developed nations' imports (Table 3).
Between 1950 and 1973, Japan's consumption of tropical hardwoods
increased 19 times, with three-quarters of the aggregate supply deriving
from Southeast Asia. Among all Japan's imports, wood now ranks as
a strong second to oil; the country depends on overseas sources for
around two-thirds of its wood, a proportion that could rise as high as
four-fifths by 1985 (some of the imports stem from North America, but
hardwood imports almost entirely derive from the tropics) (Japan Eco-

nomic Research Center, 1976; Kanamori *et al.*, 1975; Tsurumi, 1976). Hitherto Japan has looked mainly to Southeast Asia for its hardwood needs, but it is increasingly directing attention toward Latin America and West Africa.

The United States is the second largest consumer of tropical hardwoods. U.S. demand has been growing at a rate far above the country's growth rates for population and GNP. This has been partly caused by rapidly rising costs of high-quality hardwoods from within the United States, following increased interest in the country's hardwood forests for their esthetic and recreational values. A more important reason is that plywood panelling can be obtained relatively cheaply from Southeast and East Asia; over four-fifths of U.S. imports of tropical hardwoods come in the form of plywood and veneer via Japan, the so-called Philippines mahogany that originates in Southeast Asia. Between 1950 and 1973, U.S. imports of tropical hardwoods increased 9 times (until the country was accounting for about 70 percent of all tropical plywood and veneer entering world trade), and by the year 2000 they are projected to double again.

The nations of Western Europe account for about one-third of the developed world's imports of tropical hardwoods, an amount that is projected to increase by about 75 percent by the year 2000. Most of the timber derives from West and Central Africa, though within the last few years there has been a marked expansion in hardwood imports originating from Southeast Asia.

By far the major source of tropical hardwoods to date has been Southeast Asia (Table 4). Between 1950 and 1973, the region increased its exports 24 times, until it was accounting for three-quarters of international trade in tropical hardwoods. Latin America, with around 3 times as many hardwood stocks as Southeast Asia, currently produces only 10 percent of the world's hardwood timber, and exports very little, due to the remote location of many of its hardwood forests. West and Central Africa export only about one-third as much as Southeast Asia. Plainly, however, the progressive depletion of Southeast Asia's forests will cause much greater exploitation pressure to be directed toward the two TMF regions that have hitherto supplied little to international hardwood trade, namely Amazonia and Central Africa. As harvesting technology allows loggers to extract timber from localities that are currently considered inaccessible because of such factors as difficult terrain or remoteness, and as processing technology enables more heterogeneous types of hardwoods to become acceptable on commercial markets, both Amazonia and Central Africa can be expected to increase their share of the hardwood timber trade.

TABLE 3 Consumption of Tropical Hardwood Timber: Past, Present, and Projected (million m³)

Country/Region	1950	1960	1970	1973	1980	1990	2000
Japan	1.5	4.6	20.1	28.9	35	38	48
United States	0.8	2.2	5.1	7.2	10	15	20
Europe	1.9	6.2	10.5	17.2	21	27	35
Total three importing regions	4.2	13.0	35.7	53.3	66	80	95
Tropical producing regions	21.0	34.0	42.6	46.5	66	117	185
Rest of world	1.0	2.1	4.2	9.0	13	18	23
TOTAL	26.2	49.1	82.5	108.8	145	215	303

SOURCE: FAO, 1978; Pringle, 1976.

TABLE 4 Supply of Tropical Hardwood Timber: Actual and Projected (million m³)

Region	1950 Production	1950 Export (%)[a]	1973 Production	1973 Export (%)	1980 Production	1980 Export (%)	1990 Production	1990 Export (%)	2000 Production	2000 Export (%)
Tropical Africa	4.7	1.5(32)	16.5	11 (67)	20	12(60)	25	9(36)	35	10(29)
Latin America	15.5	0.8 (5)	20	3 (15)	32	4(13)	60	7(12)	118	28(24)
Southern and Southeast Asia	14.3	2 (14)	72.5	48.5(67)	93	65(70)	130	82(63)	150	80(53)
TOTAL	34.5	4.3(13)	109	62.5(57)	145	81(56)	215	98(46)	303	118(39)

[a] Figures in parentheses are percentage of production given to export.

NOTE: As tropical developing countries themselves start to consume more of their hardwood output, there will be (except in the eventual case of Latin America) a smaller share available for export to developed countries. At the same time, developed countries' demand will steadily expand. So there will be compounded pressure to exploit tropical hardwood forests.

SOURCES: Pringle, 1976; other FAO documents.

CONTRIBUTION OF TROPICAL MOIST FORESTS TO INTERNATIONAL
TRADE IN SOURCES OF PAPER PULP

While global consumption of hardwood products is expected to continue to expand, it is paper products for which the greatest growth in demand is projected. TMF contain relatively few stocks of the conventional source of paper pulp, *i.e.,* softwoods. But the international paper trade now expects to depend on TMF for much of its raw materials, as a consequence of recent changes in forestry technology. Until the mid-1970s, it was thought that TMF, with their multiplicity of hardwood species, could not readily be pulped after the manner of softwoods. But new production processes now allow wood chips from some 100 selected TMF tree species to be simultaneously converted into pulp (U.S. Forest Service, 1978). TMF, comprising some 55 percent of the world's forests, currently produce only about 7 percent of the world's paper and paperboard—a percentage that could shortly start to grow rapidly.

During the period 1950–1970, world output of paper products increased from 40 to 130 million t for a growth rate twice that of population. If long-term trends continue, world demand could rise from its present level of around 180 million t per year to 400 million t by the year 2000, and to twice as much again after only a further two decades (Jahn and Preston, 1976; Pringle, 1977). The developed world now uses almost 160 million t of pulp a year, the developing world little over 20 million. An average developed world's citizen consumes an annual amount of over 155 kg of paper and paperboard (in the United States, 325 kg), while a developing world's citizen is unlikely to use more than 5 kg. (Many a citizen of Indonesia and Nigeria may not even account for 1 kg, roughly half of one copy of the Sunday edition of the *New York Times*.) If consumption continues to grow as in recent years, the developing world is projected to expand its consumption roughly 3 times, as compared with a 2¾-times increase on the part of the developed world; thus by far the largest share of total consumption will remain with the developed world.

Whereas many nations of North America and Western Europe are self-sufficient for paper pulp or even produce a surplus, Japan is heavily dependent on foreign sources, almost half of its pulpwood now coming from overseas. Following recent increases in prices of U.S. softwood chips, Japan is turning to Southeast Asia and tropical America for hardwood chips, which now supply over half of its pulpwood-chip needs (Shimokawa, 1977).

Even though their consumption rates are presently very low, developing countries are strongly motivated to develop sources of paper pulp. They currently import the great bulk of their supplies, at a 1975 cost of $2 billion—worth almost two-thirds of developing countries' exports of tropical timber. To give an idea of low-level demand in developing countries, and of the amount by which it could expand, total newsprint consumption in 14 Asian countries, including all the most populous ones except China, now totals around 600,000 t per year, or less than Canada's. Not only does demand for paper increase with growing human numbers, it expands much more as a consequence of growing human aspirations. In particular, the spread of literacy serves as a powerful stimulus to demand—and in many developing countries, lack of paper is causing serious setbacks to education and communications. Within another decade, there will be a further 150 million consumers of paper in developing countries; by the year 2000, Southeast Asia is expected to need 5 times as much paper as in 1974. Indonesia, after paying out $92 million for pulp imports to meet 85 percent of its needs in 1977, feels strong incentive to use its own forest resources as a pulp source.

ECONOMIC VALUE OF TROPICAL WOOD TRADE

Between 1954 and 1976, tropical wood exports increased in value from $272 million to $4.2 billion. This represents a growth rate far faster than that for global trade in all forest products. Tropical wood exports now amount to around 4 percent of the value of all the developing world's exports excluding petroleum, making it one of the five most important export earners among major commodities produced by the developing world. In fact, tropical wood is now one of the fastest growing exports of the developing world, earning about as much revenue as sugar, cotton, or copper.

Yet, substantial and expanding as these export earnings are, trade in tropical wood nevertheless amounts to only about 15 percent of global trade in forest products. The Congo and Finland have land areas and forest estates roughly the same size, yet in 1973 the value of Finland's forest exports was 60 times greater than the Congo's. The six main countries of the Amazon Basin, plus French Guiana, Guyana, and Suriname, possess 2.7 ha of forest per person, compared with a world average of about 1 ha, yet they import more forest products by value than they export.

ECOLOGICAL IMPACT OF COMMERCIAL LOGGING

Due to the diversity of tree species in tropical forests, coupled with the reluctance of international timber markets to take more than a small proportion of wood types available, the commercial logger is inclined to harvest very selectively, taking a few choice specimens with disregard for the rest—a "creaming" operation. Of Amazonia's many thousands of tree species, only about 50 are widely exploited, even though as many as 400 have some commercial value. Africa exports only 35 principal species (albeit twice as many as in 1950), with 10 accounting for 70 percent of the total (Erfurth, 1976). In Southeast Asia, loggers focus on less than 100 tree species, with exports consisting mainly of only a dozen or so (Sumitro, 1976; Whitmore, 1975).

So when a patch of TMF is exploited, only a few trees, often less than 20 of 400 per ha, are taken. Yet the logging operation can leave many of the remaining trees damaged beyond recovery—far more than would be the case in a temperate-zone forest—because TMF trees are strongly linked together with vines, lianas, and other climbing plants, sometimes as many as 2,000 per ha and some of them 200 m long (Ewel and Conde, 1976). Commercial trees are often limited to the tallest which, benefiting from the sunlight, develop crowns as widespread as 15 m. When one of these giants is felled, it is likely to break or pull down several others with it. Furthermore, tropical trees are highly susceptible to attack by pathogens; as a result, a seemingly minor injury, such as a patch of bark torn off, can leave a tree vulnerable to irreparable damage. Logging roads and haulage tracks, sometimes averaging as much as 10 km for each km² of forest exploited, can, together with dumping zones and lands for logs, account for 10–30 percent of the forest area (Burgess, 1973).

Repeated surveys in Southeast Asia reveal that average logging leaves between one-third and two-thirds of residual trees damaged beyond recovery (Hadi and Suparto, 1977; Kartawinata, 1975; Suparto et al., 1978; Tinal and Balenewan, 1974). In addition, almost one-third of the ground may be left bare, in many instances with the soil impacted by the heavy machinery (Burgess, 1973). With greater care, the damage could be reduced by half. But less destructive exploitation would raise timber prices for the end-product consumer—something that the main markets (developed nations) are unlikely to accept on the grounds that it would be unduly inflationary.

Clearly, logging impact varies from area to area. In some places, the consequence is only light modification of the forest, while in other places it amounts to gross degradation. If the logging is highly selective, *e.g.*, for mahogany, it is quite possible that the forest may never return to its original composition. If high-grading is less selective, it will still take many more than a few years for natural regeneration to fill the gaps caused by the removal of timber trees (G. Hartshorn, personal communication, Tropical Science Center, Costa Rica, 1979).

WOOD CHIPS

Forestry technology has recently developed processing methods that enable tropical hardwoods to be pulped in a single mixture (Chudnoff, 1976; Richardson, 1978). In Colombia, some 100 species are used in one operation, subsequently supplying 40 percent of the kraft and linerboard. In Papua New Guinea, a joint hardwood chip mill, established in 1974, accepts over 200 species at once. Similar operations are under way in Brazil, Indonesia, Malaysia, the Philippines, and Thailand. Since the techniques can not only be applied to sound trees of any sort, but can be used to salvage defective trees and dead standing timber, it can expand the yield of a hardwood forest tract by as much as an additional 300 percent of usable wood (Keays, 1974).

Thus the extreme heterogeneity of TMF no longer presents a problem to the forest exploiter who seeks to manufacture wood pulp. This represents a welcome breakthrough not only for Japan, with its large and growing demand for wood chips from overseas, but also is of potentially enormous benefit to tropical-forest countries themselves, with their ever faster growing need for wood pulp.

Furthermore, some observers look upon this "any-tree/all-tree" harvesting, also known as full-forest harvesting, as an innovation that could represent some sort of salvation for TMF, at least so far as certain forms of wood exploitation are concerned. By enabling intensified production of wood products in a few selected areas, it could relieve extensive harvesting of wood from large tracts of forests. But other observers are inclined to believe that it could amount to a two-edged sword. Under this technique, a patch of forest is not exploited selectively, on a sustained-yield basis; segments are exploited entirely, once and for all. But, if a harvested forest is then replaced by a man-made forest, this intensive use both of the original forest and of the land on which it stood may help to confine timber harvesting to limited localities. Alternatively, full-forest harvesting can be conducted in scattered blocks, or in strips possibly up to 200 m wide (although no experimental studies in tropical forest management have shown 200 m to be the upper limit of clear-cut strips), whereupon the surrounding tracts of undisturbed forest will eventually enable the exploited zone to regenerate.

However, this sophisticated harvesting technique can work two ways: It can either hold out better prospects for many sectors of untouched forest, or it can presage total conversion for many sectors.

PLANTATIONS

In a few localities of the tropics, forest plantations are being established. These plantations now comprise around 85,000 km² (Lanly and Clement, 1979; Persson, 1975). Of this total, almost 40,000 km² are in Latin America (over half in Brazil), and the rest split between southern and Southeast Asia, and West and Central Africa.

To the extent that man-made forests supply the quantities and types of wood required by world markets, they reduce the pressure to exploit primary forests. So fast-growing are some plantation tree species (notably *Eucalyptus* spp., *Gmelina arborea,* and *Pinus* spp.) that a 500-km² plantation can readily produce 1 million m³ of marketable timber per year, a volume that could be obtained only from 10 times as large an area of natural forest (Johnson, 1976, 1977). However, only 5,000 km² or so of additional plantations are established each year—only one-third as many as would be required to supply enough wood to relieve extreme exploitation pressures on TMF during the course of the next two decades.

In any case, tropical forest plantations are not without problems. They can prove costly to establish, $200–400 per ha. In common with many monoculture crops, they tend to attract diseases and pests that are numerous and varied. When plantation trees are harvested, they may take a large stock of nutrients with them, requiring ever growing amounts of fertilizer to maintain productivity.

The greatest expanse of tropical plantations, some 25,000 km², is in Brazil, one of the world's most impressive forestry accomplishments (Muthoo *et al.,* 1977; Pringle, 1976). Less than 1,000 km² are located in Amazonia, with the rest in southern Brazil, where 13,000 km² comprise broad-leaved species and over 10,000 km² comprise conifers. In 1975, Brazil consumed 1.9 million t of paper, an amount that is expected to reach 4 million t by 1985. Although Brazil is now among the world's 10 leading pulp producers, it imported 700,000 t of pulp and paper in 1974, worth $349 million (Potma, 1976). As a result of its plantation program, established in the mid-1960s, Brazil aims to produce enough pulp to meet its own needs by the early 1980s, and, by the year 2000, Brazil plans to have an annual surplus of 20 million t of pulp for export to other countries of Latin America (worth, at present prices, $5.5 billion) (Ekström, 1976). This long-term program will require an additional 40,000 km² of plantations. During the 1970s, the average price of land for reforestation in some of Brazil's heavily populated southern areas has increased 11 times, so there is strong incentive to look for opportunity elsewhere—notably in Amazonia, where there are scheduled to be 10,000 km² of plantations by 1985. Nonetheless, even if all additional plantations of the next two decades were to be located in Amazonia, they need affect less than 1.5 percent of the present forest expanse.

From the standpoint of safeguarding primary TMF, the most appropriate strategy is to establish plantations in forest territories that have already been exploited and have become poor-quality secondary forest, degraded grasslands, or areas that have been overburdened by forest farmers. There are 440,000 km² of such misused lands in Indonesia alone—an area larger than the country's designated protection forests. A number of pioneer tree species, notably *Albizia* and *Terminalia* spp., can be made to grow satisfactorily in such areas. Regrettably, an outcome of this sort is generally precluded by at least two factors. First, a plantation entrepreneur seeks to locate his concession within an extensive tract of primary forest, so that he can exploit the hardwood timber to capitalize his plantation. Secondly, already cleared forestlands are generally occupied by settlements of one sort and another, and it is politically difficult to uproot them in order to plant trees.

A further problem arises, one that could severely reduce the expanse of plantations to be established anywhere in TMF countries. This concerns the scale of investment that will have to be made available for plantations (plus associated processing industries) if they are to make a sizable contribution to tropical timber supplies during the foreseeable future. FAO and World Bank estimates run as high as $3 billion per year over the next two decades. In face of investment requirements of this magnitude, TMF countries are increasingly looking toward the foreign investor: Half of Latin America's total sales of paper and paperboard have recently been accounted for by affiliates of U.S. timber corporations (Gregersen and Contreras, 1975); and Brazil has just reached agreement with 11 Japanese companies for a $1 billion, 4,000-km² pulp project. Yet foreign investors are not moving into the field of tropical plantations as fast as they might. They are not sufficiently assured concerning security of prices for their products, or security of tenure for their holdings. Each inflationary upheaval in world currency systems, and each nationalization of a foreign enterprise in a tropical country, defers the day when enough plantations will be established to relieve the more excessive timber exploitation pressures on TMF. Considering that plantations require a lead time of at least 10 years before they start to produce wood in bulk, stabilizing a favorable politico-economic environment for the foreign entrepreneur is an urgent requirement.

5 Role of Cattle Raising in Conversion of Tropical Moist Forests

Cattle raising plays a substantial role in conversion of tropical moist forests (TMF) in tropical Latin America; in Brazilian Amazonia and in Central America, it plays the dominant role. This factor seems likely to grow rapidly in the years ahead, both in total volume and in proportion to other conversion factors in Latin America. This will be due mainly to the demands of the international beef trade; the bulk of additional beef produced will not be consumed by citizens in the countries concerned but will be exported to the developed world. Cattle raising in TMF is dealt with here from a standpoint different from that of Chapter 9 (Regional Reviews: Latin America). It is analyzed for what it reveals of ecologic-economic linkages among the international community. These resource relationships between, *e.g.,* the United States and Brazil, are expected to become increasingly important.

Between 1950 and 1975, the area of man-established pasture in Central America more than doubled, almost entirely at the expense of primary moist forests. The numbers of beef cattle also more than doubled, though the average beef consumption on the part of Central American citizens actually declined, the surplus meat being exported to North America among other developed-world markets. Between 1966 and 1978, 80,000 km² of Brazil's Amazonian forests were converted into 336 cattle ranches supporting 6 million head of cattle, under auspices of the Superintendency for Development of Amazonia (SUDAM). In addition, some 20,000 other ranches of varying size have been established. Cattle raising is now the dominant cause of forest conversion in

Brazilian Amazonia, and its effects could well increase. Originally, Brazil hoped to become the world's leading beef exporter by the early 1980s, but it does not seem likely that it will reach this goal. Indeed, Brazil remains a net importer of beef, because management of many, if not most, of its pasturelands has not met expectations. Similar initiatives, though not so expansive, are being implemented in the Amazon territories of Colombia and Peru, fostered in certain instances by the Inter-American Development Bank, the World Bank, and the UN Development Program. Many ranches become unprofitable within less than 10 years, because the productivity of artificial grasslands declines. But a rancher can generally obtain another patch of forest to clear, thus practicing a new and broad-scale variation of shifting agriculture.

A main stimulus for this outburst of cattle raising is the growing demand from markets in the developed world for "noninflationary" beef (Table 5). On the one hand, people in North America, Western Europe, and Japan want to continue increasing their consumption of beef, and the demand for beef, according to projections of the Food and Agriculture Organization of the UN (FAO), will rise more rapidly until at least 1990 than for any other food category except fish. On the other hand, cattle owners in many countries of the developed world have recently found it insufficiently profitable to produce additional beef, so there has been rapidly growing inducement for developing countries to fill the gap. In terms of marketplace prices, these developing countries are often well placed. Due to low costs of land and labor, grass-fed beef can be produced in tropical Latin America at only one-quarter the price of similar beef in the United States; beef imported from tropical Latin America into the United States in 1978 averaged $1.47/kg, compared with a wholesale price of $3.3 for grass-fed beef produced in the United States. Hence the steadily climbing volume of beef imported by the United States from tropical Latin America: 111 million kg in 1971 and 133 million kg in 1976, for an annual growth rate of 4 percent. True, these imports amount to only around one-quarter of all U.S. imports of beef, most of the supply coming from Australia and New Zealand, but as a factor contributing to conversion of Latin America's TMF, this international beef trade is far from trifling.

Equally important, the price of U.S. beef has been rising far faster than the overall cost of living. Of all grocery items contributing to inflation in the United States, beef is considered a prime indicator. In 1975, a Montana steer was selling for $0.63/kg at the packing plant; by early 1979, the price had risen to over $1.50. During the first 3 months of 1979, retail prices for beef climbed by 9 percent (to $4.90/kg), and they are expected to climb an additional 25 percent by the end of the

TABLE 5 Central America and Brazil: Beef Production and Exports

Country	Area (km²)	No. of Cattle		Beef Produced (t)ᵃ		Net Beef Exports (t)		Per Capita Consumption of Beef (kg per year)	Pasture (km²)		Forests and Woodlands (km²)	
		1961	1978	1961	1978	1961	1978	1978	1961	1975	1961	1975
Brazil	85,119,700	57,900,000	99,500,000	1,369,000	2,370,000	35,500	140,000	19.3	1,318,800	1,700,000	5,268,000	5,100,000
Costa Rica	50,700	951,000	2,010,000	21,800	71,500	7,100	43,600	15.7	9,690	15,558	28,480	25,180
El Salvador	21,390	1,141,000	1,274,000	20,700	32,300	—	7,300	6.6	6,060	6,700	2,300	2,500
Guatemala	108,890	1,134,000	2,417,000	35,600	88,400	1,500	23,900	10.6	10,390	8,900	84,000	58,000
Honduras	112,090	1,411,000	1,700,000	17,600	50,000	3,300	29,300	5.8	20,000	20,000	71,000	71,000
Mexico	2,022,060	17,668,000	28,800,000	375,000	1,020,000	35,700	29,100	15.3	738,200	670,000	806,200	716,000
Nicaragua	130,000	1,291,000	2,787,000	27,600	76,300	8,300	42,300	15.5	17,100	18,500	64,320	61,500
Panama	75,650	763,000	1,385,000	21,600	55,700	—	4,900	26.3	8,990	11,500	41,000	41,000
United States	9,363,120	97,700,000	116,000,000	7,425,800	11,197,900	454,100	970,000	55.9	2,612,350	2,150,000	3,076,000	3,044,000

SOURCE: U.S. Department of Agriculture, 1978.
ᵃt = metric tons.

year. In fact, prices for U.S.-produced beef are not likely to stabilize until the end of 1980, and are not likely to decline appreciably until 1982. This is because the national herd, which totalled 132 million head in 1975, has been allowed to decline to around 111 million head by late 1978, on the grounds that it was becoming unprofitable for cattlemen to maintain their former inventory of stock. Now that the high beef prices encourage cattlemen to rebuild their herds, it will take at least 3 years (due to the lengthy production cycle) before the national herd recovers its mid-1970s size.

Since beef from tropical Latin America is grass-fed, it is considered suitable for only a limited sector of the U.S. beef market—the fast-food trade with its hamburgers, frankfurters, and other processed-meat products. As it happens, this is the fastest growing part of the food industry in the United States. From the early 1960s, fast-food chains have boomed, until they were growing in the mid-1970s at 20 percent per year, or 2½ times faster than the restaurant industry overall. Over half of all sales are now accounted for by only eight fast-food corporations, notably the major hamburger chains. During the course of 1979, hamburger prices are expected to grow by at least 20 percent. Faced with price jumps of this scale, the U.S. Administration decided to step up beef imports by 7.6 percent in June 1978 and by a further 5 percent in early 1979. Although these additional imports contribute less than 1 percent to the country's consumption of beef, the government estimates that they will trim a nickel off the price of a hamburger—and hardly any other initiative can do as much to stem inflation.

Therein lies the connection between difficulties of the U.S. domestic economy and the demise of TMF in Central America and Amazonia. The price of a U.S. hamburger does not reflect the total costs, and especially the environmental costs, of its production in tropical Latin America; and the American consumer, seeking best-quality hamburger at the least price, is not aware of the ramifications in forest zones thousands of kilometers away.

This topic has been dealt with at some length here, since "the hamburger connection" looks likely to supply ever greater pressures to convert additional TMF during the next few years at least.

6 Role of Firewood Cutting in Conversion of Tropical Moist Forests

Firewood cutting appears to rank as only a marginal factor in conversion of tropical moist forests (TMF). True, it is thought that almost one-half of all wood cut worldwide each year is used as fuel, over four-fifths of it in the developing world (Arnold, 1979; Arnold and Jongma, 1978; this report, Chapter 3). But only a small part of this firewood is taken from TMF, and a still smaller part from primary TMF. In many parts of most countries, firewood is obtained mainly from savannah woodlands, scrub and brush patches, and local woodlots. In India, for example, it has been found that people living inside or adjoining forests meet their total firewood requirements from the forest; in areas within 10 km of forest boundaries, about 70 percent of the firewood comes from the forest; while beyond 10 km, the use of firewood from the forest steadily diminishes until at about 15 km it is almost nil. A similar pattern of use is reported from a number of other countries.

However, this situation is changing in many parts of the developing world. While one person can, generally speaking, obtain an adequate supply of firewood without damaging the environment from the equivalent of ½ ha of average forest, woodland, or scrub, it is more usual that, in order to exploit supplies close at hand, as many as 15 persons may be taking wood from 1 ha—an excessively concentrated rate, and one unsustainable of forest well-being. This means that local supplies rapidly become exhausted, and people look further afield. This trend is likely to accelerate: As human populations expand, many residual sources of firewood become quickly subject to increasing overexploitation, and they will disappear at ever more rapid rates. Already

48

there is a compensatory trend. In a number of countries, large-scale commercialization of the firewood trade is directing exploitation pressures toward far-distant sources, as it becomes financially worthwhile, *e.g.*, charcoal manufacturers transport their supplies from forests in one part of a country to markets in another part of the country, sometimes hundreds of kilometers away. This trend is already pronounced in such countries as Thailand. The Bangkok conurbation, with its 5 million inhabitants, derives much of its charcoal supplies from forests in remote sectors of the country (Lekagul and McNeely, 1978).

Of approximately 1 billion people living in the TMF biome (a very rough estimate, proposed only to gain a measure of the problem's dimensions—see Table 1 of Chapter 3), some 200 million people are believed to live within or on the fringes of forests. So far as can be ascertained, each of these people consumes an average of 0.5–1.3 m³ of firewood per year. In addition to this local use, substantial amounts are taken to serve commercial markets in far-off urban areas. As a crude assessment, one could say that the total may amount to some 150 million m³ of wood taken for fuel per year. Regrettably, insufficient information is available as to whether forest areas can sustain an annual harvest of this size; it may amount to once-and-for-all usage. Until we have a more detailed grasp of the situation, there seems little point in trying to come up with even a best-judgment evaluation of the situation, especially insofar as firewood cutting presently appears to be a marginal factor in overall conversion of TMF.

However, three further points can be made.

IMPACT OF THE FIREWOOD PROBLEM ON AGRICULTURE

Shortage of firewood has an adverse effect not only on forests but on rural economies in general. As a substitute for firewood, some 400 million t of cow dung are reputed to be burned each year in developing countries of Asia and Africa alone (Spears, 1978). Each ton of cow dung that is burned instead of used as fertilizer means a loss of around 50 kg of potential grain output. As problems of food production increase in these countries, there will be progressive pressure to exploit whatever sources of firewood are available, even at the cost of transportation over what now appear to be excessive distances.

WASTE OF POTENTIALLY USABLE FIREWOOD

To date, most of the large amounts of wood felled each year by forest farmers is almost invariably sent up in smoke, rather than dispatched to market. The volume could be as much as 500 million m³ of potential firewood each year. As the firewood trade becomes increasingly commercialized, there could be eventual prospect that these vast amounts of wood can be put to use, thus reducing firewood-harvesting pressures on forests.

SUPPLEMENTARY SOURCES OF FIREWOOD

A start is being made on establishment of farm woodlots and local-community tree blocks, to supply firewood. According to the World Bank (1978), the aggregate area required for the developing world, at an annual output of some 10 m³ of firewood per ha, will amount to 600,000 km². Establishment costs run to $100 per ha, so the total amount of investment required is some $6 billion. Regrettably, the present pace of plantation establishment is not nearly sufficient, and by the year 2000 there could be at least a further 250 million people in developing countries without firewood for their minimum cooking and heating needs (Spears, 1978).

7 Monitoring of Conversion Trends of Tropical Moist Forests

The need for ongoing monitoring of conversion trends in TMF is great. Only through continuous assessment can we remain aware of how fast the biome continues to lose its forest cover, which countries are likely to suffer severe deforestation, and which of the richest and most diverse areas are most threatened.

Fortunately it is becoming easier to document conversion processes in the TMF biome. Satellite imagery, side-looking radar, aerial photography, and other forms of remote sensing now offer opportunity to inventory extensive areas in a short space of time, often at remarkably low cost. During the past 5 years and especially during the past 2 years, advancing technology has produced both quantitative and qualitative improvements in techniques available.

ONGOING SURVEYS

As described in the Regional Reviews, Chapters 9–11, a number of countries have already published in-depth results of their remote sensing activities. The two leading countries are the Philippines and Thailand. Several other countries have instituted comprehensive remote sensing programs, and their findings should become available within the near future, in a few instances by the end of 1979 and in several instances by the end of 1980. Fortunately they include the country that possesses by far the largest extent of TMF, Brazil, and one of the two next largest, Indonesia (the other, Zaire, is still planning its

51

program, and will not move to an implementation phase for some time yet). In addition, Colombia, Venezuela, and possibly Peru will shortly make available the results of their surveys. This means that, within the relatively near term, some two-thirds of the biome will be covered through comprehensive inventory and mapping surveys.

POSSIBLE SURVEYS ON THE PART OF DEVELOPMENT AGENCIES

As the main source of satellite-sensing technology, the United States extends appreciable support through its Agency for International Development (AID) for remote sensing in a number of TMF countries. It has been through this financial and technical support that the Philippines and Thailand were enabled to launch their broad-scale programs in the mid-1970s. AID is now assisting several other countries in like manner, however, AID can offer support only to those countries that specifically wish it. Not all countries of the TMF biome are yet inclined to look in this direction.

Among other bilateral development agencies, the Canadian International Development Agency makes substantial contributions to certain countries for remote sensing of their forest resources, notably Colombia and Indonesia. Japan may enter this field shortly, with some emphasis on countries of Southeast Asia (partly in view of the strategic relevance of the region's timber stocks to Japan's economy).

As for multilateral agencies, at least three UN bodies are active in this field. UNESCO, through its Man and the Biosphere Program, has maintained a 10-year interest in TMF—though primarily from a standpoint of scientific research of ecosystem processes, rather than through action-oriented activities such as inventorying and monitoring. This latter role has been assigned to the Food and Agriculture Organization of the United Nations (FAO) as the UN agency with primary responsibility for forestry. FAO, in conjunction with the UN Environment Program (UNEP), has recently started work on a Project for Tropical Forest Resources Assessment, the main purpose being

to assess, through study of existing documentation and local observations, supplemented by appropriate Landsat-image analysis of areas that lack useful documentation, the present state of tropical forests and woodlands as well as the rate and patterns of their depletion and degradation (J. P. Lanly, personal communication, Food and Agriculture Organization, Rome, Italy, 1979).

Part of FAO's procedural intention has been to use as a foundation an earlier "Pilot Project on Tropical Forest Cover Monitoring" in four countries of West Africa (Baltaxe and Lanly, 1975). However, this Pilot

Project, due to be completed in 1977, was subject to at least eight delays before it could be finally terminated—due not so much to deficiencies on FAO's part as to unanticipated management problems in the countries concerned. It would not be unrealistic to suppose that the present FAO/UNEP project may take longer than its proposed schedule (mid-1980). Furthermore, the FAO/UNEP project is subject to a basic constraint: It can be carried out only in accord with the wishes of the countries involved. As Member States of the United Nations, these countries help determine the project's objectives, management procedures, and technical methodology. This means that the FAO/UNEP project depends, in large measure, on the amounts and sorts of information that individual countries choose to make available. As indicated in Chapter 1, this information can vary greatly in both quantity and quality. While this does not mean that FAO and UNEP cannot engage in evaluation of statistical material forwarded to them by TMF countries, ultimately they are bound by the wishes of the Member States in question.

FUTURE SURVEY RESEARCH

Further surveys are needed as an extension of this short-term survey that has already been commissioned by the National Research Council. More work of this sort need not be construed as alternative to the options proposed in the above section. On the contrary, they would complement the research activities of development agencies. The surveys would draw on their findings (as has the present survey), while depending primarily on published results of countries such as Brazil, Colombia, Indonesia, and the Philippines. However, this second approach would allow the findings from whatever source to be appraised through independent analysis.

Were further research to be undertaken along these lines, it would be inappropriate to envisage a simple extension of the present survey. In order to gain sufficient insight into conversion processes that are overtaking the TMF biome, it is certainly not necessary to make detailed inquiries in all of the nearly 40 countries of the biome. On the contrary, future investigations could be limited to countries with at least 100,000 km² (at least 1 percent) of TMF cover, namely Cameroon, Congo, Gabon, and Zaire in Africa; Bolivia, Brazil, Colombia, Ecuador, Guyana, Peru, and Venezuela in Latin America; and Indonesia, Malaysia, Papua New Guinea, the Philippines, and Thailand in Southeast Asia. These 16 countries contain 70–75 percent of the biome. True, it would leave out a number of countries with not insignificant tracts of TMF, notably French Guiana, the Ivory Coast, Madagascar, and Suriname; perhaps these four countries could be included as "special cases." An alternative approach could be focusing on countries with at least 100,000 km² of the rainforest, richest TMF forest ecotype; this would reduce the list to Brazil, Colombia, Ecuador, Gabon, Guyana, Indonesia, Malaysia, Peru, Venezuela, and Zaire, covering some 80–85 percent of rainforest in the TMF biome.

If investigations were limited to the 20 countries first considered, or the 10 rainforest countries, this would greatly reduce the amount of research required. Furthermore, and as indicated above, some seven or eight of the countries listed in each of the two groups, including the largest and one of the next two largest, are expected to produce detailed documentation of their forest cover, derived from remote sensing surveys, by late 1979 or early 1980. Thus a survey along the lines proposed could be developed as a limited-scope, intensive analysis. It could probably be accomplished through a simple 6 man-month effort, or through 3 man-months per year as an ongoing activity.

SCOPE OF REMOTE SENSING SURVEYS

A number of countries now recognize the value of remote sensing surveys of their TMF resources. Remote sensing appears to offer much scope for comprehensive and systematic documentation of TMF cover. It is relatively inexpensive and its accuracy is acceptable. It is a useful technique both for initial inventorying of forest resources and for ongoing monitoring of changes that overtake forests. Three main types of remote sensing are considered here: Landsat, side-looking radar, and aerial photography.

Landsat

The Landsat system comprises satellites that continuously orbit the earth. They relay information concerning the earth's surface to ground-based receiving stations. The main advantage of the Landsat system is that, for many applications, it provides more useful, more timely information of a regional nature, at lower costs, than can be obtained through any other data-collecting system. (For some details of Landsat, especially as applied to forest surveys in tropical developing countries, see Aldred, 1976; Hildebrandt and Boehnel, 1979; Miller and Williams, 1978; Pettinger, 1978; Sadowski, 1978; Sayn-Wittgenstein *et al.,* 1978; Strahler *et al.,* 1978; Wacharakitti and Miller, 1975).

Two Landsat satellites, working in unison, now orbit the earth 14 times each day at an approximate altitude of 920 km. On each orbit, they scan a strip of the earth's surface 185 km wide, with a 14 percent overlap with previous and successive strips at the equator (somewhat broader overlaps at higher latitudes). A Landsat "image," containing approximately 7 million picture elements (pixels) or minimal-area data points, covers 34,225 km². Each satellite returns to the original orbit every 18 days, recording a set of images over the same area. Thus any one area of the earth's surface could be surveyed by Landsat once every 9 days, meaning that virtually any part of the earth's surface can be sensed up to 40 times a year.

Each orbit takes 103 minutes. Moreover, images are taken under conditions of virtually fixed solar illumination, since they are recorded at the same local time (9:30 A.M.) each day, and they are taken from a vertical perspective. These two factors also assist with interpretation, especially as concerns identification of vegetation patterns.

It should not be supposed, however, that the Landsat sensors are continuously activated. Except for the United States and for certain areas within range of ground-receiving stations, frequent repeat coverage is rarely achieved. In fact, many tropical areas have been imaged only a few times since the Landsat program began in 1972. It was decided, fairly early in the program, that the sensors and tape recorders should be used sparingly, especially over foreign areas, in order to extend satellite and sensor longevity. Hence coverage of the TMF zone to date is intermittent at best.

Another major problem for satellite sensing in many tropical regions is the prevalence of cloud cover. For example, cloud cover over southern Sumatra, between September 1972 and 1973, ranged from 30 to 90 percent, with a median of 70 percent. In the case of the Philippines, it has not been possible to obtain the 30 Landsat frames required to survey the entire country within a single year. By contrast, the forest resources of Thailand, being located in a zone with less cloud cover, can be readily sensed within 1 year—a marked improvement over earlier techniques such as aerial photography, which, largely because of cost, did not permit a complete survey to be conducted more often than once every 10 years.

Satellite imagery's relatively low resolution requires complementary ground-truth checks. These are on-ground investigations that, in the case of TMF, supply spot-check details of forest cover information that correlates what is sensed from space with what actually exists on earth. Generally conducted as a stratified random sampling, ground-truth checks usually document the following categories of information, among others: type of forest, *e.g.*, evergreen mixed deciduous; stand attributes, *e.g.*, crown density, tree height, median girth; forest disturbance, *e.g.*, none, light or heavy cutting, fire damage, agricultural clearing; and macro-relief classification, *e.g.*, flat land, undulating or rolling land, hilly land, aspect. It is not uncommon for several hundred ground-truth checks to be made per Landsat image. For example, in northern Thailand over 500 checks were made in an area of 107,011 km² (Boonyobhas and Klankamsorn, 1976), or 170 checks per Landsat scene. Clearly, it is neither practical nor necessary to comprehensively check each section of a Landsat image, but only focus on localities where Landsat information is most likely to be fallible.

Landsat sends its information to a ground-receiving station in digital form that can be handled by computers. Landsat records reflected electromagnetic energy in four wavelength intervals—visible green, visible red, and two near-infrared intervals. Through analysis of Landsat data, one hopes to distinguish features of the earth's surface, identifying them through their characteristic reflectance patterns or spectral signatures. In identifying forest cover, the most useful Landsat band for multispectral scanning data is band 5 (visible red light). In this band, land cover patterns are most easily distinguished. Forest cover is usually dark in tone, while other land cover types, *e.g.,* agricultural land and grassland, as well as urban areas, are often lighter in tone (Figure 1).

Since the spectral response of vegetation on Landsat images is dominated by the constituents of canopy cover, Landsat can offer forest information such as vegetation cover and density. Differences in vegetation density are governed by parameters such as tree height and crown diameter, which means that Landsat might differentiate forest areas into different density classes. For example, dense forest is characterized by darkness and evenness of tone, with evergreen forest appearing as one of the darker tones; deciduous forest, by contrast, shows up during the dry season in a lighter tone. Primary forest patches that have been cleared and replaced by predominantly secondary-growth forest are characterized by variable, indeterminate gray tones, according to how much regrowth has become established; when the secondary forest has reached about 10 years of age, Landsat can no longer be used to consistently differentiate secondary growth. Also, rates of forest regression can be determined by multitemporal comparisons of the same geographic area (Figure 1).

Beyond this, however, Landsat varies in its capacity to classify forest cover. Hardwood and softwood communities can be distinguished with 60–70 percent accuracy (Dillman, 1978; de Steigueir, 1978). With respect to species-specific forest classification, however, Landsat yields only 48–64 percent accuracy, which is below the level required for most mapping procedures. However, if an interpreter has a knowledge of individual ecological preferences of tree species, acquiring knowledge of habitat conditions for forest tracts as a form of collateral data can often differentiate between species and stands with similar spectral characteristics, through their individual habitat preferences. In Peruvian lowland Amazonia, for example, Landsat data can be used to map Aguaje palm (*Mauritia flexuosa* L.) stands that appear to correspond closely to swampy conditions. Similarly, other conditions, such as permanently flooded forest, forests subject to temporary flooding, nonflooding alluvial forests, and hill forests, can be identified (Danjoy and Sadowski, 1978). Most mangrove areas in Southeast Asia prove recognizable from Landsat images, though the great variation in mangrove canopy cover, together with the heterogeneity of species composition, makes it virtually impossible at present to categorize the mangrove stands according to species; instead, Landsat can perform only a diagnosis of the presence of mangrove stands (Bina *et al.*, 1978).

The instantaneous field of view of Landsat is approximately 80×80 m; thus, features must occupy at least a few hectares to be consistently recognizable. Cleared shifting cultivation plots can be distinguished if they are sufficiently large and contrast with surrounding forest areas. Regrettably—since shifting cultivation is by far the most pervasive form of forest conversion (see Chapter 3)—Landsat proves less capable of recognizing plots after they have been planted with crops; the new vegetation cover tends to merge with surrounding forest.

A particularly valuable feature of the Landsat system is that its repeated coverage provides information on changing land-use trends in forest zones. In other words, it provides a first-rate opportunity to monitor dynamic phenomena, notably changes in vegetation patterns. Brazil, which has a ground-receiving station of its own, utilizes Landsat to monitor its program for controlled development of large portions of Amazonia's forests, especially with respect to expansion of cattle ranches. In fact, the National Institute of Space Research in Brazil finds that routine systematic use of Landsat is the only economical way of enforcing the terms of government-assistance contracts and of controlling the volume of tree felling in accord with the 50 percent rule (a rule that limits the amount of forest to be felled on a concession site to 50 percent of the standing timber) (Hammond, 1977).

In 1981, Landsat D will be launched. Through its thematic mapper, it will yield spatial resolution predicted at 30 in., 2½ times better than current Landsat MSS sensors; in combination with improved spectral resolution, the thematic mapper will greatly increase Landsat's capacity to map forest features in finer detail. In fact, the system will be able to discriminate features on the earth's surface as small as 0.08 ha. A multispectral scanner will also be included to provide continuity with

FIGURE 1 Landsat images from January 6, 1973 (above), and January 18, 1976 (opposite), graphically illustrate the progressive elimination of forest cover from a portion of southern Thailand adjacent to the Gulf of Siam. In this multitemporal comparison, MSS band 5 is useful in distinguishing between forest vs. non-forest cover. Black areas on the land surface represent forest cover; lighter areas (gray and white) represent cut over areas, which are either in permanent agricultural plots, or have reverted to vegetation other than dense forest.

earlier Landsats. With data from Landsat D, there is potential for identifying cultural features such as very small clearings and logging roads.

In sum, Landsat offers great potential for monitoring changes in tropical forests because of its low-cost, synoptic, repetitive coverage. Countries have the option to choose from simple (manual) to sophisticated (digital processing) techniques of Landsat image analysis, enabling each country to satisfy national limitations of available funding, trained personnel, and project difficulty. Uses can include monitoring existing forest cover for alterations due to shifting agriculture and forest exploitation, which would lead to improved management of forests and adjacent croplands.

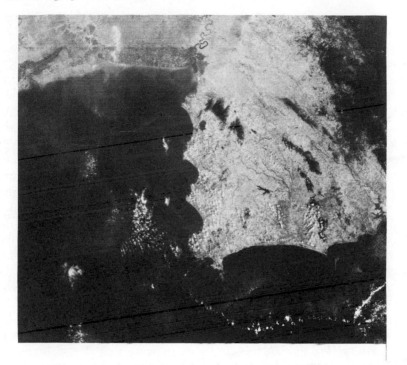

Side-Looking Radar

Remote sensing can also be accomplished through a technique known as side-looking imaging radar (Nielsen and Aldred, 1978; Trevett, 1978). Sensors are mounted on high-flying aircraft from whence they transmit microwave pulses at an angle to the flight-path. These pulses interact with a swath of terrain several kilometers in length, and are reflected back to the sensor, where they are recorded on magnetic tape or film. The patterns of radar images show land forms and terrain in detail, as well as other major features of the landscape being sensed, including details of vegetation patterns. Soil type is usually inferred from interpretation of geology, land form, and vegetation type, and not interpreted directly. In general, radar sensing from high-altitude aircraft offers a resolution potential intermediate between that of Landsat and high-altitude aerial photography.

Like satellite sensing, side-looking radar collects data from large areas in a short period of time. Unlike satellite sensing (and unlike aerial photography), it can be acquired under virtually any weather and light conditions. These advantages are especially significant in equatorial regions where frequent, even daily, build-ups of cumulus clouds often preclude satellite sensing and aerial photography.

The most extensive use of side-looking radar has been in Brazil, where Project RADAM (Radar Amazonia), begun in 1970, has documented land cover in detail. The project covered 4.6 million km² of northern Brazil by the end of 1977, including the whole of Amazonia and part of peripheral areas in the northeast. Surveys were conducted by Caravelle jets crisscrossing Amazonia at about 10,000 m altitude and at a speed of 850 km per hour. These investigations were backed up by ground-truth checks: 3,000 sites in Amazonia were explored by helicopter, and many more by river boat. Project RADAM has allowed Brazil to prepare its first accurate land-form maps for Amazonia, with some surprising revelations. For example, a major new tributary of the Amazon hundreds of kilometers long, mountain ranges far removed from their supposed locations, and an area of forest reserve that turned out to be open savannah have been discovered (Hammond, 1977). And maps of the geology, soils, vegetation, and potential land use from the survey are helping Brazil to develop the vast resources of the Amazon basin in a rational manner.

A similar effort, though on a far more limited scale, is being mounted in Nigeria, to obtain a radar-based vegetation survey of large parts of the country. Preliminary observations indicate that the technique is particularly appropriate for dense vegetation cover in central and southern parts of the country, where the last forest tracts survive (Trevett, 1978).

Radar imagery also offers good resolution. By assessing image characteristics such as tone, texture, size, shape, and arrangement, an interpreter can identify land forms, topographic features, vegetation communities, water bodies, and major cultural features such as urban areas and transportation networks. Within vegetation communities, radar returns indicate gross average heights of different formations, and, to less extent, variations in vegetation density. This means that radar imagery proves particularly useful for mapping forest cover. Especially important for TMF, radar imagery can distinguish differences in physiognomic forms, notably closed-canopy and open-spaced forests, and variations thereof. It can even pick out clearings made by shifting cultivators.

Aerial Photography

Aerial photography in its various forms is a useful tool for many aspects of forest survey, especially as a back-up for Landsat image analysis. It can be used to classify forest communities; it often provides species-specific information that lies beyond the resolution capabilities of Landsat satellites with respect to most TMF cover (Aldred, 1976; Omakupt, 1978; Pettinger, 1978; Sayn-Wittgenstein *et al.*, 1978; Smit, 1978; Synnott, 1977).

For detailed mapping and charting, low-altitude photography (from a height above ground level of 9 km or less) is used. For photographic reconnaissance applications, medium-altitude aircraft are used, flying at 9–15 km, equipped with photographic equipment. For broad-area mapping, high-altitude planes are used, at heights of more than 15 km above the ground, carrying high-resolution wide-angle cameras and multiband cameras.

Aerial photography techniques allow certain characteristics of forest cover, *e.g.*, crown shapes, to be recorded (Sayn-Wittgenstein, 1978). In temperate zones, aerial photography documents tree crown diameter and density, and tree heights, which information permits calculation of standing timber volume. In tropical evergreen forests, however, the exceptional species heterogeneity makes for poor correlations between crown characteristics and stem dimensions. Moreover, only the overstory crowns of a multilevel canopy can be resolved. As a result, it is difficult to resolve ground-level aerial photography of tropical evergreen forests. But newly developed techniques may allow tree crowns in tropical evergreen forests to be measured, and even species to be identified. In tropical deciduous forests, aerial photography can be used to identify the main species and vegetation types, and to calculate tree densities and cover.

Aerial photography is particularly helpful in providing information on shifting cultivation in TMF. It can usually be used to differentiate three categories of shifting-cultivator impact: cultivated fields, relict grasslands including fallow patches, and secondary forests of various ages. However, it can only be used with moderate success to differentiate between secondary forests derived from shifting cultivation on the one hand, and low forest on poor ecological sites on the other hand (the man-made clearings tend to have straight edges that can often be distinguished). Aerial photography also may not be useful in distinguishing between man-made secondary forest and secondary forest deriving from natural disasters such as flooding and cyclones.

Aerial-based photography studies are not only more time consuming than satellite sensing, but they can be several times more expensive. For example, a Landsat survey in northern Thailand required 39 frames to be interpreted, plus ground-truth checks occupying four men for 60 days, at an average cost of $1.20 per 100 km². Aerial photography for the same survey would have required 3,652 photographs, and occupied 20 men for 210 days, at an average cost of $9.50/km².

8 Regional Review: Southern and Southeast Asia and Melanesia

This very extensive region is generally considered to incorporate rather over one-third of the tropical moist forest (TMF) biome. A good part of it, insular Southeast Asia (Indonesia, Malaysia, Papua New Guinea, and the Philippines), features roughly 950,000 km² of rainforest—an area that is, biotically speaking, one of the richest zones on earth, and is, commercially speaking, one of the most attractive zones for timber exploitation. It is here that an exceptional amount of ecological diversity is undergoing exceptional depletion.

This is not to say, of course, that the monsoonal (seasonally deciduous) forests of the region do not have their own intrinsic interest, both to the scientist and to the logger. But these monsoonal forests of continental Southeast Asia (Burma, India, Indochina, and Thailand) do not compare either in richness or in commercial value with the rainforests of insular Southeast Asia.

From an economic standpoint, the most prominent trees of the region are the dipterocarp family of trees (Dipterocarpaceae), totalling several hundred species. Supplying high-quality timber that is unusually light and suitable for plywood and veneer, the dipterocarp forests have been widely exploited since World War II, and particularly since 1960. This trend has been due mainly to the developed world's growing demand for tropical hardwoods, now earning, according to the Food and Agriculture Organization of the United Nations, well over $2.5 billion per year for Southeast Asia. In 1978, when the region exported 22 million m³ of logs and 7 million m³ of processed timber, it accounted for 86 percent of all exports of tropical hardwoods. Moreover, being located close to the most populous region on earth (1.8 billion people live within 5,000 km of Singapore), Southeast Asia can look forward to a vast future market with all that implies for expanding pressures to exploit its remaining stocks of primary forests.

AUSTRALIA

Several patches of TMF are found along Australia's east coast in Queensland, in a 65-km-wide belt between the coastal ranges and the sea. Much if not most of it can be characterized as rainforest. But in terms of ecological richness and biotic diversity, it is an impoverished formation compared with the rainforest of Southeast Asia. The number of plant genera south of the ocean gap between Australia and New Guinea is 340, only slightly over half as many as the 644 north of the gap (Van Steenis, 1950). In short, TMF formations on either side of the demarcation line represent distinctive floristic regions.

The largest tract of Queensland TMF, extending from 16 to 19 degrees S, is centered on Cairns. Further south toward latitude 21 degrees, a little evergreen rainforest is found on mountains, in relict patches that are of special interest because of their high concentrations of primitive and taxonomically isolated species and genera. South of 21 degrees S, semi-evergreen rainforest is found in mountain areas; the region also features some monsoon forest (marginal semi-evergreen rainforest), the determining environmental factor apparently lying not with rainfall alone but with soil fertility. (This brief review is based on Australian Conservation Foundation, 1975; Douglas, 1975; Routley and Routley, 1973; Specht *et al.*, 1974; Stocker *et al.*, 1977; Webb, 1968, 1978; Webb and Tracey, 1978; Whitmore, 1975.)

Of the 7,000 km² of forestlands controlled by the Queensland Forestry Department, most still feature forest, albeit in various stages of disturbance. In fact, all except about 660 km² has been logged at least once since European settlement, and much of the forest at low and medium elevations has been repeatedly logged for the past 100 years. The volume of timber extracted has steadily declined during the past three decades, and many authorities believe that logging of rainforests will soon come to an end altogether, after clear-felling has virtually wiped out lowland rainforest wherever man can introduce a tractor. Moreover, lowland forests have not only been heavily exploited for their timber, they have been taken over for sugar plantations and dairying among other types of agriculture. True, there is less pressure now than a few years ago to convert forests to agriculture, due in part to depressed market prices prevailing for dairy products and beef cattle. In fact, current economic trends seem to favor intensification of activities on forestlands already cleared, as opposed to expansion into new forest areas. When the economic climate improves, however, there will probably be renewed pressures to open undisturbed forest to agriculture, and a further pressure to accommodate mining interests.

It is difficult to ascertain how much TMF, and especially rainforest, originally existed in Australia. The Rainforest Ecology Section of the Commonwealth Scientific and Industrial Research Organization states that it can answer neither that question nor that for current conversion rates even in the broadest terms. As a rough estimate, however, many observers believe that rainforest in north Queensland originally covered about 11,700 km², of which about 6,000 km² now remains, albeit in various states of disturbance.

Fortunately, a good deal of rainforest, especially of key types, is being brought under protected status. The National Parks and Wildlife Service, which controls 1,080 km² of rainforest, hopes to have a further 300 km² set aside shortly. A particularly encouraging trend is to set aside islands of relict rainforest in remote localities, e.g., in the Cape York peninsula.

BANGLADESH

Bangladesh, 142,721 km², contains 23,240 km² of "state forestlands," of which only about 13,260 km², 9.3 percent of national territory, are forested. Such, at any rate, is the estimate of the Bangladesh Department of Forestry (1978), which does not indicate the basis for its statistical assessment. Plainly, however, population pressure has reduced the country's forests to a residual form of land use, i.e., land that has been left over on agricultural margins.

Bangladesh lies almost entirely in the semi-evergreen rainforest zone (Choudhury et al., 1978; Whitmore, 1975, 1976). About 6,000 km² of this forest type occur in the Chittagong Hill Tracts. There is also a narrow belt of unknown area of evergreen rainforest along the steep rugged hills inland from Chittagong. At the mouth of the river Ganges is a 6,000-km² block of mangrove tidal forest, the largest such tract in the world, known as the Sundarbans. Finally, there is a 1,000-km² patch of alluvial forest on the low-lying plains, dominated by Shorea robusta, much cut in the past and now poorly stocked.

Around 11,500 km² of forests have been designated as forest reserves. These areas are restricted primarily for timber exploitation, though they are subject to much attrition through various illicit forms of land use, such as illegal logging and squatter settlement.

A major factor in the status of the country's forests is shifting cultivation (Alim and Imam, 1978). The practice affects some 9,600 km² of forestlands, and is becoming especially prevalent in the evergreen and semi-evergreen hill forests of Chittagong. According to a 1974 enumeration survey, almost 510,000 people are involved, of whom 406,550 are tribal hill people. As a consequence of shifting cultivation, or *jhuming,* much valuable tree growth has been eliminated in both the forest reserves and the unclassified state forests. Through population growth and improper land use, fallow cycles have been reduced from 20 to 3 years, with the result that crop yields steadily decline, and with a further result that fallow periods are reduced even more. The overall consequence is that forest ecosystems become extensively degraded. An effort is now being made to persuade shifting cultivators to turn to *taungya*-type agroforestry at sites within the forest reserves. The government is also attempting to settle cultivators through integrated community farming projects. Meantime, however, forests in the central and northern parts of the country are reputed to be declining, primarily through shifting cultivation, at a rate of 80 km² per year.

As for the Sundarbans mangrove forest, it supplies livelihood, either directly or indirectly, for one-third of the country's populace. In fact, almost two-thirds of the forest is now regularly exploited for fuel, poles, and other wood uses, while part is now being clear-felled to feed a newsprint factory at Khulana. In addition, the forest has been badly damaged in recent years by cyclones. Yet mangrove forests are such a notable ecological feature on a world scale that, according to a UN Educational, Scientific, and Cultural Organization/Food and Agriculture Organization of the United Nations Regional Seminar on Mangrove Environments in late 1978, Bangladesh deserves to become the site for an international research center to study mangrove forest ecosystems.

BRUNEI

Brunei, 5,743 km², lies on the northwest coast of Borneo between Sumatra and Sabah. Estimates are available of the forest estate only, since no inventories have been taken. About 4,300 km², or almost 75 percent of the land area, are believed to be still covered with relatively undisturbed primary forest, including most types of rainforest. Secondary forest is reputed to cover 1,170 km², and cultivated land and settlements 250 km².

The interior of Brunei is characterized mainly by lowland evergreen rainforest (Hunting Technical Services, 1969; Whitmore, 1975, 1976, 1978). Brunei's position at the heart of the Sunda Shelf region accords it an exceptionally diverse flora, with mixed dipterocarp forests probably more species-rich than similar forests elsewhere.

The country's oil fields provide tax revenues well in excess of government expenditures, so there is little incentive to exploit timber resources to generate foreign exchange. In fact, timber is harvested only for domestic consumption, except for export of small quantities of Ramin.

The main form of disruption of the primary forests—and this is a low-impact factor—is shifting cultivation. Around 2,000 families, or roughly 16,000 people, are believed to practice shifting cultivation. They grow subsistence crops such as hill paddy, maize, tapioca, and various sorts of vegetables, accounting for about 10 percent of all agricultural production. These peasant communities are concentrated mostly along rivers, and in the few hilly localities where they cause serious soil erosion. The amount of forestland they occupy is not known; but if it is assumed that each of 2,000 families uses 10 ha, the area in question amounts to 200 km², or less than 5 percent of the country's forest estate.

BURMA

Of Burma's 696,500 km², around 365,000, or 52 percent, is reputed to be still forested (Asian Development Bank, 1976; Government of Burma, 1977, 1979; Wint, 1978; World Bank, 1976).

Spanning nearly 30 degrees of latitude, Burma contains a wide range of climatic, topographic, and edaphic variants. According to the Forestry Department (which does not indicate how it arrives at its estimates), forest ecotypes include the following: mixed deciduous (the principal source of teak, *Tectona grandis*), 146,000 km²; evergreen dipterocarp, 54,750 km² (much of it approximating open woodland); deciduous dipterocarp, 54,600 km²; montane, primarily temperate evergreen above 1,000 m, 76,650; coniferous, 18,250; mangrove, 7,300; swamp, 3,650; and lowland evergreen rainforest in pockets of lower Burma, 3,650. Of these ecotypes, the main category, mixed deciduous, can be broadly subdivided into moist upland mixed deciduous forests, on north-facing slopes, containing the best teak stands in terms of quantity and quality; dry upland mixed deciduous forests, on south-facing slopes, containing inferior teak stands; and lowland mixed deciduous forests, on alluvial plains and lower foothills, containing some teak and hardwood associations. Of these subtypes, the last is likely to decline most rapidly, because its lowland location facilitates its increasing conversion to agriculture. Montane forests, including temperate evergreen and hill evergreen forest subtypes, are of commercial value mainly insofar as they supply genetic resources, notably for tropical pine species; moreover, they are generally difficult of access, so they are unlikely to be extensively logged in the foreseeable future. Evergreen forest types contain valuable dipterocarp stands, and other than teak provide the principal source of hardwoods currently harvested in Burma, but stocking densities are much lower than those of the more homogeneous dipterocarp forests of insular Southeast Asia.

By far it is the teak stands that are commercially most valuable. Now that Thailand no longer exports teak, Burma, with at least 75 percent of the world's remaining stands of teak, has a virtual monopoly of international teak markets. To date, however, lack of industrial infrastructure and problems of insurgent activities have not permitted extensive exploitation of the teak resource. Exploitation is still primitive; elephants are more numerous than tractors, skidders, and trucks combined. When logs are floated along the rivers from remote teak forests to Rangoon, a process that can take as long as 2 years, one-third are stolen, mostly by insurgents, for sale in Thailand. In 1977, teak production rose to 331,000 t (in contrast with the 919,000-t output for other hardwood), but exports amounted to only 84,000 t, much below the level of the early 1970s.

Despite its limited scale, forestry contributes more than 25 percent of the country's foreign exchange earnings. This proportion is likely to increase following the signing of an agreement with the Japan International Cooperation Agency for a $4.5 million logging project in the Changta Forest Reserve.

To safeguard its forest resources, the government has established a network of forest reserves, increased slightly in area in 1977 to reach 99,197 km². But many of these reserves are located in territory controlled by insurgents, so they are inadequately policed. Also to safeguard the forests, the Forestry Department has recently established a Forestry Research Institute at Yeizen, to conduct research on forest inventory, yield, management, silviculture, forest biology, conservation, biometrics, and other aspects of forestry.

The principal disruptive factor in the forests appears to be shifting cultivation, especially in the hill areas of the north and northwest. Of 5.7 million people living in hill regions of the five northern states— Kachin, Kayah, Karen, Chin, and Shan—some 2.9 million, or 8.8 percent of the national populace, practice various forms of shifting cultivation, raising rice and vegetables among other main crops. According to the Forestry Department, around 1,420 km² of primary forest are markedly modified if not transformed through shifting cultivation each year (Wint, 1978).

INDIA

India contains 749,000 km² of legally classified forest, or 22 percent of the national territory. Of this area, 570,000 km² have been officially designated as "effective forest zone." But only 260,000 km² can be considered to be adequately stocked forestlands (Champion and Feth, 1968; Persson, 1974; Rao, 1978; Whitmore, 1975, 1976). These remnant forests comprise 21,040 km² of evergreen rainforest, 8,340 of semi-evergreen rainforest, 102,000 of moist deciduous forest, and 138,750 of dry deciduous forest. The wet and moist forests are confined to patches along the Himalayan foothills in Assam, a narrow belt along the western Ghats, and relicts in the Andaman Islands and possibly in the Nicobar as well.

These forests, and especially the various forms of moist forest, are being progressively disrupted and depleted as a result of two principal factors. One is population pressure, notably in the form of landless peasants who encroach on the perimeters of forests. The second is shifting cultivation, which is believed to affect some 80,000–100,000 km². But, according to the Report of the National Commission on Agriculture (1976), "No dependable statistics are available on the magnitude of the problem, *i.e.*, the number of persons and families, and the total area of land, involved." The problem is thought to be most acute in the northeast, where it has caused serious degradation of forests.

According to the National Remote Sensing Agency, the government has been conducting conventional aerial photography and airborne geophysical surveys for the past 10 years. Landsat sensing began, on a research and development basis, in the early 1970s, and was operationally implemented in 1976. Vegetation and bioclimatic maps of the entire country and its natural resources, based on Landsat data, will be available early in 1980.

INDONESIA

Indonesia comprises over 13,000 islands, of which about 3,400 are inhabited, strung out in a 5,000-km chain astride the equator between Asia and Australia. This location gives the country special importance from the standpoint of biogeographic zones by linking two distinctly different continental biota.

Indonesia is reputed to cover 1,905,154 km²—"reputed" because it proves so difficult to make an accurate measurement of the country's area (comprising, as it does, thousands of geographical entities) that official figures offered for national territory vary by as much as 5 percent from the figure given. Similarly, the forest cover is still asserted to amount to 1,220,000 km², though this figure, while cited in Indonesia's Country Report to the World Forestry Congress in Jakarta, October 1978, is derived from 30-year-old assessments. How much forest actually survives in 1979 is apparently unknown, and it is difficult to find any authoritative observer who will hazard a "guesstimate." The best that can be said here is that several major activities—notably shifting cultivation, commercial logging, and transmigrant settlements—have caused marked modification of large tracts of forest, and entirely eliminated several extensive sectors. According to a consensus of responsible and experienced opinion in Indonesia (1975, 1978), the amount of primary forest remaining can now be considered to be well below 1 million km², and probably as little as 850,000 km², conceivably as low as 800,000 km². It is all the more regrettable that adequate data are not available, insofar as one can fairly assume, in broad terms, that Indonesia comprises roughly half of all TMF in Southeast Asia and almost 10 percent of the entire TMF biome.

Forest Types

Within such a vast country, there are substantial variations in climatic patterns. The wettest zones coincide roughly with the Sunda and Sahul continental shelves, while in the center of the archipelago lies a zone of seasonally dry climate (at least in the lowlands), extending from northern Sulawesi and the Moluccas to the Lesser Sunda Islands. In accord with these broad climatic zones, there are significant floristic divisions, with the flora becoming progressively more species-poor eastward and southward before becoming richer again in Irian Jaya. The most important divergence lies in the tendency for dipterocarps to dominate most lowland forest formations in the Sunda region, but to occur only very locally in the Sahul region. (This review is based on Benetahuan, 1974; Chandrasekharan, 1977; Director-General of Forestry of Indonesia, personal communication, 1978; Indonesia Government, 1975, 1978; Kartawinata and Atmawidjaja, 1974; Meijer, 1973, 1975; Sadikin, 1978; Whitmore, 1975, 1976.)

By far the most extensive forest formation is evergreen rainforest, the forest type that is ecologically richest for the scientist and commercially most attractive for the logger. Before the forest-exploitation drive began in the mid-1960s, evergreen rainforest probably accounted for at least three-quarters of Indonesia's forest cover, but now the proportion may have declined markedly, insofar as this forest formation has borne the brunt of Indonesia's forest development efforts, while other formations, *e.g.*, montane forests, have not been nearly so much affected. Semi-evergreen rainforest occurs in intermontane areas of major mountain ranges of Sumatra, and of southeastern Kalimantan and Irian Jaya, and also in the dry central zone of seasonally dry climate. Some montane forest is to be found in the more elevated sectors of Kalimantan and Irian Jaya, while in the latter region there is even some subalpine forest.

Regrettably, there is not even general authoritative information concerning the nature and extent of these forest formations. All that can reasonably be stated here is that of Kalimantan's 539,500 km^2, almost three-quarters are reputed (on the basis of possibly out-of-date statistics) to still feature forest of one sort or another; of Sumatra's 479,500 and Sulawesi's 182,900 km^2, over half; and of Irian Jaya's 421,900 km^2, almost three-quarters. As for land-use classification, production forests, *viz.*, lowland forests suitable and available for timber exploitation, have been designated as occupying 470,000 km^2; while protection forests—*viz.*, forests mainly located in hilly areas of over 500-m elevation, and on slopes of greater than 30 percent, hence less accessible to the logger and important for watershed catchments—are officially stated to total 245,400 km^2. In practice, however, the advent of sophisticated timber-harvesting equipment now allows hill territories and steep terrain to be exploited; in some localities, logging extends to 1,500-m elevations. This means that the legal division between production and protection forests is little observed on the ground.

Including 180,000 km^2 scheduled for early conversion to permanent agriculture (but not counting another 50,000 km^2 scheduled for eventual conversion), the amount of forest that is now officially available for timber exploitation totals 650,000 km^2—or around half of the area that is officially classified as forestland, and probably over three-quarters of forested lands that actually remain.

Shifting Cultivation

One of three major factors contributing to the regression of Indonesia's forests is shifting cultivation. It is believed to be a dominant land-use pattern in most of Kalimantan and Irian Jaya, and frequent but not dominant in Sumatra, Sulawesi, the Lesser Sunda Islands, and the southern fringe of Kalimantan (Whitmore, 1975). At least 12 million people are believed to be involved, not only traditional tribal groups but also landless peasants. Although the cycle of shifting cultivation varies considerably from area to area, it is becoming steadily shorter in all areas, because of population growth and exhaustion of long-used croplands; all too often, the cycle can be maintained for only two rotations at most, after which the cultivator is obliged, due to soil exhaustion and declining crop yields, to move on and break new ground. Most of the forestlands that have been thus degraded by shifting cultivation and by excessive past clearing have now become impoverished secondary types of forest, or have been overtaken by *alangalang* grassland (*Imperata cylindrica*). The best estimates, albeit very rough ones (and this aspect is stressed), suggest that between 280,000 and 370,000 km² of former forest have now been accounted for through shifting cultivation, of which 160,000 km² are considered to be in critical condition. The zone in question is believed to be expanding at an accelerating rate, though regrettably no worthwhile statistics (even order-of-magnitude estimates) are available. The figure frequently advanced in government documents, 2,000 km² each year, is here rejected as a gross underestimate. There is good cause to consider the figure of 12 million shifting cultivators as reasonably credible; this may be said to correspond to at least 1.5 million families. If each family is clearing an additional 1 ha per year, and if only one of these 10 additional ha cleared each year fails to regenerate into forest cover, this trend alone would account for 15,000 km² of forest eliminated each year.

Timber Exploitation

In the mid-1960s, soon after President Suharto came to power, Indonesia decided to increase exploitation of its timber resources. Finding it lacked the finance and technology to do the job itself, it looked to foreign enterprise and capital. The 1966 Investors Incentive Act offered many attractions to overseas corporations, including guaranteed repatriation of investment, tax holidays, duty-free import of equipment and auxiliary goods, accelerated depreciation rates on capital investment, compensation in the event of nationalization, and government financing of some infrastructure development such as aerial surveys and forest roads. The result has been an influx of foreign timber corporations, notably from Japan, the Philippines, Singapore, South Korea, Taiwan, and the United States.

By early 1978, timber corporations had applied for, and had generally taken out, 683 concession agreements (with a total investment of $1.3 billion). These concessions account for approximately 675,000 km², virtually all accessible lowland forests (W. Meijer, personal communication, University of Kentucky, Lexington, 1978), plus some supposedly protection-forest sectors in upland areas. Although the amount actually exploited to date is limited (no authoritative statistics are available on how much, largely because government foresters have to supervise an average area of almost 2,000 km² each), conservative estimates suggest that lowland forests of Sumatra and Sulawesi are likely to have been logged out within 5–10 years, Kalimantan and most of the smaller islands within 10–15 years, and Irian Jaya within 15–20 years. Given that present rates of exploitation could accelerate progressively, these predictions could be shortened. In view of the importance of presenting reliable and responsible estimates of how fast Indonesia's lowland forests may be harvested, the above figures were checked with a variety of experienced observers in Indonesia, and were strongly supported.

Since broad-scale exploitation began, timber exports have boomed. In 1965, Indonesia exported 140,000 m³ of logs, worth $2.8 million; during the 1970s, except for a lapse during the global economic recession of 1975–1976, annual exports have stood at 15–18 million m³ (around two-thirds of all logs cut), and the aim is to reach 20 million by 1980 and 30 million (out of 50 million cut) by 1990. The country's foreign-exchange earnings in 1978 surpassed $1 billion, or 30 percent of all earnings from non-oil exports.

A logger expects to take at least 10–15 trees per ha. Given the disruptive impact of logging practices (Hadi and Suparto, 1977; Inansothy, 1975; Kartawinata and Amadidjaja, 1974; Sumitro, 1976; Suparto et al., 1978; Tinal and Balenewan, 1974), this level of harvest leaves between one-third and two-thirds of the residual forest damaged beyond recovery, and as much as 30 percent of the ground exposed. In these circumstances, there is little prospect of the forest regenerating itself within a harvest cycle of 35 years, which is supposed to allow a forest to be sustained. In order to prevent over-exploitative harvesting, the government requires that a logger cut only trees of 60-cm diameter or more; yet a visit to the log ponds of several major corporations at one of the main export centers, Samarinda in East Kalimantan, revealed that many smaller trees are taken. Some concessions are logged within 4 years, instead of the agreed-upon 20 years; others may last more than 20 years. However, present trends show that more areas have been converted than were originally planned or shown by official sources

(W. Meijer, personal communication, University of Kentucky, Lexington, 1979). Because of insecurity in inflationary money markets, and general political instability, international timber corporations are inclined to go for a cut-and-run operation, sometimes looking no further than 10 years. Thus disruption of primary forest is generally severe, with virtually no effort to rehabilitate the residual forest.

Transmigration Program

Of Indonesia's present population of 142 million, Java supports around 95 million on its 132,470 km² (the size of New York State), only 7 percent of the entire country. This means that the island has an average density of over 700 people per km², by contrast with a density in Kalimantan of less than 10 and in Irian Jaya of only 2. As a measure of the strain that Java's population pressure places on the country's economy, Indonesia imports around 2.6 million t of rice (around 10 percent of its total grain requirements) per year, or roughly one-third of all rice available on world markets.

In order to convey some of the excess numbers from Java (also from the neighboring islands of Madura and Bali) to other parts of the nation, the government has launched a transmigration program (Chambers and Sobur, 1977; Guinness, 1977; Hanson, in press; Hanson and Koesoebiono, 1979; 1978; Mustaffa, 1978; Sobur *et al.*, 1977). The program is especially directed toward 50,000 km² of coastal swamplands in southeastern Sumatra and southern Kalimantan, which are considered to offer potential for tidally irrigated rice cultivation; and toward the lowlands of Central Sulawesi, which are scheduled to receive some 300,000 people during the next 5 years.

The original aim was to move 50,000 families per year from the three overpopulated islands in question. Each family would receive about 5 ha of land, meaning that 2,500 km² of land in the outer islands would be newly settled each year. In the event, only 50,000 families were moved during the entire planning period 1974–1978—a rate of migration that does not remotely keep up with Java's annual population increase of 2,600,000. The present aim is to move between 100,000 and 250,000 families per year, until 2 million families, or 12–15 million people, have been translocated. Under the present program, each settler family receives 1–5 ha of new land, which means that the program will entail settlement of between 20,000 and 100,000 km². However, fair-quality agricultural land of all sorts on the outer islands is believed to account for less than 5 percent of total land area; and most of the best agricultural zones have already been occupied. As a result, many of the transmigrants find themselves obliged to take up a shifting cultivator's life, which amounts to a more extensive mode of using forestlands.

There is no stability, in fact, regarding land-use planning or development direction, which makes it probable at present that much land is being converted into agriculture in some provinces faster than in others. The target is around 42 million ha (420,000 km^2) for conversion to agriculture by the year 2000 to supply food for 250 million people at a level 1.5 times the present (W. Meijer, personal communication, University of Kentucky, Lexington, 1979).

In summary review of these three factors that are ostensibly generating marked impact on Indonesia's primary forests, it can generally be concluded, qualitatively speaking, that the rate of conversion of primary forests must be appreciable, to say the least. But to assert anything further would be premature, until such time as authoritative quantitative information becomes available.

Resource Surveys and Inventories

Fortunately, adequate documentation of Indonesia's forest estate should become available within the near future, as a consequence of several recent survey initiatives. In early 1977, the Indonesia National Institute of Aeronautics and Space started to implement a $60 million, 5-year remote sensing program with the aim of accomplishing integrated resource mapping of the entire country by the end of 1983 (Asmoro et al., 1978; Wiraotmodjo, 1978). At the same time, the National Coordination Agency for Surveys and Mapping has launched a National Resource Survey and Mapping Project, which will provide 1:50,000-scale photographs for the country; the photomaps are to be overprinted with geologic, pedalogic, forestry, agricultural, and land-use and land-capability data. In addition, the Directorate of Forest Planning, through the Food and Agriculture Organization of the United Nations (FAO) and bilateral-agency support, has accumulated 61,000 aerial photographs, allowing land forms to be interpreted for some 295,000 km^2; preliminary results should become available by the end of 1979. Finally, an FAO expert in forest inventorying has been assigned as of early 1979. These various initiatives all mean that Indonesia should be able to present a more accurate and authoritative assessment of its forest resources by 1980.

According to a trial survey over 3,000-km^2 Lombok Island, Indonesia's remote sensing program can achieve detailed inventorying of several vegetation classes, including primary forests, secondary forests, bush and shrublands, coconut plantations, dry ricefields, irrigated ricefields, and water bodies. When checked against ground-truth investigations, classification accuracy (statistical) of the various land categories has ranged from 63 to 93 percent, and the mapping accuracy (positional) from 51 to 93 percent, with classification accuracies of 90 percent for primary forest, 75 percent for secondary forest, and 70 percent for coconut plantations (Kalensky *et al.*, 1978).

Protected Areas

In view of the progressive conversion of its primary forests, Indonesia is planning to increase the amount of forest estate under protected status. The present network of parks and reserves covers about 37,000 km², comprising 166 units that range in size from a 1-ha locality with a single fig tree to over 8,000 km² in the Gunung Leuser Reserve. The government aims to expand this network to a total of 100,000 km² by 1983, and it envisages that most additional parks and reserves will be in forest zones, with a large proportion in Irian Jaya (many of them, however, in poor-grade forestlands). Regrettably, many of the present protected areas amount to little more than "paper parks." Over half of the 166 units are game reserves, in which wildlife is theoretically protected, but "management of the forests" (in reality, exploitation of timber) is permitted. The rest are nature reserves, fully protected by law, but, as in the case of game reserves, often sites of much logging and shifting cultivation. For example, two-thirds of the Kutai Reserve's 3,000 km² have been logged or otherwise disturbed.

On a more positive side, a number of recent measures offer hope for a new era in Indonesia's forestry and conservation efforts. The Third National Development Plan 1979–1983 includes four major forestry programs: formulation of regional sector plans, based on evaluation of land-use capabilities and resource inventories; conservation of soil, water, and wildlife; improvement of forest exploitation, including timber production, and forestland management for multiple use and reforestation; and agroforestry initiatives, to meet village energy needs and to coordinate community forestry with transmigration schemes. Even if only a part of these programs is implemented, this will represent an advance over the past, when planning has scarcely looked in these directions. Moreover, signs of a new approach can be detected in several substantive moves since mid-1978: Parliament has established a National Environment Policy, under which "the exploitation of natural resources must be conducted in a comprehensive manner so that the human environment is not damaged and future generations are accounted for.'' The new government agency responsible for this mandate, the Ministry of Environment and Development Control, is headed by Dr. Emil Salim, a University of California-trained man who has direct access to President Suharto. In addition, the Directorate of Nature Conservation and Wildlife Management may be upgraded, its budget has been increased to $2.4 million a year, and it is now headed by Mr. Lukito Darjadi, who demonstrated his capacities when organizing the World Forestry Congress in Jakarta in October 1978.

KAMPUCHEA (CAMBODIA)

According to an inventory undertaken by the U.S. Agency for International Development (AID) in 1960–1962, the forest area of Kampuchea (formerly known as Cambodia) then amounted to 131,735 km², or 73 percent of national territory. Of this forest cover, 96,000 km² could be considered to be commercially exploitable (Persson, 1974). A partial survey a few years later put the forest cover at only 87,249 km² (Williams, 1965). Regrettably, no further statistical estimates have been attempted. All that can be reasonably said here is that some 40 percent of the forest cover is probably made up of deciduous monsoon forest, including dry dipterocarp forest, in the plains of the north (where they undergo extensive burning during the lengthy dry period); and about 30 percent is made up of hill evergreen rainforest, located in the southern uplands and along the Annamite Chain in the east.

Like the other countries of former Indochina, Kampuchea's forests have experienced much modification over a period of many centuries, until little of the present forest cover can be characterized as primary forest (Bethel and Turnbull, 1974; Cliff, 1966; Dwyer Mission, 1966; Kernan, 1968; McNeely, 1978; Nuttonson, 1963; Rollet, 1962; Wharton, 1966, 1968; Williams, 1965).

Beyond these general statements, it seems that nothing substantive can be said about Kampuchea's forests.

LAOS

In 1965, approximately 160,520 km² of Laos' 236,328 km² were officially classified as forests (Williams, 1965). At various stages in the 1970s, the government has asserted that 140,000 km² are still forested—some 40 percent at altitudes between 500 and 1,000 m, and some 40 percent above 1,000 m (McNeely, 1978; Persson, 1974). Evergreen forests, both lowland and hill forests, are considered to cover 27,000 km²; they are found in the moister parts of the Annamite Chain, and especially in the Sekong Valley bordering the Bolovens Plateau, together with a few patches along the Mekong River. Deciduous forests—including, at elevations between 700 and 1,000 m, some 700 km² of good teak forests—are considered to cover 80,000 km²; they are mainly located in the south around Pakse, and in much of the area between Vientiane and the Burmese border. Mixed deciduous forests, scattered in various localities, are estimated to cover 20,000 km². In addition, pine forests, typically found on sandy soils at elevations of 600–1,400 m, are believed to cover 10,000 km². Finally, bamboo forests amount to roughly 6,000 km².

However, a number of observers state that a large proportion of these officially designated forestlands are not good-quality forests (Bethel and Turnbull, 1974; McNeely, 1978; Nuttonson, 1963; Wharton, 1968; Williams, 1965). Much of the closed high forest has been degraded to open woodlands and even to bush growth. In the higher elevations of the northern part of the country, hill evergreen forest, *i.e.*, above 1,000 m, has been replaced by grassland as a consequence of soil exhaustion on the part of maize- and opium-growing hill tribes. Pine forests, which used to cover much of the Plain of Jars, have been grossly reduced through military activity, and this entire subtype may now amount to only 3,000 km² (Mekong Committee, 1978). A recent satellite/aerial photography survey map (Mekong Committee, 1978) indicates that forest cover is now well below the 60 percent of national territory officially cited by the Forest Department, and may well approximate to no more than 40 percent. A recent U.N. Development Program/U.N. Industrial Development Organization (UNDP/UNIDO) report (1977) estimates that well-stocked forest totals only 46,000 km² at most.

A major factor in the status of the country's forests has been the long-established role of the subsistence forest farmer. As many as 3 million of the country's 3.5 million people depend on subsistence agriculture of various sorts; and of these, at least 1 million are hill-dwelling farmers who practice shifting cultivation in forestlands, often on steep terrain. Not surprisingly, few forest lands remain that have not been markedly affected by shifting cultivation at some time in their past. Not only do cultivators clear patches of forest, but they set fires that subsequently run out of control; and it is wildfires that have accounted for extensive destruction of primary forests, especially in the drier zones. Of today's forests, shifting cultivators are reputed to till at least 7,500 km² at any one time, and to maintain 72,500 km² under ever shortening

TABLE 6 Malaysia Land Classification, 1977 (km²)

Land Category	Peninsular Malaysia	Sarawak	Sabah	Total
Total land area	132,343	124,190	71,129	327,662
Forest already converted to agriculture and other development purposes (urban areas, etc.)	57,216	17,103	9,341	83,660
Remaining forest	72,153	97,087	61,488	230,728
Logged-over forest and forest disturbed by shifting agriculture	34,484	34,426–41,400	26,967–30,500	95,877–106,372
Undisturbed forest	37,669	55,687–62,661	31,000–34,521	124,356–134,851
Forest scheduled for eventual conversion to agriculture	21,080	26,885	20,805	68,770

NOTE: The statistics for peninsular Malaysia can be considered accurate within 5 percent; those for Sarawak and Sabah are less, possibly much less, reliable.

SOURCE: Government of Malaysia, 1976, 1978; forestry authorities' personal communications, 1978.

cycles of fallow. Through this overexploitative pattern of shifting cultivation, some 3,000 km² of forest are estimated to be destroyed each
year (Persson, 1974; UNDP/UNIDO, 1977).

In addition to the pervasive role of shifting cultivation, Laos' forests
have been depleted by unduly wasteful logging operations during the
course of many decades, especially in the lowland evergreen and upland teak forests.

Clearly, however, little substantive data, particularly quantitative
data, exist concerning the present status of Laos' forests.

MALAYSIA

Malaysia, 327,662 km², consists of three parts: the peninsula, 132,343
km²; Sarawak, 124,190 km²; and Sabah, 71,129 km². Of the peninsula,
72,000 km², or 54 percent of total land area, were still forested in late
1977; of Sarawak, 97,087 km², or 78 percent; and of Sabah, 61,488 km²,
or 86 percent (Table 6).

The peninsula, or western Malaysia, comprises 11 states of the original federation before the secession of Singapore and the accession of
Sarawak and Sabah, the latter two states now known as eastern Malaysia; the states of the peninsula, while enjoying considerable local auton-
omy, coordinate with the Federal Department of Forestry in Kuala
Lumpur, whereas Sarawak and Sabah have their own Departments of
Forestry. Marked ecological divergences exist between the peninsula
and the off-shore states. In addition, the peninsula has established itself as the world's leading exporter of processed tropical hardwoods,
whereas Sarawak and Sabah follow the pattern of most TMF countries
in that they still export mostly raw logs; thus the forest economies of
western and eastern Malaysia differ markedly. The three sectors of the
federation are considered separately.

Peninsular Malaysia

The forest economy of peninsular Malaysia is more developed than that
of virtually any other TMF country. Because of this degree of development, the forests have been documented in detail and the base data are
maintained through tri-monthly returns from each of the states to the
Department of Forestry in Kuala Lumpur. This practice allows up-to-
date information to be made available on forest extent and status
for the peninsula as a whole and for each of the states (Tables 6
and 7)—information that, according to a variety of authorities, can be

TABLE 7 Forest Distribution in Peninsular Malaysia by States, 1977 (km²)

State	Land Area	Total Forest-land	Proposed Permanent Forest Estate (under federal government)	Unproductive Permanent Forest Estate (safeguarded for water-shed needs)	Productive Permanent Forest Estate			Stateland Forests		
					Undis-turbed Forest	Logged-Over Forest	Total	Undis-turbed Forest	Logged-Over Forest	Total
Pahang	35,950	27,210	15,443	5,635	2,785	7,023	9,808	4,487	7,280	11,767
Kalantan	14,925	11,112	8,980	3,795	1,963	3,222	5,185	1,066	1,066	2,132
Perak	20,996	10,335	10,135	4,919	2,764	2,452	5,216	—	200	200
Tengganu	12,950	8,806	5,788	1,958	1,292	2,538	3,830	—	3,018	3,018
Johore	19,786	5,289	4,164	173	2,197	1,794	3,991	90	1,035	1,125
Kadak/P. Pinang	10,454	3,994	3,784	1,501	874	1,409	2,283	—	210	210
Others	17,282	5,407	3,850	1,220	855	1,775	2,630	95	1,462	1,557
TOTALS	132,343	72,153ᵃ	52,144	19,201	12,730	20,213	32,943	5,738	14,271	20,009

[a] Reduced from 83,000 km² documented by the National Forest Inventory of 1972. This represents an average decline of almost 2.67 percent per year, to be compared with a current rate of 3.95 percent.

NOTE: These figures can be considered accurate within 2½ percent.

SOURCE: Government of Malaysia, 1978; forestry authorities' personal communications, 1978.

considered reputable. This statistical background makes it possible to analyze the situation here in reliable detail.

The vegetation of peninsular Malaysia typifies evergreen, dipterocarp-dominated rainforest. (This analysis is drawn from Aiken and Moss, 1975; Chandrasekharan, 1976; Daniel and Kulasingam, 1974; Economic Commission for Asia and the Far East, 1975; Government of Malaysia, 1976, 1978; Nor and Tang, 1973; Rahman, 1976; Singh, 1973; Soepadmo and Singh, 1973; Whitmore, 1975, 1978; Yong Hoi-Sen, 1979; author's observations, 1976, 1978.) The forests are probably complex and species-rich with exceptionally diverse flora and fauna. Local forest variants occur only in three areas: in the northwestern sector of the peninsula, where an ecotonal forest type merges into the semi-evergreen forests of Thailand; along coasts and rivers where mangrove and peatswamp forests flourish; and in localities where edaphic and topographic factors give rise to, *e.g.*, heath forests, limestone subtypes, and forests on ultrabasic soils.

At the time of independence in 1957, 74 percent of the peninsula, or almost 100,000 km² of 132,343 km², was forested. By 1971, this proportion had fallen to 61 percent; and by 1977, to less than 55 percent—of which only a little over half can be considered to be undisturbed forest. The depletion has been primarily due to timber harvesting. In particular, and because of their commercial value, the peninsula's lowland evergreen rainforests have been heavily exploited for at least two decades, until almost half of them have now been logged. In addition, a number of multi-use development projects, notably the Jengka Triangle, Phang Tenggara, and Johore Tenggara, have excised substantial blocks. Of other forest types, hill forests on the western side of the peninsula have been exploited, and those on the eastern side are now undergoing logging after being made accessible by a new road across the Main Range near the Thai border. Heath forests have been selectively logged, whereupon they show little potential for regeneration due to their sclerophyllous species and their nutrient- and moisture-poor soils; instead they degrade to *padang* or savannah. (Unlike virtually any other major areas of Southeast Asia, shifting cultivation and forest farming are not a factor in peninsular Malaysia. In fact, the amount of forest believed to have been eliminated through this cause is put at a mere 160 km² [Jamil, 1978]).

Timber Exploitation   As mentioned, peninsular Malaysia has gone far to develop its forest industries. Between 1967 and 1973, log output more than doubled, and some 85 percent of the timber is now processed before export. In 1976, exports totalled 3.2 million m³ worth $370 million.

This volume of timber harvesting has had a marked effect on the lowland forests, some 34,500 km² of which have now been logged. All timber extraction is carried out by contractors, most of them small-scale operators. During the 1960s, when agricultural clearing operations started to accelerate, a large number of operators became active, who, because of their limited capital investment, were primarily concerned with rapid redemption of their mortgaged equipment. As a result, and despite Department of Forestry's controls, logging operations have tended to be wasteful: according to the Department of Forestry's *Economic Bulletin* for August 1976, logging residues rise as high as 2.8 million m³ per year, with a potential export value of $50 million.

Much of the problem lies with the fact that forestry development in Malaysia is not the responsibility of the federal government. Rather, it rests with state governments. The states tend to view forests as a residual resource or a "capital bank" through which they can finance various forms of socioeconomic development. So in state forests, which comprise 3.8 percent of timber-producing forests, logging regulations are more liberal and less strictly applied than in federal forest reserves. The result has been an outburst of little-planned and uncontrolled forest exploitation. Parallel with this trend has been an urge to excise more and more undisturbed forest for permanent agriculture, the agricultural program being used as an excuse to liquidate amounts of forest capital that are far in excess of what is required to meet strictly agricultural needs. The consequence is that forestry authorities at all levels are not able to plan development strategies for sustainable exploitation, since forestlands can be excised at virtually no notice for alternative forms of land use; in many instances, forest areas that have been successfully regenerated, or even subject to enrichment planting, have been summarily assigned to nonforestry purposes.

Agricultural Development   The federal government is committed to a major program of agricultural development. According to the Economic Planning Unit under the Prime Minister's Office, agriculture now generates around 1 million jobs for the peninsula's populace of 10 million people, whereas forestry provides only 30,000 jobs. So from the standpoint of employment—a politically important issue in virtually any developing nation—agriculture can be construed as a more "worthy" form of land use than timber-producing forestry, even though the long-term economic returns and environmental benefits of forestry may be competitive.

Agriculture has already claimed 29,000 km², or 22 percent, of the peninsula. Another 20,000 km² are scheduled, under the Land Capability Classification system, for eventual conversion, 13,000 of them within the next few years (3,000 km² in Tengganu, 2,700 in Pahang, 1,800 in Johore, and 1,200 in Perak). The principal form of permanent agriculture envisaged is rubber and oil-palm plantations.

This means that 37 percent of the peninsula's land area, and around 35 percent of the original forests, have been adjudged to be suitable for ultimate conversion to agriculture and agro-industries. Since agricultural development is best accomplished in lowlands, most of the remaining lowland evergreen rainforests are likely to be steadily eliminated within the next two decades and conceivably within just one more decade. In fact, the only remnant patches of lowland forest to survive will almost certainly be limited to parks and reserves, which, according to present estimates, are not likely to exceed the 6,044 km² already established and a further 3,000 km² envisaged. In short, the 52,000-km² permanent forest estate will consist almost entirely of hill forest.

Under the present program for agricultural development, as detailed in the Third Malaysia Plan 1976–1980, the rate of conversion is set at roughly 570 km² per year. The actual rate of forest clearing in proposed agricultural lands during the past 5 years, however, has averaged 2,850 km² per year, far beyond the amount that can be usefully absorbed by agriculture—and representing an annual decline in the total forest estate of almost 4 percent. This rate has arisen because of the attitude of the states toward forests as capital resources, to be liquidated in the "broader interests" of their overall economies.

Present Status and Future Prospects of the Peninsula's Forests   Within the past year, the Department of Forestry has recognized that prevailing exploitation patterns for the peninsula's forestlands are likely to exhaust the available forest resource within a decade at most (Government of Malaysia, 1978). As indicated above, the amount of forestland considered suitable for conversion to permanent agriculture and agro-industries amounts to just over 20,000 km², of a present forest estate of 72,000 km². The remaining forestlands, currently considered unsuitable for sustained agriculture, will be assigned to a permanent forest estate of almost 52,000 km², or 39 percent of the peninsula's land area.

Not all this permanent forest estate will be given over to productive forestry. Because of environmental and biological factors—for example, the need to conserve water catchments, and to protect rare fauna and flora—at least 19,000 km² of the permanent forest estate will consist of "unproductive forests," notably forests in montane areas and in broken country, and on steep terrain and on other adverse sites where timber cannot be economically harvested. This means that timber harvesting will be limited to "productive forests" within the permanent forest estate, amounting to almost 33,000 km². Of this area, however, 20,200 km² have already been partially or fully harvested, and of this only about 12,100 km² can be reharvested (or subjected to salvage felling); the remaining 8,100 km² require special management, including silvicultural treatment, to restore their timber-producing potential, or almost 4 times as much as has been so treated in the past 21 years.

During the years 1971–1976, 22,250 km² of forest have been opened for logging and conversion to agriculture—the great majority, 16,600 km², in state lands. In 1977 and 1978, the average rate of harvesting and clearing has risen to 4,400 km² per year. Forests that are considered to be loggable within the foreseeable future amount to 12,100 km² of reharvestable forest, 12,730 km² of undisturbed forest in the productive permanent forest estate, and some 13,000 km² of forest scheduled for conversion to agriculture within the next few years, or a total of 37,830 km². In other words, the peninsula will not be able to maintain the present level of exploitation without exhausting its available forest resources within less than 10 years.

This all means that, as Mr. Datuk M. Mohamed, Deputy Prime Minister and Chairman of the National Forestry Council, has pointed out, peninsular Malaysia could face a serious shortage of timber by the end of the 1980s. To meet domestic consumption needs of 1990, let alone to supply the forestry industrial capacity that has already been established, peninsular Malaysia may have to import virtually as much timber as it is now exporting. By contrast, a longer-sighted policy for the peninsula's forests postulates that the exploitation rate be reduced from a 1970s average of 3,880 km² per year to 550 km². Under this alternative strategy, the forest resource would be liquidated only when it was absolutely required for agricultural development, thereby prolonging the flow of timber until well into the next century.

Sarawak

With a land area of 124,190 km², Sarawak still possesses 97,087 km² of forest of one sort or another, amounting to 78 percent of the state's territory (Table 6) (Government of Malaysia, 1976; Whitmore, 1975, 1976). At least, this is the situation as revealed by official statistics. But according to a range of experienced observers, much of the remaining forest cover has been disturbed to varying degree, and the amount of primary forest remaining can be considered to be rather less than the officially declared amount, 62,661 km².

Throughout most of the interior, typical vegetation is lowland evergreen dipterocarp rainforest. Until the early 1970s, this forest formation covered around 62,000 km². How much remains in undisturbed form following the rapid expansion of logging in recent years is not known with accuracy; but several workers who have years of experience in the area report that the primary forest cover has been much reduced. Along the eastern boundary of Sarawak, running north-south, is a narrow belt of montane rainforest, covering about 10,000 km²; above 450-m elevation, dipterocarps tend to decrease until they disappear altogether above 1,200 m where they are replaced by conifers, oaks, and chestnuts. Although the state's topography tends to be rugged, hills are low-lying for the most part, and true hill forests amount to only a little over 10,000 km². Other forest types include peatswamp, formerly covering almost 13,000 km² but now markedly modified for the most part following exploitation; and a few patches of mangrove forest survive along the coast.

Forests rank second only to petroleum as a major source of foreign exchange. In 1977, log production reached 4,883,000 m³, of which exports accounted for 3,470,000 m³ (together with 231,600 m⁸ of sawn wood) worth $203 million. These export earnings amounted to around 16 percent of the state's total export revenues.

To sustain this forest economy, 31,080 km² have been constituted as permanent forests, to be managed by the Department of Forestry for timber production and environmental protection. However, the forest estate is declining in both quantity and quality, mainly due to over-exploitative timber harvesting on the part of legitimate forestry enterprises and a growing number of illegal fellers, and to a large community of shifting cultivators. In fact, some authorities believe that as many as half of the total populace of 1.25 million persons are engaged in shifting cultivation, accounting for some 26,400 km² or 21 percent of the state's land area. Logged-over forest, according to official statistics, amounts to 8,026 km²; but recent reliable reports suggest the amount could be twice as much, and expanding rapidly. If one assumes that the area of logged-over forest amounts to some 15,000 km², and adds this to the area of shifting cultivation, the total amount of disturbed forest can be put at 41,400 km², which leaves undisturbed forest to total 55,687 km² (and even this calculation can be considered conservative). Crude as these reckonings may be, and dependent as they are upon a range of sources of varying reliability, they are advanced solely in order to gain a "working idea" of the current forest situation in Sarawak. As a further measure of exploitation patterns and trends, the licensing system for timber harvesting has been recently removed from the Department of Forestry and placed with the Office of the Prime Minister; by mid-1979, virtually all lowland rainforest had been given out to timber concessionaires. Timber extraction is often carried out carelessly, leaving the residual forest unnecessarily damaged, and often effectively eliminated as an economic entity for future logging.

According to a Land Capability Classification survey, a large portion of Sarawak is considered suitable for conversion to permanent agriculture, in fact 26,885 km² or almost 28 percent of the state's land area. How this vast territory is to be exploited for agriculture is not made clear; the most likely possibility that one can envisage is an influx of foreign capital and technology, through multinational corporations, in order to implement large-scale, extensive agricultural enterprises. At all events, only minor patches of forest have so far been taken for permanent agriculture. These agricultural plans, however, in conjunction with the stepped-up rate of timber exploitation, incline the observer to the conclusion that Sarawak will not hesitate to engage in widespread exploitation of its forests and forestlands, possibly beyond the capacity of the forests to sustain their present composition and well-being.

Sabah

Of Sabah's 71,129 km², 61,488 km² or 86 percent are reputed to be still under forest cover of one type or another, albeit with varying degrees of disruption in large areas (Fox, 1972; Meijer, 1970; Whitmore, 1975, 1976; the Forest Research Center Sandakan, Sabah Forest Development Authority, reputable observers, personal communications). At least, these figures represent the situation as documented by official statistics. The degree of authenticity that can be attributed to these data, and the reservations that the reader might prudently hold, are much the same as for Sarawak.

Although Sabah's vegetation is becoming better known, not much has been published on the various forest formations. Indeed, only fragmentary accounts have been published of the various forest formations. It seems probable, however, that until recent times much of the state was covered with evergreen rainforest, of a kind that was exceptionally imposing in stature, though slightly less rich in species than similar forests in peninsular Malaysia and Sumatra (Whitmore, 1975). The last large remaining patch of this exceptional forest type is now confined to the east coast, where it is being rapidly exploited for timber. In other sectors of the east coast, especially in areas of seasonally dry climate, a few patches of semi-evergreen rainforest may be found. In several lowland localities, forests on ultrabasic soils are widespread, also in a few montane areas such as Kinabalu; in certain circumstances, this forest type appears similar to lowland evergreen rainforest, while in other areas the structure and flora of the forest community are distinctively diverse (Whitmore, 1975). The forests of the west coast have already been widely logged, or replaced by shifting cultivation. Statewide, at least 44 percent of the forests—some observers say 50 percent or more—have been disturbed by logging, and more predominantly, by agricultural development and shifting cultivation.

The timber industry is central to Sabah's economy. It contributes around 50 percent of the GNP, and 55 percent of export earnings (of which raw logs constitute 98 percent). Timber production in 1977 reached almost 12 million m³, with exports earning $440 million. Yet despite the exceptional importance of the forestry industry in the state's economy, the system of forest reserves includes only 23,857 km² as commercial forest and 4,720 km² as protection forest, a total of 28,577 km² that amounts to only 46 percent of the state's remaining forests. Moreover, 20,805 km² of forest are considered to offer agricultural potential, and are scheduled for eventual conversion to agriculture and agro-industry; and over 7,000 km² of these conversion-scheduled forestlands are located within the forest reserves. Since Sabah's human populace, not yet 1 million, cannot supply the agrarian skills necessary to undertake permanent agriculture on such extensive scale, the development will be conducted by joint ventures (entailing foreign capital and expertise) in conjunction with local entrepreneurs. Many forestlands have already been opened up for cocoa and palm-oil plantations.

Sabah's policy with respect to its forests was formerly to manage the resource on a 80–100-year rotation, producing a harvest while sustaining the forest through a few outsize long-term timber concessions. This policy has recently been changed, and now the forests are being rapidly felled with the aim of maximizing immediate revenues. So accelerated has the rate of forest harvesting become that timber exports are earning a per capita income of $500 per year for each of the state's 920,000 citizens (Pringle, 1976). In point of fact, each of the 311,682 shareholders of the Sabah People's Trust received a 1978 dividend of $40, payable from net profits of log sales deriving from 8,540 km² of forest vested for 100 years in the organization known as the Sabah Forest Foundation, whose gross sales are currently estimated at about $50 million per year. But a number of experienced observers suggest that the present speeded-up rate of harvest may exhaust Sabah's exploitable lowland forests within only another 5 years.

As a partial gesture to offset this somewhat overexploitative approach to its forest resource, Sabah is undertaking two new initiatives. First, it is progressively reducing log exports by 50 percent between 1976 and 1981, in order to foster local processing and forest industries. Secondly, the state is aiming to restore tree cover to 11,750 km² of former forestlands that have been denuded or reduced to grassland through shifting cultivation. But the present commitment calls for a tree planting schedule of only 80 km² per year.

MELANESIA

Melanesia comprises several groups of islands, of which the major ones are Fiji, New Caledonia, New Hebrides, and the Solomon Islands. In climatic terms, virtually the whole area is suited to forest growth, especially evergreen rainforest (though the forest structure is less lofty than in Malaysia, and biomass is lower). Indeed it is probable that before the arrival of man, forest covered the whole of Melanesia except for certain ultrabasic localities in New Caledonia and the Solomon Islands, and the environs of active volcanoes (Schmid, 1978). Hence the name Melanesia, a word of Greek derivation meaning dark islands, probably referring to the aspect as seen by sea of a dark green rainforest mantle.

New Caledonia, 19,103 km², contains 16,000 km² of forests of one sort and another, according to the Forestry Department. But only 10 percent of the territory can be considered to feature relatively undisturbed rainforest (Thomson and Adloff, 1971), and many authorities agree that the other forests, virtually all secondary, degraded forest, are receding rapidly, as a result of bushfires, overexploitative harvesting of timber, and mineral extraction. Indeed, the Forestry Department believes that only 15 percent of the total forest cover can be classified as good timber stands; almost half the forestlands are classified as *Melaleucea* savannah woodlands.

Insofar as timber production meets only about one-third of domestic needs, there is obviously incentive to increase the rate of timber extraction. However, the official policy seems to be to forego a sustainable harvest (one that would allow the forest to maintain its current condition), in favor of a once-and-for-all liquidation of the forest capital. As a result, "it is estimated that the high forest resource will be exhausted in 30–40 years' time" (Thomson and Adloff, 1971).

This impoverishment and depletion of New Caledonia's forest cover is especially regrettable since the islands are remarkable for the distinctiveness of their flora, which demonstrates affinities with Australia, New Zealand, and New Guinea. From this standpoint, New Caledonia is much more fortunate than the other islands of Melanesia, which, by comparison, are markedly impoverished. Of New Caledonia's 3,000 plant species, around 80 percent are endemic; and like that of Madagascar, the flora contains high concentrations of primitive species that could be useful for basic biological research into evolutionary processes.

Fiji, 18,380 km², possesses, according to a 1966–1969 aerial-photography inventory plus a 45 percent enumeration of timber stocks, around 8,000 km² of forest (Berry and Howard, 1973; British Overseas Development Administration, 1970; Government of Fiji, 1977; Lembke, 1971; Oram, 1971; Overgaard, 1975; Routley and Routley, 1977). Most of the rainforests are concentrated on the southeastern sides of the islands, *i.e.*, those that are exposed to the southeast trade winds. Northwestern sectors are characterized by dry forests, savannahs, and grasslands. In upland zones, reaching as high as 1,735 m, there is some montane rainforest. Of this total forest estate, some 2,530 km² are classified as production forests, notably on the eastern half of Viti Levu, over much of Vanu Levu, and in montane areas of Kandavu Island (almost 500 km² have already been logged out); some 2,500 km² are classified as protection forests, and around 2,300 km² as noncommercial forests. Forest reserves comprise only 180 km², the greater part of the forest estate being commonly owned by *Mataqualis* (extended families). Around one-quarter of all these forests are considered to be secondary forests, due to the long-standing effects of shifting cultivation. However, shifting cultivators are now being absorbed into the sugarcane industry and other sectors of modernized agriculture.

Forestry's contribution to the economy, while modest to date, is growing. Between 1970 and 1975, exports of sawn wood and veneer increased 5.6 times. However, official policy seems to be to regard the natural forests as a resource to be mined. According to the Conservator of Forests, A. K. Oram (1971), "The balance of advantage would appear to be strongly in favour of felling and selling as much timber as possible. If it were possible to do so efficiently, it is arguable that it would be desirable to fell all of the natural timber over, say, the next five years." Since a strategy of that sort is practically impossible, a compromise approach lies in spreading out the liquidation of the indigenous forests over the next 20–30 years—and, to this end, all major forest areas have been allocated to timber concessionaires. Thus "the policy now is to regard the natural forest as a wasting resource, and to plan to meet requirements from plantations" (Routley and Routley, 1977; see also Lembke, 1971). True, the plantation program is extensive, with 100 km² of hardwoods (principally mahogany) established by 1970, and 240 km² of pines established by 1975. The pine component of the plantation program will be expanded by 40 km² per year, until a total of 750 km² has been established, by which time it is hoped that plantations will generate export earnings 10 times greater than the current level for all forest products. In view of this plantation strategy, no attempt is being made to regenerate the original forests.

The Solomon Islands, 29,824 km², contain about 23,000 km² of forest (Hansell and Wall, 1976; Hoyle, 1978; Whitmore, 1966). The predominant formation is lowland evergreen rainforest. Only the north coast of Guadalcanal, being in the rain shadow of the Tavo Range, is seasonally dry, with some gallery forests, savannah forests, and grassland. Despite the very wet climate (around 6,000 mm of rainfall per year), the forest communities are poor in species, with little regional differentiation within the archipelago, and little local endemism.

How far the lowland rainforest can be described as primary forest is an open question. Disturbance, whether by man or by earthquakes and cyclones, seems to be the preeminent factor determining different floristic types of lowland rainforests. A cyclone that hit Santa Isabel Island in 1972 caused gross injury to 329 km² of forest, from which the residual stand is not likely to regenerate within less than 50–100 years.

Since most of the forests are located in very steep and rugged terrain, only 4,000 km² are considered suitable for commercial forestry. Furthermore, over half of this tract was extensively damaged in 1972 when a cyclone struck Santa Isabel. Forestry concessions now cover a little over 1,000 km² of forests, producing 263,200 m³ of logs in 1976, almost all of which were exported to Japan. A review of forestry policy suggests that "tracts currently under commercial exploitation will last about 10 years, and in other areas will last a further 20–30 years in all. . . . The present cutting program will consume all the known resource in 30 years, i.e., by the end of the century" (Lembke, 1970). "Extensive operations in the rainforests are expected to consume the known timber resource in 20–30 years" (Routley and Routley, 1977). Already a number of small islands have been clear-felled, and the island of Gizo is threatened with similar treatment, despite the existence of an endemic bird, the Gizo White-eye (*Zosterops luteirostrosis*).

The New Hebrides, 11,860 km², are mostly covered with dense tropical rainforest (Hoyle, 1978; Marshall, 1978). However, the forests are considered to be largely subclimax by tropical standards, as a consequence of cyclones that cause extensive and severe damage every few decades. An additional disruptive factor lies with forest farming—the indigenous population was formerly dense. As a consequence of these twin factors, the lowland forests are now interspersed with scrub and grassy patches. The only extensive high forest, dominated by *Agathis obtusa*, on southeast Erromango Island, has been mostly logged, though in the southwestern and northern sectors of the island, fairly dense forests remain, as on the southern slopes of Mount William. Furthermore, much of the forest is being cleared for cattle raising, especially on Efate.

For reasons not readily discernible, the flora of the New Hebrides is markedly poorer than that of the Solomon Islands, with little generic endemism.

PAPUA NEW GUINEA

Of Papua New Guinea's 463,650 km², around 400,000 km², or around 86 percent, are still covered with forest (Crocombe and Hide, 1971; Diamond, 1978; M. J. Gardner, personal communication, Office of Forests, Boroko, Papua New Guinea, 1979; Government of Papua New Guinea, 1977, 1978; Haantjens, 1975; Lamb, 1977, 1980; Lembke, 1974; McIntosh, 1973; Paijmans, 1975, 1976; Ryan, 1972; Specht *et al.*, 1974; Webb, 1977b; White, 1973, 1976; Whitmore, 1975, 1976; Winslow, 1977; Womersley and McAdam, 1957). This means that the country contains about 22 percent of the closed forest area of the four main countries of Southeast Asia, the other three being Indonesia, Malaysia, and the Philippines.

It is only recently that wide-scale accounts of the country's vegetation have been made—and even these are inconsistent of nomenclature of forest formations. In brief, one can say that, although Papua New Guinea lies wholly within the tropics, its vegetation formations are of unusually wide variety, due mainly to its domination by a central cordillera that extends 2,400 km and rises in places to more than 4,500 m in altitude. So far as can be ascertained, only 44 percent of the country's forests are at elevations lower than 300 m, while almost 40 percent occur between 300 and 1,500 m, and the rest at still higher elevations. Not surprisingly, then, forest types range from lowland evergreen rainforest to montane and subalpine ecotypes; the country's Office of Forests recognizes seven distinct forest systems. Evergreen rainforests—which, unlike those of the Sunda Shelf region, include few or no dipterocarp stands—are widespread in both the lowlands and at elevations up to 800 m; in many localities, these evergreen rainforests are interspersed with semi-evergreen rainforests, the two subtypes being difficult to distinguish because of local rain-shadow effects that cause much complex interdigitation. The country also contains sizable tracts of seasonally dry monsoon forest that, in the driest territories, phase into savannah woodlands; these monsoon forests occur in both lowland and upland zones, notably in the southwest close to the Irian Jaya border, along parts of the southern coastal zone, and in the intermontane valleys of the central cordillera. As would be expected for a country that features the largest mountains of Southeast Asia, montane forest types include lower montane, upper montane, and subalpine forest formations.

Disturbance of Forests

Papua New Guinea's forests have been much disturbed, especially those below 1,000 m. Natural disruptions come in many forms: periodic severe droughts, volcanoes, wildfires, landslides, shifting drainage patterns, and typhoons, all of which phenomena contribute to the present situation where undisturbed climax rainforest, in its strict sense, is relatively rare.

However, a more important contribution to the generally disturbed nature of these forests derives from human activity. The country contains only 3 million people, making it the least densely populated country of Southeast Asia; but at least half the populace appears to make its living through shifting cultivation, so signs of human intervention are to be found in most parts of the country. True, almost 40 percent of the populace lives in intermontane valleys between 1,400 and 2,600 m in altitude at densities of 200 persons per km^2, and a few other concentrations are scattered along the coastlines, which means that in the remainder of the country human density does not rise above one person per km^6. But shifting cultivation is widespread and is believed to have been by far the main factor in disruption of Papua New Guinea's primary forests. According to Whitmore, 1975, citing White, 1973, "A great deal of the New Guinea lowland and lower montane rainforest, and perhaps most of it . . . shows signs of disturbance by man." Indeed, there seems little doubt that much montane forest between 1,500- and 2,600-m altitude has been eliminated by shifting cultivation. (Above the upper limit, conditions become too cold for human settlement. Below that limit, much of the forest cover has been disturbed and depleted.) As an associated factor, man-caused fire—especially fire set by shifting cultivators that then runs out of control—is responsible for much avoidable burning of primary forest: Fire reduces primary forest to secondary woody vegetation, and thereafter, through repeated burnings, to degraded secondary woody vegetation, until eventually it is converted into grassland, a formation that is maintained by fire. As a result of this process, extensive tracts of former forest have apparently been converted to savannah woodlands and grassland (in many localities, fire is believed to determine the tree line). Without man's intervention, savannah woodlands and grasslands, apparently derived from dry evergreen, semi-evergreen, and deciduous forests, would probably be rare vegetation types in the country, instead of covering some 15 percent (Haantjens, 1975).

In many places, of course, densities of shifting-cultivator communities are still so low that fallow periods suffice to allow the forest to regenerate without long-term injury. In many localities, however, densities have increased to a point where fallow periods are becoming concentrated, whereupon forest ecosystems sustain irreversible damage. Many authorities who have studied the subject believe that at least 40 percent of Papua New Guinea's forests bear the imprint of human interference; and there seems little doubt that traditional agriculture has done more to modify primary forests than has been the case for large-scale agriculture development in the form of plantations and cash crops. Rough estimates suggest that a total of 40,000 km² of forestland have been either denuded or rendered unproductive through shifting cultivation, and another 2,500 km², including at least 250 km² of primary forest, are cleared each year (Haantjens, 1975).

Timber Exploitation

As mentioned, Papua New Guinea is believed to contain about 22 percent of the closed forest area of the four main countries of Southeast Asia. But because around three-quarters of its forestlands are located in mountainous zones or on broken terrain, the area considered inaccessible totals 210,000 km². Therefore Papua New Guinea contains only about 15 percent of the operable forest area of Southeast Asia. Furthermore, these forest stocks are, by comparison with those in other parts of Southeast Asia, relatively unattractive for exploitation and management: Dipterocarp stands are rare; the wide variety of tree species is relatively unknown in commercial markets; the range in wood properties is broader than usual; log form is comparatively poor; lowland forests are often swampy, hence difficult to exploit; and timber stocking densities and commercial yields are low to very low, with merchantable log volumes generally not higher than 50 m³/ha, by contrast with

100–150 m³/ha in Malaysian lowland rainforests. In fact, the amount of forests that are known to be accessible to current harvesting technology but are not considered to be economically attractive for exploitation amount to 102,000 km². This means that total forest stocks available for commercial exploitation at present amount to only 88,000 km², reducing Papua New Guinea's share of Southeast Asia's economically operable forest volume to only about 13 percent. However, because Papua New Guinea's populace totals less than 3 million, the country supports around 640 m³ of economically operable forest per head, as compared with less than 200 in Malaysia and well under 50 in Indonesia and the Philippines.

Despite its relatively poor commercial forest endowment, the government places much emphasis on its timber export trade. Between 1951 and 1977, forest exports have increased in value more than 900 times. In 1977, log production totalled 1,113,600 m³, realizing exports of 464,400 m³ of timber (mostly raw logs), worth $31,120,000. These exports represented 4.1 percent of total export earnings, and, if copper exports are excluded, 12.2 percent.

Thus Papua New Guinea's forests contribute significantly to the national economy. Indeed, the remaining large unlogged areas are beginning to be perceived as a source of easily available income. Timber concessions have been allocated for 23,760 km² of forest, or 27 percent of total forest area classified as offering economic potential. Of these concessions, around 8,000 km² are committed to intensive sawn timber production, while a further 7,470 km² are scheduled for liquidation logging within 10–15 years. The former amounts to marked modification of forest formations; the latter leads to complete elimination of forest ecosystems. The largest logging operation is at the Gogol Valley near the north coast in Madang Province, comprising 681 km² of lowland rainforest; 22 percent of the concession is to be selectively logged, and 48 percent is to be clear-felled. About three-quarters of the clear-felled area will be assigned to forest plantations, the rest being used by 2,000 villagers for gardening, while the selectively logged area will be given over to enrichment planting (Lamb, 1977). A salient feature of the Gogol Timber Project is that it incorporates the first large-scale wood chipping operation in Papua New Guinea. This example of full-forest harvesting, together with a second such operation, converted about 20 km² of forest into 233,299 t of wood chips in 1977, all for export to Japan. Although the amount of forest in question is small, these initiatives could mark the start of a rapidly expanding trend.

As for other forms of forest conversion, industrial-wood plantations account for around 18 km² per year, and planned agriculture (plantations of oil palm, coconut, cocoa, rubber) for around 20 km² per year. These data, supplied by the Office of Forests, derive, like other forest-area statistics cited above, from an aerial photographic survey undertaken in 1977. Most of the data can be described as "reasonably accurate," *i.e.*, accurate within 5 percent.

In conclusion, it can be said that Papua New Guinea's forestry situation is changing rapidly. According to on-site observers (notably Haant-jens, 1975; Lamb, 1977), it is highly probable that large areas will be significantly altered within the next few years. Meantime, there is still considerable potential for protection of comparatively undisturbed forest, supposing that conservation initiatives take account of local economic and social constraints (especially the traditional land-tenure system). According to recent unpublished surveys by Diamond (1976) and Diamond and Raga (1977), there is opportunity, and special need, for a large nature reserve of 50,000 km², extending from the lowlands of the Fly River (containing the largest tract of relatively undisturbed lowland rainforest in the Pacific region, with many endemic species), over the central range between Telefomn and Teri, to the lowlands of the Upper Sepik. To safeguard most of the genetic wealth of the country, however, a larger network of protected areas will be needed, including a further 21 reserves totalling almost 34,000 km².

THE PHILIPPINES

Of the Philippines' national territory of 299,990 km², over 200,000 km² are accounted for by two large islands, Luzon and Mindanao, and a further 50,000 by Visayas. The remainder is divided among some 7,000 islands.

The entire country can be considered to fall within the T M F biome. A strip down the western side lies in the rain shadow of mountains down the eastern side, so the western quarter of Luzon and Mindanao can be characterized as monsoon forest. The remainder, which receives its rain from the Pacific to the east, can be categorized as true rainforest.

With a human population in mid-1979 of 47.4 million, the country has fewer forest resources per head than any other country of Southeast Asia—only 0.24 ha. This is to be compared with 0.32 ha in Thailand, 0.65 in peninsular Malaysia, and 0.8 in Indonesia.

Forest Exploitation

At the end of World War II, a large part of the Philippines, perhaps as much as three-quarters, was forested. Shortly after the country became independent, the dipterocarp forests began to be exploited. As a measure of the exceptional commercial value of these forests, an average dipterocarp stand in Philippines yields 125 m³ of hardwood per hectare, twice as much as the usual yield in Indonesia and Malaysia. A good part of the exploitation of the past three decades has been conducted by large timber corporations, which can deploy the capital investment, the professional expertise, and the technology to extract large harvests from extensive areas in relatively short periods of time.

Domestic consumption has increased total log output to just over 10 million m³ per year, taken from a present annual average of 800 km² of hitherto undisturbed forest. In 1978, commercial logging accounted for over 1,000 km² of primary forests that, in view of the capital-intensive modes of timber harvesting now in common practice, have been left in extremely degraded condition.

Still more critical to the status of the Philippines' forests has been the impact of expanding agriculture. Sizable tracts of forest are alienated to legal agriculture each year, as much as 500 km². Even more significant is the scale of "illegal agriculture," which has spread rapidly as an unintended consequence of commercial logging. When timber cutters penetrate their forest concessions with logging roads, they open the way for shifting cultivators, squatter-type farmers, and other agriculturalists who take their way of life deep into forests that have hitherto been closed to them. So serious is this pattern of peasant encroachment ment that it deserves to be considered in some detail.

Agricultural Encroachment on Forests

The Bureau of Forest Development and the National Environment Protection Council estimate that *kaingineros*, or forest farmers of one sort and another, now total 380,000 families. They are believed to occupy at least 23,000 km² of forestlands, 13,000 of them in critical watersheds. Due to growing population pressure, the traditional cultivators are being forced to reduce their fallow periods, and they are practicing a system of farming that is becoming intensive as well as extensive. The result is that forest ecosystems now receive scant chance to regenerate. Within officially designated forests, at least 10,000 km² of excessively exploited *kaingin* plots have been reduced to grassland and scrubland, while another 30,000 km² of similar lands elsewhere are thought to owe their origin to forest farmers. Somewhere between 800 and 1,400 km² of forest are similarly converted each year. Of course, the nature of the overall forestry situation means that agricultural encroachment tends to occur mostly on logged-over areas, so it is not undisturbed forest that is generally being eliminated. But forest farmers set large numbers of wildfires each year, especially in Luzon's monsoon forests where vegetation becomes highly inflammable during the dry season, November through May; the National Environment Protection Council estimates that in 1977 some 1,460 km² of forest were eliminated through this cause alone.

Forest farming is practiced by both hill tribes and lowlanders. Traditional cultivators, *i.e.*, those who have been born into the life-style and know no alternative way of supporting themselves, are no longer so numerous as two more recent categories of *kaingineros*. First, and most rapidly expanding in number, are obligate cultivators, *i.e.*, persons who originate from outside the forests and who feel compelled, for lack of land elsewhere, to try their hand at forest farming, even though they know next to nothing about the ecological constraints of the practice. Secondly, speculator cultivators are becoming increasingly important, these being persons who enjoy a sufficient source of livelihood elsewhere but take up forest farming as a commercial proposition (Castro, 1978).

To tackle the problem presented by forest farmers, the Kaingin Management Program, under the Bureau of Forest Development, proposes two courses of action. The first is to allow traditional cultivators to remain in the forests, while adapting to a stabilized form of agriculture on permanent 7-ha plots suitable for agroforestry. The second course is to relocate the recent forest settlers into areas that have already been deforested; a notable instance is the resettlement project of the Paper Industries Corporation of the Philippines, which has allocated 4–5 ha to each of some 3,320 families, who are encouraged to practice a combination of stabilized cultivation and tree growing.

These various forms of exploitation mean that, if the various categories are simply summed, at least 5,000 and possibly 6,000 or even 7,000 km² of forest are being accounted for each year. However, legally established agriculturalists and colonizer cultivators often prefer logged-over areas to undisturbed forest, which reduces the total. By contrast, the figures given are strictly demonstrable, and thus minimum, figures. For the purposes of this report, a total of 500–700 km² per year is posited. While this represents no more than an informed estimate, it is advanced in order for forestry planners to realize the scope of the problem confronting them, namely the rate at which Philippines' remaining forests are being converted away from their primary state.

Extent of Present Forests

According to a National Forest Inventory taken in 1965, the Philippines then contained 170,300 km² of forestlands, constituting 56.76 percent of the country. These forestlands were officially designated as lands of public domain that had not been alienated—a classification different from forested lands. In fact, certain of these so-called forestlands contained long-established agricultural settlements, urban communities, and other forms of nonforested development. But most of them were indeed forested, insofar as they met the official criterion of 10 percent tree or brush cover.

A further estimate in 1971 indicated that 132,721 km² or 44.24 percent could still be classified as forestlands (though an official Country Report to the World Forestry Congress in late 1978 stated that the Philippines' forestlands continued to accord with the 1965 figure). The 1971 assessment also indicated that at least 1,720 km², and possibly a great deal more, of forest were disappearing each year. The main causes of the declining situation were apparent. During the second half of the 1960s, the government had increased its rate of issuing logging licenses, and timber corporations were applying more intensive forms of harvesting while taking less and less notice of forestry regulations. In addition, shifting cultivation and other agricultural activities were claiming sizable sectors of forestlands, and were hampering reforestation of exploited areas. Recognizing that its forest resources were being increasingly degraded if not eliminated (Pollisco, 1975; Republic of the Philippines, 1976), the government decided to undertake a detailed survey through various forms of remote sensing.

The survey was carried out by the Department of Natural Resources, in conjunction with the General Electric Company Space Division of Beltsville, Maryland (Lachowski and Dietrich, 1978; Lachowski et al., 1978; Roque, 1978). The primary source of information was Landsat imagery and digital data for 1972–1976, supplemented by aerial photographs, reconnaissance flights over selected areas, and topographic maps. The whole operation was supported by ground-truth investigations to guide and verify the classification process. The entire effort has been sufficiently systematic and comprehensive for the results to be characterized as reliably accurate, i.e., (for purposes of this report) accurate within 5 percent—an assessment that was confirmed by on-site inquiries.

The survey provided a synoptic overview of total forest resources within the country. The data were classified into major forest types, including full-closure forests, partial-closure forests, mangrove forests, and mossy forests.

Results show that only 114,616 km² or 38.2 percent of the nation were still forested in 1976 (Table 8). The largest apparent portion of this forest cover, 60,119 km² or 20 percent, consisted of full-canopy forest, while partial-closure forest amounted to a further 38,000 km², or 12.7 percent. ("Apparent" because 5 percent of the overall total was categorized as obscured by cloud, hence could not be allocated to the various classes; if allocated by proportion with the 95 percent whose forest cover could be ascertained, the full-closure forest would be increased by 3,040 km², or 1 percent, and partial-closure forest by 1,930 km², or 0.6 percent.) These two categories of forest could generally be considered adequately stocked, or even densely stocked, dipterocarp forests suitable for commercial exploitation—though old-growth dipterocarp forests constitute only 35,800–39,000 km², while young-growth forests make up 31,000–35,300 km² and reproduction brush 28,000–37,500. Just over 43,000 km² of these forests are to be found in Mindanao, and almost 38,000 in northern Luzon. These interpretations are, however, considered by some observers to be on the high side. According to a think-tank agency, Population, Resources, Environment and Philippines' Future (PREPF)—a consortium of the Development Academy of the Philippines, University of Philippines School of Economics, and University of Philippines Population Institute—densely stocked forests cover only 80,999 km², or 27 percent of the country.

Furthermore, the Landsat survey reveals that the country's forests have been undergoing conversion to other uses at an average rate of around 3,000 km² per year between 1971 and 1976—a rate that appears now to have risen (according to calculations set out above) to 5,000–7,000 km² per year. This latter rate, which is likely to accelerate, would theoretically bring an end to all forests within 15–21 years. Of course, forests located in areas of steep terrain and mountainous zones may well remain beyond the scope of timber harvesters and agriculturalists for the foreseeable future, *i.e.*, some forest tracts will survive even if present exploitation patterns intensify. By the same token, however, lowland forests can be expected to undergo increasingly rapid depletion and conversion, and the Philippines government is now inclined to agree with forecasts by the Food and Agriculture Organization of the United Nations, the Asian Development Bank, and the UN Economic Commission for Asia and the Far East, among other international agencies, to the effect that all accessible dipterocarp forests will have been logged out, or given over to nonforestry purposes, as early as 1985.

Moreover, the continuing attrition of the country's forest estate is causing much degradation of several major watersheds. In the view of PREPF, the National Economic and Development Authority, and the National Environment Protection Council, as much as 52,166 km², or

TABLE 8 Forest Areas of Philippines as Measured by Landsat (km²)

Island or Region	Total Land Area	Land Cover Category					Forest Cover by Region (and %)
		Full-Closure Forest	Partial-Closure Forest	Mangrove Forest	Mossy Forest	Forest Obscured by Clouds	
Luzon	116,254	21,777	14,064	109	—	5,788	41,738 (35.9)
Mindanao	101,998	24,119	11,358	398	16	7,217	43,108 (42.3)
Palawan	14,896	6,757	3,123	349	—	870	11,099 (74.5)
Mindoro	10,245	2,722	1,874	67	45	309	5,017 (48.9)
Visayas	56,606	4,744	7,757	138	—	1,015	13,654 (24.1)
TOTAL (and % of country)	299,999	60,119 (20)	38,176 (12.7)	1,061 (0.4)	61 (0.02)	15,199 (5.1)	114,616 (38.2)

NOTE: These data can mostly be considered to be accurate within 5 percent.

SOURCE: Lachowski and Dietrich, 1978; Lachowski et al., 1978; Roque, 1978.

17 percent of the country, must be reforested, in order to safeguard watersheds, reduce soil erosion, and supply other environmental services. At the same time, the Bureau of Forest Development accepts that projected supplies from second-growth forests and present plantations will be far from able to meet even domestic needs, let alone foreign markets, by the year 2000 (Bureau of Forest Development, 1977; Dung, 1975; Population Center Foundation, 1978; Revilla, 1976).

In face of these prognoses, the government has determined that forest cover should amount to 125,000 km^2, or 42 percent of the country, in order to safeguard economic and environmental interests. To this end, the government plans to establish, during the next two decades, some 25,000 km^2 of man-made forests, or an average of 1,250 km^2 per year (about 14,000 km^2 for watershed management and other environmental reasons, and 11,000 km^2 for commercial wood). But existing plantations amount to only 3,000 km^2, and the recent rate of reforestation averages only 175 km^2 per year (Tagudar, 1978). Moreover, this reforestation program will supply a maximum of 13.6 million m^3 of logs per year at maturity, whereas projected demand for domestic needs alone is likely to rise to at least 17 million m^3, leaving a timber shortfall of 3.4 million m^3.

Thus conservation of forest resources has become a priority issue in the Philippines' development policies. President Marcos, having declared that the state of the country's forests constitutes a national emergency, has created a Presidential Council for Forest Ecosystem Management and has established a National Environment Code. These two initiatives have several objectives: to achieve a holistic ecosystem approach to forest resources management; to prevent irreversible injury to forest ecosystems; to restore degraded forest ecosystems; to conserve watersheds; and to encourage agroforestry. In an effort to reduce the overexploitative logging of remaining forests, the export of logs is to be progressively restricted, and eventually phased out; foreign-exchange earnings from the timber trade will be safeguarded through greater emphasis on export of processed forest products rather than raw logs.

In addition, the country is to maintain an ongoing survey of its forest resources. In late 1976, the government established a National Resources Management Center, and in late 1977 a National Cartography and Photogrammetry Committee. The Center undertakes research in remote sensing technology, including satellite imagery analysis, airborne multispectral scanning systems, computer-assisted analysis of satellite data, and side-looking airborne radar; while the Committee implements a nationwide program of aerial photography and cartography. Through these two measures, the government plans to conduct continuous inventory of its forest resources, together with monitoring studies of forest productivity, watershed health, and the status of protected areas such as national parks.

SRI LANKA

Of Sri Lanka's 65,584 km², 24,400 km² are still classified as forestlands. But adequately stocked forests amount to only around 17,000 km², or 26 percent of national territory, compared with at least 50 percent and possibly 65 percent reputedly forested in 1950 (Cruz, 1973; Department of Forestry of Sri Lanka, 1978; Persson, 1974; Whitmore, 1975, 1976).

Lowland evergreen rainforest, receiving at least 2,500 mm of rainfall per year, and featuring a good number of endemic dipterocarp species, is restricted to a 1,590-km² tract in the southwestern part of the island. Lower and upper montane rainforest account for about 670 km². The rest (87 percent) of the forest cover is made up of dry-zone low-quality forest.

Roundwood production, derived primarily from forest reserves totalling 952 km², amounts to 250,000–265,000 m³ per year, of which slightly less than half is made up of industrial timber, the rest being firewood and poles. The amount of disruption that this exploitation causes for primary forests is roughly equalled by the disruption of shifting cultivators, who, during the past 30 years, are reputed to have degraded some 10,000 km² of forests. The government is attempting to gradually reduce the impact of shifting cultivation through *taungya*-type agroforestry, *i.e.*, traditional type of forestland agriculture that combines growing of trees with food crops.

If plans for conversion of forestlands to agricultural use are implemented, only 12,134 km² of forest will be left, two-thirds in forest reserves and one-third in protected areas such as national parks. Within these land-use planning constraints, the government is taking measures to protect representative areas in all climatic zones of the country, primarily through UNESCO's (UN Educational, Scientific, and Cultural Organization) Man and the Biosphere Program. The program's aim is to establish 21 reserves, including the Sinhraja Forest Reserve, for a total of 425 km².

THAILAND

Much up-to-date and authoritative information has recently become available for Thailand. This country therefore receives detailed treatment here, as an example of the systematic analysis and inventory that are required for all countries of the TMF biome.

Thailand's 519,953 km² can be divided into five regions: The North is made up mainly of highlands and steep mountains surrounding fertile alluvial valleys. The Northeast comprises a generally low-lying zone, plus the Korat Plateau. The Central Region constitutes the Chao Phraya Plain around Bangkok. The East consists largely of a broad coastal zone, with a hilly hinterland. The South comprises a long narrow peninsula extending toward Malaysia.

In historic times there was forest within 100 km of Bangkok. Other signs indicate that much of the country was once forested, the principal exception being the natural savannahs of the Northeast. The present forests cover as little as one-quarter of the country. The valuable teak (*Tectona grandis*) forests, for which Thailand was once famous, are now virtually restricted to the North and to patches along the border with Burma. Although the highlands of the North still support large tracts of forest, they are being extensively and rapidly reduced by shifting cultivation and agricultural settlement. In the Northeast, forests are largely restricted to a depleted fringe along the border with Cambodia and Laos; in particular, the Korat Plateau is characterized by severe conflicts between forestry and agriculture, with agriculture becoming widespread in many parts. The East, being mostly flat and suitable for farming, has lost much of its forest in the past few decades and especially during the 1960s and 1970s. Only the South still retains major forests (with a significant surplus of industrial timber and firewood), though even these are being ever more rapidly degraded, if not destroyed, through shifting cultivation, squatter settlement, and illegal felling. Being wetter than other parts of the country, the South features its own distinctive vegetation formations, notably evergreen rainforests.

Natural vegetation, in the sense of vegetation where man's influence has been slight or nil, has been eliminated from most of Thailand. The activities of hunters and slash-and-burn agriculturalists, both of whom have been active in Thailand's forests for several thousand years, have disturbed if not disrupted most forests, many of them several times (Wharton, 1968, cited by Lekagul and McNeely, 1977). The long-term human impact is probably responsible for the notoriously low stocking densities (the amount of timber available for lumbering) of Thailand's forests, averaging little more than 40 m³/ha, and ranging from 75 to 100 m³/ha in the South's evergreen rainforests to only 15–35 m³/ha in the Northeast's dipterocarp deciduous forests, as compared with 100–150 m³/ha in similar forest ecotypes in other countries of Southeast Asia.

Forest Types

Thailand features two main groups of forest types: evergreen, account-ing for about one-third of remaining forests, and deciduous, accounting for almost two-thirds (Lekagul and McNeely, 1977; McNeely, 1977; Mungkorndid, 1978; Mungkorndid and Eadkao, 1978; National Re-search Council, 1976; Smitinand, 1977; Whitmore, 1975). The first group includes three major types—lowland evergreen, hill evergreen, and coniferous—while the second group includes mixed deciduous and dry deciduous dipterocarp. Of course, these are not highly distinct classifications: An evergreen forest may feature many deciduous trees; a deciduous forest may contain some evergreen trees (especially in the lower shrub layer); and an evergreen forest may be converted to de-ciduous forest through a change in climate or human influence. Crude as these classifications are, they are the best available in the absence of a systematic ecological analysis. The only methodical attempt at a classification has been that of Holdridge *et al*. (1971), who proposed a system of 15 life zones for the country, based on bioclimatic param-eters. Until this Holdridge methodology is put into practice, there is little option but to use the traditional, generalized, and unquantified typology of the Royal Forest Department of Thailand.

The second most extensive of these forest types, the lowland ever-green, is the most diverse and complex, making it the most valuable from the standpoint of biological research. From a commercial stand-point, however, the most valuable type is still the mixed deciduous, with its residual teak stands.

Lowland Evergreen   This forest type, accounting for around 30 per-cent of Thailand's forests, occurs in localities below 1,000 m, and with an annual rainfall of at least 2,000 mm fairly evenly distributed through-out the year. These forests once covered much of central and southern Thailand, together with low-lying valleys of the North, but now they have been reduced to scattered fragments. The farther south, the more prominent the dipterocarps, until communities begin to resemble those of Malaysian forests. The southernmost sector of the peninsula exhibits the least seasonal variation in rainfall, which accounts for a subtype of lowland evergreen forest, evergreen rainforest, that covers about 3,500 km^2. In the remaining parts of the southern peninsula, and reaching as far north as about 11 degrees N, with a slight extension along the hills of the Burma border, is a second subtype, semi-evergreen forest. Limited to areas below 1,000 m, this subtype covers about 1,000 km^2. By far the dominant form of lowland evergreen forest is the moist evergreen subtype, typically found mixed with bamboo, some deciduous formations, and scattered fire-climax grasslands. Occurring on the wetter parts of several mountain ranges and along northern stretches of the Mekong River, it covers roughly 30,000 km².

Hill Evergreen This forest type occurs above 1,000 m, and in areas where annual rainfall exceeds 2,000 mm and is fairly evenly distributed throughout the year. Comprising 3,000 km² or so, it is found mainly in the North, and often located in areas inaccessible for exploitation of commercial timber. However, it is much subject to shifting cultivation by hill tribes and to squatter settlement by other forest farmers: during the past decade, these forests have been ever more rapidly eliminated through increased migration on the part of hill peoples, and through growing pressure from Thai farmers moving upwards from the lowlands.

Coniferous This forest type is generally found on sandy soils at elevations of 400–1,400 m, and especially between 700 and 1,000 m, in the highlands of the North and on the Korat Plateau. There are also a few groves in the plains and along the coasts. Altogether they total a mere 2,500 km². In some areas they reveal the controlling effects of fire, and in a few localities they constitute a fire climax. Formerly widespread in several parts of north, northeast, and central Thailand, significant remnants are now found only in the North, and along the southern borders of the Northeast. They offer great potential for pulp production and resin tapping.

Mixed Deciduous Found in areas with 1,250–2,000 mm of annual rainfall and marked by well-pronounced wet and dry seasons, this forest type grows on a variety of soils both in the plains and in the hills up to 1,000 m. Accounting for around one-quarter of Thailand's forests, this type is still widespread throughout the country, particularly in the North. It is strongly affected not only by rainfall limitations but by burning practices, to the extent that some of the forest tracts are now characterized by fire-resistant forms. As in Burma and Laos, certain of the moisture variants contain a good proportion of teak; the teak forests have been extensively logged and frequently burnt, until typical climax associations are now to be found only in inaccessible localities.

Dry Deciduous Dipterocarp Accounting for roughly two-fifths of Thailand's forests, this forest type replaces the mixed deciduous where annual rainfall drops below 1,250 mm and the dry season lengthens to

6 months, though certain communities appear to be edaphic as much as climatic variants of the mixed deciduous. The type constitutes around two-thirds of the forests in the Northeast, while extensive tracts also occur in the northern part of the Central Region. The forests tend to occur on sites that are particularly suitable for cassava and kenaf, which makes them vulnerable to clearing by both itinerant and settled farmers. Fairly open formations in their natural state, burning and clearing are rendering these forests similar to savannah woodlands interspersed with forest patches.

Other Forest Formations   In addition to these five main types of high forest, there are a few other forest formations. For example, mangrove forests are still fairly extensive (though much depleted), notably along the western peninsula coast where they are unusually luxuriant, plus smaller patches along the eastern peninsula coast, and a few relict fragments in the tidal swamps around river mouths in the Gulf of Thailand (Aksornkoae, 1978; Sukwong *et al.*, 1975; Vibulsresth *et al.*, 1975). Unlike the situation in several other parts of Southeast Asia, where demand for mangrove poles and charcoal has virtually eliminated mangrove forests, Thailand's mangroves still survive in moderate-sized patches. Some 1,775 km², or over half the remaining mangrove forests, are to be exploited through full-forest harvesting for wood chips.

Regional Review

Of Thailand's five regions, the North is by far the largest, comprising 171,775 km² or one third of the country. Around 40 percent is still densely forested (Table 9), though only limited areas remain undisturbed. Around another 30 percent of the North consists of former forest that has been so heavily logged or burned that it now amounts to savannah woodland or even open grassland (Chunkao *et al.*, 1976; Kunstadter *et al.*, 1978; Miller *et al.*, 1978; Nualchawee and Miller, 1978; Omakupt, 1978; Morain and Klankamsorn, 1978; Wacharakitti and Morain, 1978). Despite their degraded state, the North's forests continue to be exploited beyond the point at which the forest can maintain its integrity, currently producing 70 percent of Thailand's timber output. These forests serve a further important function by maintaining water catchments—a service that is more significant in the North than in any other region. Yet this is the region where forest cover is undergoing the most disruption and destruction through shifting cultivation and the wildfires that cultivators set. Located in the North's mountainous territory are the headwaters of four major tributaries of

Thailand's largest river, the Chao Phraya. Of the Nan basin's 13,099 km², where the largest numbers of forest farmers are concentrated, shifting cultivation has accounted for at least 5,500 km²; only 48 percent of the basin retains its evergreen forest (Morain and Klankamsorn, 1978). When all four watersheds are considered together, some 9,150 km² have been eliminated through shifting cultivation. Paddies and other croplands throughout the North totalled 48,702 km², or 28 percent of the region, in 1976.

The Northeast has retained only about one-third of its original forest (Table 9). During the past 20 years, almost 44,000 km² have been severely disrupted or eliminated, accounting for over half of the region's forests. Yet this is the area where the government feels it can do least about the problem, since insurgents, who occupy some 75,000 km² of Thailand, are principally active in the Northeast.

The East now features a mere 6,524 km² of forest, less than one-third as much as in 1961 (Klankamsorn, 1978; Wacharakitti, 1978). The rate of regression during the 1970s has been exceptionally rapid, almost 8 percent per year (Tables 9 and 10). Two of the seven provinces, Chon Buri and Rayong, are losing forest at more than 12 percent per year, while Chantaburi province, with its evergreen forest, is losing forest cover at more than 5 percent per year. The main cause of forest conversion is population pressure from agriculturalists, whose numbers are expanding at over 3 percent per year through natural increase and through immigration from areas to the north.

The Central Region, being mostly lowland plain dominated by paddies, has only scattered patches of forest. Nevertheless, despite the concentrations of population (not just in Bangkok but in several sectors of the Chao Phraya Plain), almost one-fifth of the region still supports forest (Table 9). However, the decline since 1961, when well over half was forested, is greater than for any other region except the East.

Finally, the South, being mainly made up of the peninsula extending toward Malaysia, is characterized by coastal plains with a mountain range running along the center. As noted, much of its evergreen rain-forest still survives. But the region is subject to increasing settlement, especially of the "forest squatter"; and it is being overtaken by a great expansion of rubber plantations and oil-palm estates.

Shifting Cultivation

Since the practice of shifting cultivation is crucial to the status of Thailand's forests, the topic is worth considering in some detail.

Shifting cultivation is practiced in many forest areas of Thailand,

TABLE 9 Forest Areas of Thailand as Revealed by Remote Sensing

Region	Total Land Area (km²)	Aerial Photographs, 1961		1965		Reduction in Area, 1961–1965	% Reduction, 1961–1965
		km²	% of Region	km²	% of Region		
North	171,775	116,275	67.69	106,820	62.19	9,455	8.13
Northeast	174,407	70,904	40.65	62,970	36.12	7,934	11.19
East	36,394	21,163	58.15	18,170	49.92	2,993	14.14
Central	67,189	35,660	53.07	33,710	50.17	1,950	5.47
South	70,188	29,626	42.21	27,280	38.87	2,346	7.92
TOTAL	519,953	273,628	52.63	248,950	47.88	24,678	9.02

Region	Total Land Area (km²)	ERTS-1 1972		Reduction in Area, 1965–1972 (km²)	% Reduction 1965–1972	Landsat-2 1978		Reduction in Area, 1972–1978 (km²)	% Reduction 1972–1978
		km²	% of Region			km²	% of Region		
North	171,775	95,842	55.80	10,978	10.23	68,588	39.92	27,254	28.44
Northeast	174,407	47,466	27.22	15,504	24.62	27,519	15.78	19,947	42.02
East	36,394	15,036	41.31	3,134	17.25	6,524	17.93	8,512	56.61
Central	67,189	23,970	35.68	9,740	28.89	12,398	18.45	11,572	48.23
South	70,188	18,435	26.27	8,845	32.42	16,756	23.87	1,679	9.12
TOTAL	519,953	200,749	38.61 (Aug.)	48,201	19.36 (Aug.)	131,785	25.35 (Aug.)	68,964	34.35 (Aug.)

RELIABILITY: Except for the aerial photographs of the 1960s, most of these data can probably be considered reliable within 5 percent, and all of them can certainly be considered reliable within 10 percent.

NOTE: Forest areas as documented by ERTS-1, 1972, include both productive and nonproductive forestlands (plus a few patches of scrub forest and forest plantation), whereas forest areas as documented by Landsat-2, 1978, include only productive forest areas (suitable for timber exploitation). Hence the reduction figures given for 1972–1978, 68,964 km² and 34.35 percent, are somewhat higher than is warranted by the actual situation on the ground.

SOURCE: Boonyobhas and Klankamsorn, 1976; Wacharakitti, 1978; Wacharakitti and Morain, 1978; and data disclosed to the author by Royal Forest Department, Department of Land Development, National Economic and Social Development Board, National Research Council, and other agencies during a visit to Bangkok, November 1978.

TABLE 10 Forest Depletion in Eastern Thailand

Province	Total Area in 1973 (km²)	Forested Area, 1972–1973 (km²)	Forested Area, 1975–1976 (km²)	Forested Area, 1975–1976 (%)	Decrease in Area, 1973–1976 (km²)	Decrease in Area, 1973–1976 (%)	Average Annual Decrease 1975–1976 (%)	Average Annual Decrease 1961–1971 (%)
Chachoengsao	5,446	2,624	2,131	39.1	493	18.8	6.3	(0.7)
Nakhon Nayok	2,431	585	536	22.2	49	8.4	2.8	(4.0)
Prachin Buri	12,341	5,592	4,997	40.5	595	10.6	3.5	(2.0)
Chon Buri	4,506	1,020	636	14.1	384	37.6	12.5	(4.4)
Rayong	3,977	988	628	15.8	360	36.4	12.1	(3.9)
Chantaburi	6,047	3,176	2,680	44.3	487	15.4	5.1	(1.7)
Trat	2,995	1,060	1,023	34.1	37	3.5	1.2	(3.4)
TOTAL	37,743	15,045	12,631	33.5	2,405	16.0[a]	5.3[a]	(5,9)

[a]Average obtained by dividing totals, not by summing columns and dividing by 7.

SOURCE: Klankamsorn, 1978.

with an accumulated detriment of at least 40,000 km². The actual area could be much larger, since the usual remote sensing often fails to detect cultivated patches within closed forests.

There are two main groups of forest farmers, of which only the first practices shifting cultivation as it is generally understood (Bruneau and LeToan, 1978; Food and Agriculture Organization of the United Nations (FAO), 1978; Kunstadter et al., 1978; Miller et al., 1978; Mungkorndin, 1978). These are the hill tribes, mainly located in the North. According to a 1977 census, the communities in the North comprise 2,270 villages, 55,500 households, and 336,000 persons (Chaiyapechara, 1978). In addition, the North harbors large numbers of refugees and infiltrating insurgents from Burma and Laos, who have reputedly become at least as numerous as the native people. Both of these categories farm primarily for subsistence, growing rice, maize, and vegetables, though a number of cultivators above 1,000-m altitude grow opium poppies as a cash crop. For all these communities, shifting cultivation has become a ritualized life-style, with an area of forest cleared each year in accordance with binding custom. Of course, the key question is not how much forest is cleared, but how much new forest is cleared in addition to what has already been cleared. Systematic studies, based on successive phases of aerial photography supported by ground-truth investigations, reveal that farmers have traditionally followed a rotational pattern of clearing, which has allowed them to make sustainable use of the forest environment. During the past two decades, however, population pressure has increasingly obliged them to abandon their former cyclic practices, and to clear more and more new land, often at a rate of at least 1 ha per family per year. This means that around 700,000 upland dwellers, with an average of six persons to a family, could be accounting for almost 1,200 km² of forest each year.

Still more numerous than the hill cultivators, and probably far more significant for the status of Thailand's forests, are a second group of forest farmers, the people living in the lowlands. According to a 30 percent sample enumeration survey, there are now more than 1 million of them, almost all of them Thais (Mungkorndid, 1978). Their form of agriculture is fundamentally different from that of the hill cultivators. Many of them are not forest farmers at all as the term is usually understood; rather they are landless peasants from outside the forest zone who seek a patch of public land on which to establish their temporary gardens. By contrast with the hill tribes who cultivate for subsistence, lowland farmers cultivate primarily to generate a cash income. With a life-style that is more that of itinerant squatters than shifting cultivators of the traditional sort, they hack away at the forest fringe, plant cassava and maize for a year or two, and then push still further into the forest. This allows a wave of follow-on agriculturalists to establish themselves on the cleared lands with various forms of larger-scale commercial crops such as sugarcane. Thus the forest gets no chance to regenerate, and the original ecosystem is eliminated entirely and for good. An average family of six persons is believed to clear at least 10 *rais,* or 1.6 ha per year. This means that 1 million people are accounting for at least 2,667 km^2 of forest each year—a figure that closely accords with the minimum estimate of FAO (1976) of 2,550 km^2. Some of the follow-on agriculturalists believe that to generate a cash income of $1,000 per year, a farmer needs to work at least 20 *rais,* or 3.2 ha; a few operate anywhere between 15 and several hundred ha.

These calculations indicate that the forest cleared annually by forest farmers of all types could approach 4,000 km^2.

This great and growing threat to Thailand's remaining forests has drawn the attention of the government. Yet the government is reluctant to tackle the problem by invoking the full power of the law, since this could encourage many forest farmers to seek security with insurgent communities. In any case, the government does not exercise sufficient control throughout the North, where the problem is most pronounced, because of guerrilla activity and border troubles with Burma and Laos; but it is trying a strategy based on forest villages (Boonkird, 1978; Samapuddhi, 1975). The aim is to collect forest farmers in discrete localities, and to stabilize their patterns of cultivation. One system, the Forest Village Project, executed through the Royal Forest Department, seeks to relocate squatters from watersheds. Each family resettled is given 2.5 ha of land for housing and crops. A second approach, the Forest Village System, implemented by the Forest Industry Organization, tries to stabilize the life-style of shifting cultivators, through agroforestry in the Organization's reforestation areas. Each family is allotted 0.16 ha on which to build a homestead, plus 1.6 ha each year in the reforestation area; and each forest village comprising 100 families is furnished with basic services. The farmers are encouraged to practice *taungya* agroforestry, with prospect of cash remuneration for trees planted—the trees being mainly timber and firewood species in the North and Northeast, and sometimes rubber in the East and South. A special problem is the opium growers in the North, who have been receiving $200–300 per year for their crop. They are being encouraged, through the Crop Replacement Program of the Watershed Management Division, to abandon their poppies in favor of vegetables, upland fruits, sesame, coffee, tea, and other substitute cash crops.

Rates of Forest Conversion

In 1971, Thailand established the National Remote Sensing Program, working in coordination with the Royal Forest Department, the Department of Mineral Resources, the Department of Land Development, military agencies, several research institutes, four universities, and FAO. A number of foresters were trained in remote sensing techniques in the United States and Europe. From this start, Thailand has developed a systematic effort for continuous remote sensing of its forest resources (Boonyobhas and Klankamsorn, 1974, 1976; Klankamsorn, 1978; Morain and Klankamsorn, 1978; Mungkorndid and Eadkeo, 1978; Sabhrasi *et al.*, 1978; Wacharakitti, 1978; Wacharakitti and Morain, 1978). The program depends largely on Landsat imagery plus some aerial photography, backed up by ground-truth investigations.

The main results are presented in Tables 9 and 10. The information from the early 1960s, taken from aerial photography, is only moderately reliable, but the satellite-derived data of the 1970s, backed up by extensive ground-truth checks, can be considered to be generally accurate within 5 percent. As indicated by the baseline data (taken from a countrywide survey using aerial photography and ground checks), Thailand's forest estate in 1961 covered 273,628 km^2, or 52.62 percent of the Kingdom. By 1973, the comprehensive remote sensing program revealed that the forest cover had declined to 200,749 km^2, or 38.6 percent. In other words, during a period of 12 years a total of 72,879 km^2 of forest had been lost. Moreover, the figure of 38.6 percent included a number of small-scale cultivation plots in the forests that were too small for Landsat to pick up. So the 1973 figure has been regarded as a maximum figure for the forest estate. More recent data indicate that by mid-1978, the undisturbed forests (productive forests suitable for timber exploitation) had further declined to 131,785 km^2, or 25.4 percent of the country. This represents a decline of 141,843 km^2 since 1961, or 51.8 percent of the former forest cover. Low as these 1978 figures are, they are supported not only by the National Remote Sensing Program but by the National Economic and Social Development Board and the National Research Council. Certain government publications still speak of forest cover around 38 percent, but, in the view of virtually all authorities whom the writer consulted in the country in late 1978, the true forest area is "certainly" and "significantly" less than these occasional out-of-date pronouncements.

The data for the period 1973–1978 suggest that an average of almost 13,800 km^2 of forest are being grossly disturbed or cleared each year, well over twice the rate of 6,075 km^2 per year for the period 1961–1973.

While a figure of 13,800 km^2 for the present annual rate of conversion sounds high, it is supported by other calculations. According to Lekagul and McNeely (1978, citing Backer and Openshaw, 1972) a survey of industries, manufacturers, contractors, households, and other wood users in 1970 indicated that consumption of wood and wood products in 1970 was 55.63 million m^3 (of which firewood accounted for 88.1 percent). This figure is to be compared with a Ministry of Economic Planning estimate of total requirements for roundwood in the national economy of 63.5 million m^3 per year. Lekagul and McNeely consider that the total volume of wood per hectare of forest would probably not average more than 72 m^3, a low figure reflecting long-term exploitation of the forests. Even if one were to assume that all wood was being utilized (FAO, 1976, estimates that about 30 percent should be added to removals to arrive at a standing volume equivalent), the amount of forest area required to supply 63.5 million m^3 in 1970 would have been 8,820 km^2. To this logged-over area must be added around 4,000 km^2 for shifting cultivators and other sorts of forest farmers (FAO, 1976, suggests that the figure could easily be as high as 5,000 km^2). This produces a total area of forest cleared in 1970 of 12,820 km^2. Extrapolating at a rate of 2.7 per year, attributable to population growth alone (apart from expanding technology of exploitation among other factors), this would mean that the amount cleared in 1978 would have amounted to 15,866 km^2. This figure is comparable with the figure of 13,800 km^2 obtained through analysis of remote sensing data.

Forest clearing at the lower rate indicates that remaining forest stocks will theoretically be exhausted within only another 10 years. The actual situation will almost certainly work out rather differently, insofar as a few forest areas, notably in steep mountainous zones, will probably remain inaccessible to exploitation despite advances in forest exploitation technology; and a few areas will be protected as national parks. Moreover, there will be regional differences in exploitation patterns, with the North, Northeast, and East, which are now being exploited well beyond their capacity, becoming critically deforested, whereas the South, with its evergreen rainforests, could avoid gross disruption and depletion for a few more years.

In face of this critical prospect, the government is taking steps to amend its forestry policies and practices. Already the country has to import logs from Malaysia and Indonesia, and is negotiating for further supplies from Burma and Laos. In late 1977, the government imposed a complete ban on exports not only of logs but of rough-sawn timber; and it is considering a ban on all forest operations for a period of 5 years, even though this would require the importation of logs worth

$850 million per year to meet domestic demand alone. Much forest destruction is caused by highly organized poaching of valuable tree species, especially teak (a single teak log can be worth well over $100), and each year some 20–40 forest guards are killed in gun battles with illegal loggers. To counter this poaching, a constitutional initiative recently empowered the government to impose extreme penalties, including summary execution of convicted violators, and a number of persons have been sentenced to 30 years in jail.

As a policy objective, the government wishes 40 percent of the country to be forested. To achieve this objective, an extensive reforestation and afforestation program has been planned. The aim is to expand the present program of establishing plantations, about 300 km² per year, to 3,200 km², during the present 5-year planning period (though the present rate of establishing plantations has yet to be achieved). All in all, forest plantations, including firewood plantations, officially amount to 9,450 km², of which 571 are teak and 530 are pine. But some observers believe that planting has been no more than 10 percent effective, and certain plantations have been damaged by fire, so official data are considered uncertain at best.

In addition, a network of national parks and wildlife reserves has been established, and is being continuously expanded. At present they cover 35,505 km², or 6.4 percent of the country. Regrettably, these protected areas are by no means safe. The largest such area, the Khao Yai National Park, is being depleted at a rate of about 0.5 percent per year—a rate that is, however, a good deal better than that for the environs at almost 4 percent.

Finally, Thailand is formulating a National Conservation Plan. The National Environment Board and the Royal Forest Department, in conjunction with FAO, the International Union for Conservation of Nature and Natural Resources, and the UN Environment Program, is developing a comprehensive strategy for the country. The government is aware that a human population that has reached 46.2 million in mid-1979, and is still growing at around 2.3 percent, is likely to exert progressive pressure on the country's natural-resource base, and especially on its forests.

VIETNAM

Vietnam, 329,426 km², comprises what was formerly known as North Vietnam, 158,687 km², and South Vietnam, 170,739 km². In the sector that was formerly North Vietnam, there are reputed to be, according to UN reports in late 1978, 118,800 km² of forest cover. However, this forest estate includes only around 14,000 km² of what can be termed moist forests, mainly in the southern part and in the mountain zone near the Laos frontier. No further information is available about these forests.

In the sector that was formerly known as South Vietnam, there was reputed to be, in 1965 and hence before the recent military activities, around 108,000 km² of forest cover (almost all hardwood forests), including 36,200 km² of moist forests (Persson, 1974). Much of this forest cover included lowland evergreen forest as a predominant ecotype in parts of the Mekong Plain, stretching into the Annamite Plain. There was also some hill evergreen forest in the Annamite Chain, especially in the southern sector; and some mangrove forest in the Mekong Delta.

Even in the mid-1960s, it was probable that very few primary forests remained in the lowlands, and such patches as were sometimes so designated would probably have been better termed aged secondary forests. This situation could probably be accounted for by two main factors. The first was the impact of agricultural communities during the course of many centuries (Bethel and Turnbull, 1974; Cliff, 1966; Dwyer Mission, 1966; Karlberg, 1976; Kernan, 1968; Mekong Committee, 1978; Southeast Asia Development Advisory Group, 1973; Swanson, 1975; Wharton, 1968; Williams, 1965). The overall pattern has been summarized by Bethel and Turnbull (1974): " . . . there is little disagreement among competent observers that the forests have been heavily used by man for centuries and that they depart a great deal from the form and structure of the original virgin forest." It appears that the forests have been extensively and repeatedly exploited for temporary agriculture by successive generations of forest farmers. In addition, the lowland forests, and especially those of the Mekong Delta, have been widely converted, especially during the last 100 years, into permanent crop lands.

In 1872, the Delta area under rice cultivation amounted to 1,700 km²; stimulated by demand from foreign markets, the area increased by 1908 to 12,680 km², following which the area increased by 1961 by a further 2,700 km². During this period, the populace is estimated to have grown from 1.7 million to almost 20 million people (Owen, 1971).

Present-day forests of what was formerly South Vietnam continue to be disrupted and depleted by shifting cultivation. There is progressive degradation of forests in the Central Highlands, where around 5 million people, composed of as many as 60 individual tribes and leading a mainly semi-nomadic life, have fundamentally modified many forest ecosystems. The total area of forest affected by shifting agriculture, with varying degree of alteration, may now be as much as 80,000 km².

A far greater cause of forest injury, however, has stemmed from the recent war (Flamm and Cravens, 1971; National Academy of Sciences, 1974; Orians and Pfeiffer, 1970; Stockholm International Peace Research Institute, 1976; Westing, 1971). During the years 1965–1971, a total of 62.3 million l of herbicides were sprayed onto forests and crops. The impact of this military activity, together with bombing and shelling of forest areas, has resulted in much defoliation and cratering, together with some change in species composition of many forest communities. It is estimated that somewhere between 20,000 and 50,000 km² of forest have been damaged to varying degree, if not destroyed outright (plus another 3,000–5,000 km² in what was formerly North Vietnam). The most seriously affected forest type has been the mangrove forests, of which about 2,600 km² of 7,200 were sprayed, with a 100 percent kill impact in many localities; no regeneration or recolonization is to be found yet (presumably because of the viviparous characteristics of most mangrove species), and forest ecologists believe that this ecotype may require 20 years to reestablish itself.

According to a UN Development Program (UNDP) mission in November 1977, and Food and Agriculture Organization of the United Nations (FAO) observers in 1978, some 65–70 percent of the forestlands of former South Vietnam are in need of restoration. These are now reputed to be only 0.5 ha of forest per inhabitant, as compared with rather more than twice as much in Kampuchea, and almost 10 times as much in Laos. The principal aim of the Ministry of Forestry, established in June 1976, is to steadily rehabilitate the war-damaged forests over the course of the next 20–25 years. As an interim alternative, the government is undertaking a forest inventory, and preliminary results may become available by the end of 1980. In 1978, the government estimated that operable forests amounted to only 29,000 km² in the whole southern sector of Vietnam, and that timber requirements were 4–8 times higher than production. To meet this situation, the government is trying to establish 12,000 km² of forest plantations, and to double the output of industrial wood to 3.5 million m³ by the end of 1980.

9 Regional Review: Tropical Latin America

Intro

Tropical Latin America is reputed to contain around 5 million km² of tropical moist forests (TMF), or well over half of the entire biome. Of this extent, some 4.7 million km² occur in South America, and some 300,000 in Central America and the Caribbean.

By far the most important sector is in Amazonia, herein defined as the forested parts of the 7.8 million-km² drainage. Of this vast forest tract, some 85 percent is considered to be dense lowland rainforest, thus constituting the great bulk of rainforest in the TMF biome. To give an idea of the extent of Amazonia, it covers an area roughly equal to the United States east of the Rockies; were it politically independent, it would be the ninth largest nation on earth. Over three-fifths of Amazonia lie in Brazil, making up over two-fifths of the country; and of the seven other countries that share the zone, Bolivia, Ecuador, and Peru have over half their national territory in Amazonia.

Without doubt Amazonia is, biologically speaking, the richest area on earth. It contains at least 50,000 known species of higher plants, or one in five of all such species on earth. Figures for animal species are comparable: For example, it features one in five of all bird species. In addition, it features many centers of species diversity, some 16–18 of which have been tentatively identified (Prance, 1977, 1978, in press; Wetterberg et al., 1976; Wetterberg and Padua, 1978). These areas, and other localities of exceptional ecological value, are dealt with in the country profiles that follow.

117

BOLIVIA

Of Bolivia's 1,074,428 km², various kinds of forest account for a total area that is roughly estimated to be 300,000 km². Of this, a tract of some 179,000 km² in the northeastern sector of the country reputedly consists of Amazonian hylean ecotype. However, according to a recent reconnaissance through Landsat imagery, supplying adequately reliable information, *i.e.*, accurate within 10 percent, tropical moist forest is restricted to the Department of Pando and the Province of Vaca Diez, and totals no more than about 80,000 km² (Bryers and Goulds, 1978; Orlando *et al.*, 1975; Persson, 1974; Stolz, 1977).

To date, this lowland moist forest sector has been subject to little exploitation. The entire area contains only 70,000 people, of whom 40,000 are located in three urban settlements. Some selective logging has taken place in the 10,500 km² of *varzea* forest, but, since the harvest is confined to only two tree species, it exerts very slight impact. Shifting cultivation has expanded slowly or very slowly, though it is now increasing along recently constructed roads. Cultivated land amounts to some 800 km², 70 percent of which consists of cattle ranches and cash-crop plantations of citrus, cacao, and coffee. Thus the great part of the TMF sector can be considered virtually undisturbed moist forest.

However, the Bolivian government is now planning to resettle appreciable numbers of farmers from the *altiplano*. In conjunction with this initiative, the government also seeks to foster broad-scale cattle ranching. Through the medium of the Anglo-Bolivian Land and Cattle Company, with reported financial support from several developed nations, Bolivia proposes to sell 10,000 km² of forestland as an immediate goal, and another 75,000 km² within the foreseeable future, to 150,000 white settlers whom it hopes to attract from southern Africa. In order to promote these development activities, the government is establishing several highways in the forest zone, and this will, in the view of observers from the Food and Agriculture Organization of the United Nations in Bolivia, soon show a decisive impact on forest areas.

BRAZIL

Of Brazil's 8,511,965 km², roughly 3,570,000 km², or 42 percent, lie in Amazonia. A large proportion of this Amazonian region, some 2,860,000 km², is believed to be still covered with lowland moist forest. In addition, roughly 500,000 km² can be categorized as transitional forest, while as much as 300,000 km² have little or no forest.

This means that Brazil contains a far greater portion of the TMF biome than any other nation—roughly 3 times more than each of the next two largest nations, Indonesia and Zaire (see *e.g.*, Berutti, 1978; Falesi, 1974; Goodland and Irwin, 1975; Meggers *et al.*, 1975; Muthoo *et al.*, 1977; Pires, 1978; Prance, 1977, 1978, in press; Reis, 1978; Smith, 1976; Sternberg, 1975).

Brazil also possesses a strip of remnant forest, much of it rainforest, along its Atlantic coast. Formerly covering a much larger area than at present, the strip now runs approximately from Brazil's northeastern salient into the Atlantic Ocean, south almost reaching Rio de Janeiro. This strip is not continuous; and it varies considerably in width, from only a few kilometers in the northern part of the state of Rio Grande do Norte, to about 80 km in northern Pernambuco, with similar variations further south. From the onset of Portuguese colonization, these dense moist forests have been heavily and repeatedly logged for industrial timber and for charcoal; and extensive sectors have been cleared away altogether in order to make way for sugarcane plantations and other cash crops. Only occasional relict patches now survive in pristine form, *e.g.*, in southern Bahia, northeastern Alagoas, and southeastern Pernambuco. One section of this rainforest, located in the state of Bahia, a heavily populated area, is being eliminated primarily through lumbering operations to make way for cocoa and coffee plantations (Mori and Silva, 1979). The gross regression of this forest tract is all the more regrettable insofar as it features much intrinsic interest from biological and ecological standpoints. In its warmer, low-lying areas, it features a fair number of Amazonian plants, and in its elevated localities it harbors representatives of Brazil's southeastern flora. But the forest also contains a large proportion of endemic species, and physiognomically it is far different from both the Amazonian and the southeastern regions. Fortunately the Brazilian government has recently decided to purchase from private owners a large part of the remaining primary forest. The purchase is all the more welcome since, from the perspective of the TMF biome overall, very few areas feature such exceptional scientific value while surviving in such reduced and precarious state.

As for Amazonia, it appears that—so far as can be determined from vegetation surveys and mapping programs, such as the radar-sensing RADAM (Radar Amazonia) project—as much as 85 percent of the Amazonian forest constitutes the richest of all TMF formations, *viz.*, lowland rainforest. This is not to say, of course, that all areas in Amazonia receive abundant year-round rainfall. The western part of Amazonas state can be described as having a perhumid climate, and the same for another area on the coast of Amapá in the northeast; each receives

3,000–3,500 mm of rainfall per year. Across much of the southern part of the basin runs a broad belt of slightly seasonal climates, including most of the forest south of the Amazon River, with Manaus near its western edge and extending eastward as far as Belém; much of this forest receives only 2,000 mm of rainfall or so, with a 1–3-month dry season with less than 60 mm per month. Along the northern boundary of the basin, notably in Roraima, there is a more accentuated dry season; and the same for parts of the southern boundary zone, notably in. Mato Grosso. Roughly speaking, perhumid climates feature evergreen rainforest, and seasonal climates feature semi-evergreen rainforest.

The forest expanse can be divided in another fashion. Whereas the great bulk of the forest, perhaps as much as 95 percent, occurs on so-called upland territory, or *terra firme* (Pliocene sedimentation from Amazonian inland lakes, presently covered with forest), there are two other zones, neither of them extensive as compared with the whole of Amazonia but each covering tens of thousands of square kilometers: the *varzea* (floodplain of the Amazon River, annually inundated) floodplains, and the *igapo* swamp forests located at the edge of the *terra firme*. Of the *terra firme*, or dense forest, around 65–75 percent consists of tall forest cover, while 10–15 percent consists of low forest cover; the latter, located mainly between the Tocantins and Madeira rivers and in the Rio Branco valley of Roraima, is distinguished by less biomass, fewer lianas, and more palm communities, notably babassu. Montane forests total scarcely 1 percent of the region.

Despite an extensive colonization program, Amazonia still contains only 5 percent of Brazil's 119 million people. An area as large as the Sahara, it is as thinly populated (outside urban areas) as the Sahara. At the same time, it contributes less than 5 percent to Brazil's GNP. The region's forests contribute only 10 percent to Brazil's output of industrial timber. The region also contains the world's largest reserves of high-grade iron ore, plus appreciable deposits of several other minerals, roughly estimated to be worth at least $50 billion. In a country with the largest foreign debt of any nation on earth, now well over $40 billion, many political leaders have been inclined to look upon Amazonia as a viable asset going to waste, lacking only capital investment, technology, and entrepreneurship. In the past few years, however, a number of prominent Brazilians have been urging caution in opening Amazonia, in order that maximum long-term benefit may be derived from exploitation of the region's vast resources.

This situation has promoted an outburst of development during the 1970s. Various exploitation strategies have been attempted, notably highway building, smallholder settlement, cattle ranching, and timber exploitation (each of which will be considered in more detail below). It is becoming increasingly apparent, however, that efforts to open this vast forest zone are not so straightforward as had once been hoped. Thus the pattern of development is varied, and will almost certainly continue to be so. This makes a comprehensive assessment difficult at best, while a prognosis for the future is still more problematic. Nevertheless, considering the prime importance of Amazonia's forests to the entire TMF biome, it is worthwhile here to attempt a brief appraisal of the situation, in whatever preliminary and approximate terms.

Moreover—and the point is stressed—this review should not be construed as any implied critique to the effect that the Amazonian forests are best left untouched. Clearly, there are many reasons why Brazil should wish to develop and exploit its Amazonian resources. The question is, what is the best way to achieve use of these vast resources that can be sustained by the forests and be of greatest benefit to the people concerned, both now and in the future?

Agricultural Settlements

As its original measure to develop Amazonia, Brazil embarked on an ambitious program to crisscross the region with roads (Alvim, 1977; Beukenkamp, 1975; Cox, 1977; Goodland and Irwin, 1975; Kirby, 1976; Kleinpenning, 1975; Moran, 1976; Pandolfo, 1978; Rosende, 1977; Smith, 1976, 1978). The TransAmazon Highway, begun in 1970, was to have extended for around 6,000 km, and subsidiary roads were scheduled to total another 12,000 km. But difficulty with settlement schemes has caused the road-building program to be slowed throughout the region, and suspended in certain areas.

Along the roads of this highway system, a 50-km belt of forestland was designated for agricultural development through smallholder settlements. The settlers were supposed to come mostly from Brazil's famine-stricken northeast with its 37 million impoverished people; Amazonia was to become, in the words of former President Medici, "a land without men for men without land." But the settlement program was soon adapted to entail an immigration of only 100,000 persons per year (roughly one-tenth of the annual increase of the northeast's population, and, in fact, less than half of the immigrants came from the northeast. Settlers were offered 100 ha of land plus other inducements, yet only a small portion of the 100,000 expected families eventually arrived. By 1975 the total of 50,000 colonists had almost stopped growing. Many homesteaders tried to grow unsuitable crops; many were immobilized by disease; and soils almost invariably proved poor. A good number of settlers abandoned the plots allocated to them, and turned to various forms of shifting cultivation and informal forest farming—the type of uncontrolled settlement that was to be expressly avoided. Fires started by these subsistence peasants and allowed to run wild account for many thousands of square kilometers of forest every year.

All in all, it is now reckoned (according to government officials in Manaus, Belém, and Brasília, February 1979) that less than 7 percent of the planned settlement can be called successful. Due to a plethora of problems, including those mentioned above, together with widespread soil erosion and threats from hostile forest tribes, government support for the settlement program has fallen off, and officials are looking closely at adverse ecological repercussions of the initiative. The upshot is that development funding for the agricultural settlement program has dwindled, and construction of certain of the highway's subsidiary roads has been halted for the time being. Meantime, agricultural areas are believed to have accounted, during the period 1966–1975, for 35,000 km² of forest, and the highway building program for 30,000 km² (Pandolfo, 1978).

It seems likely that a more realistic settlement program will focus on soils of greater fertility within Amazonia. The periodically flooded zones, the *varzeas*, with their rich alluvial deposits, amount to only 60,000 km² of Amazonia, yet they could support a rich agriculture for large communities of smallholder agriculturalists. They are well suited to fast-maturing crops such as beans and corn and especially to crops which favor floodplains such as rice (experimental plantings, *e.g.*, at Jarilandia, indicate that worldwide record yields of 9 t per ha are feasible through two crops per year). Some authoritative agronomists even believe that the *varzea* zones could eventually rival the great river-based agricultural systems of the past, such as those of China, Egypt, India, and Mesopotamia. Moreover, the *varzeas* do not exhibit such biotic complexity or diversity of species as the *terra firme* forests, so if they were to be converted to broad-scale agricultural settlements, the loss in terms of rich forest formations would not be so marked as has been the case to date with smallholder settlements in the interfluvial zones. It should be noted, however, that the fruits of the *varzea* forest are the sole food source for many Amazonian fishes. Large-scale conversion of *varzea* forest to agriculture would have a very detrimental effect on frugivorous fish populations, which in turn could reduce the availability of edible fish that are a staple food for people living along the rivers.

Meantime, the emphasis in Amazonian agriculture has shifted almost entirely away from small-scale pioneers, and toward large agro-business entrepreneurs, most of them cattle-raising operations.

Cattle Raising

A major cause of forest conversion in Brazilian Amazonia is cattle raising (Davis, 1977; Irwin, 1977; Kirby, 1976; Myers, 1979; Osbourn, 1975). It is probably the primary cause already, and appears likely to constitute the prime factor for the foreseeable future (unless, as a result of recent proposals, it is overtaken by timber exploitation). The process entails clearing of the forest in order to establish man-made grasslands, so the original ecosystem is entirely eliminated.

In addition to the fundamental motivation of wishing to develop and settle its Amazonian territories, Brazil has another reason for fostering cattle raising: the nation has an eye to the world's growing beef shortage. According to the Food and Agriculture Organization of the United Nations (FAO), global demand for meat is projected to rise during 1975–1990 more rapidly than for other foods except fish. To meet this growing demand with its soaring prices, Brazil is determined to become one of the biggest beef exporters in the world. In 1973, Brazil possessed 95 million head of cattle, a total surpassed only by the Soviet Union and the United States. By 1980, or shortly thereafter, Brazil had expected to double its 1973 output of meat and to rank as the world's number one beef exporter (a goal that is far from materializing due to poor-level management of most of the country's pasturelands, within Amazonia and elsewhere).

A prospective rancher, like other investors in Amazonia, is protected by generous terms. He can import certain forms of equipment into the country duty-free. Until recently, he received a 50 percent rebate on his income tax on activities elsewhere in Brazil, though this proportion is now being reduced, possibly to as low as 25 percent. A foreign investor can repatriate his profits and his capital. Moreover, clearing away the forest need not be costly; if a rancher employs hand labor to fell and burn the forest, costs run to only $125–250 per ha; and if he employs casual family labor, he need offer no more remuneration than opportunity for the family to take off one food crop from the forestland concession before leaving the area planted in grass for the new rancher's cattle. Thus there have been many entrepreneurs ready to try their hand at cattle raising in Brazil's Amazonian forests, even though experience to date shows that it is a questionable form of land use.

According to the Superintendência do Desenvolvimento da Amazônia (SUDAM) (C. Pandolfo, personal communication, SUDAM, Belém, Brazil, 1978), from 1966 to 1978, 80,000 km² of Amazonian forestlands were converted to cattle pasture in the form of 336 ranching projects under the auspices of SUDAM, together with some 20,000 other ranches of varying size. This total area is more than has been accounted for by smallholder settlement and other agricultural colonization, by highway construction and related activities, and by timber extraction; and of these economic sectors, cattle raising, although possibly the least appropriate since poorly productive and hardly sustainable (though given the financial incentives, highly lucrative), is expanding most rapidly. Roughly speaking, half of these ranching enterprises have been located in northern Mato Grosso, and around 28 percent in southeastern Pará, plus an appreciable number in Rondonia and Acre. In southeastern Pará, cattle raising is now the dominant form of agricultural land use. The average size of a SUDAM-sponsored ranch is 2,275 km², supporting 16,132 head of cattle, at a stocking rate of almost 1.5 ha per head. Large ranches of well over 2,000 km² comprise only 1 percent of all cattle raising operations.

An increasing number of ranching enterprises are foreign owned, not that they make up a large proportion of the ranch lands, in fact less than 1 percent, but they are significant as a measure of Brazil's readiness to harness foreign capital to promote its development of Amazonia. A U.S. consortium of the Brescan-Swift-Armour-King Ranch holds around 720 km² in eastern Amazonia, with an investment of $6 million, while other U.S. corporations include Twin Agricultural and Industrial Developers, Hublein and Sifco Industries, Anderson Clayton, United Brands (as the John Morell Company), Gulf and Western, and Goodyear. Additional foreign enterprises, among others from the industrialized nations, include Mitsui, Tsuzuki, Spinning and Nichimen, and Grubo Bradesco from Japan; Liquigas from Italy; Volkswagen from West Germany; and George Markhof from Austria. Investment on the part of the 12 largest enterprises totalled $21 million by the end of 1977, except for Volkswagen with $35 million. Volkswagen holds a concession of 1,400 km² in southeastern Pará, of which half is to be converted into pastureland; by mid-1976, the company had burned about 100 km² of forest, enough for a herd of 10,000 cattle, the eventual aim being to increase the grasslands to 700 km² for a herd of 120,000 cattle. Large as this Volkswagen enterprise might sound, it is far from the biggest ranch. Liquigas holds 5,000 km²; COPEARA (a banking consortium, including both foreign and domestic banks), 3,000; Lunar Delli, over 5,000 km²; Cetenco (a São Paulo construction company), 3,000 km²; and Compania do Rio Brado, 6,550 km².

As mentioned, experience to date indicates that cattle raising in moist forestlands can prove a doubtful venture (Hecht, 1980; Kirby, 1976; Osbourn, 1975; Smith, 1978). Not only are stocking rates low, but steers require 4 years to attain a weight of 450 kg for slaughter. Soils quickly become exhausted of nutrients, and pastures feature poorer and poorer grass unless they receive ever growing amounts of fertilizer. In addition, in the warm humid climate (some localities receive over 3,500 mm of annual rainfall), there is a problem of toxic weeds that invade as the soil becomes compacted; as a result, some ranches have lost one-fifth of their cattle holdings. In fact, many ranches have already been abandoned, and at least 200 look likely to become unprofitable after only 5 years. Of 25,000 km² of pasture established since 1960 along the Belém-Brasília highway, about 5,000 are in an advanced stage of degradation (Serrão *et al.*, 1978).

All in all, stock raising seems to be one of the most difficult of agricultural enterprises in Amazonia. SUDAM intends to authorize no more cattle ranches in the evergreen rainforests, only in the forestlands with seasonally dry climates (C. Pandolfo, personal communication, SUDAM, Belém, Pará, Brazil, 1979). Nevertheless, there seems to be little doubt about Brazil's commitment to expanding its cattle-raising strategy for Amazonia. When a ranch becomes exhausted, the owner can readily move on to a fresh patch of undisturbed forest. Wasteful as this may be, compared to shifting cultivation practiced by smallholder forest farmers, Brazil seems to have little hesitation about fostering this kind of development on the grounds that there are plenty of untouched forests to support the ranching industry for many years to come. According to various reputable authorities in several centers of Brazil the prospect as of early 1979 is that many more areas of forest will be converted to artificial pasture during the next several years at least; and if any measure of success is forthcoming, this could become the dominant form of land use in an appreciable part of Amazonia by 1990. Of course, this is no more than a forecast, and no details are available to indicate, however roughly, the potential scale of forest clearing that could be entailed. The prospect is mentioned here merely as a qualitative indication of what could well lie ahead for Amazonia's forests. Ironically, Brazil could almost certainly derive much more animal protein through exploitation of its Amazon river system, which, with over 2,000 known species of fish, drains one-fifth of all the earth's freshwater. Indeed, preliminary estimates suggest that Amazonian fish could supply Brazil's entire requirements for animal protein, and produce a surplus for export.

Timber Exploitation

Over 80 percent of Brazil's growing wood volume is estimated to occur in the Amazonian forests, with hardwood stocks valued by RADAM at over $1 trillion. To date, Amazonia has contributed only marginally to Brazil's timber output. Brazil anticipates that tropical hardwood forests elsewhere, notably in Southeast Asia and West Africa, and currently supplying 85 percent of the world market, will be exhausted by the year 2000, if not well before. So Brazil believes that Amazonia's timber resources could serve to ease the nation's huge and growing foreign debt. In addition to export opportunities, the domestic market for industrial wood is projected to increase over 4 times by the year 2000. Thus the rationale for expanded exploitation of Amazonia's timber stocks (Alvim, 1977; Bruce, 1976; Cox, 1977; Muthoo, 1978; Nyyssonen, 1978; Palmer, 1977; Pandolfo, 1978; Potma, 1976; Reis, 1978; Rudolph et al., 1978; Schmithüsen, 1978).

Amazonia's dense *terra firme* forests, covering 2,860,000 km², have timber stocking rates that average 178 m³ per ha, compared with only 130 m³ in dense forests of southern Brazil, 20–80 m³ in the *cerrado* (savannah region of Brazil having a more or less continuous layer of xeromorphic grasses and sedges with a discontinuous layer of low trees and shrubs), and 30 m³ in Amazonia's *varzea* forests. Under present logging and transportation patterns, timber harvesting in Amazonia is limited to about 100 m on either side of navigable rivers and even less on either side of roads, meaning that hardly 1 percent of the dense forest zone has been considered operable to date. With improved technology, logging areas are expected to expand to about 500 m on either side of rivers and roads, making some 430,000 km² of Amazonia, or 15 percent, accessible. These potentially loggable areas are estimated to contain, at stocking rates of 175–180 m³/ha, some 7,516 million m³ of potentially commercial timber—almost half of all such timber available in the country. However, only 25 tree species are generally acceptable on commercial markets at present, reducing the timber stocking rate to as low as 60 or even 40 m³/ha, thus reducing the accessible and actually commercial timber stocks to a total of 1,933 million m³.

According to planning projections by Brazil's forestry agency, Instituto Brasileiro de Desenvolvimento Florestal (IBDF), Amazonia is expected to produce, by the end of the century, around 27 million m³ of industrial wood per year, or nearly 9 times the present amount. This level of output will be feasible, at harvesting rates of only 18 m³/ha, from around 195,000 km² of dense forest.

In order to plan for this expanded zone of forest undergoing timber exploitation, IBDF has proposed that some 400,000 km² be earmarked for potential exploitation, in 12 selected areas scattered throughout Amazonia. The proposal envisages that forest areas be assigned to concessionaires through "risk contracts," arrangements under which the government would share in any profits but would not incur losses

(Schmithüsen, 1978). At the same time, SUDAM has proposed (Pandolfo, 1978) that at least 800,000 km² be set aside as forest reserves for eventual timber exploitation.

Meantime a huge amount of wood—much of it commercial timber—is wasted when patches of Amazonian forests are cleared for nonforestry purposes, notably smallholder agriculture and cattle ranching. The total area in question is put, very roughly, at a minimum of 10,000 km² per year. Because of the scattered distribution of agricultural and stock-raising ventures, and given the constraints of commercial factors, it would not be easy to dispatch even a moderate proportion of this timber to market. To date, however, the amount is less than 0.5 percent of timber available following felling operations, the remainder—perhaps as much as 40 million m³ of commercial timber per year—going up in smoke.

To carry out its ambitious plans for forest exploitation in Amazonia, Brazil intends to rely heavily on foreign investors. A number of multinational timber corporations are already active in Amazonia. They include National Bulk Carriers, Georgia Pacific, and Atlantic Veneer of the United States; Eldal of Japan; and Bruynzeel of Holland (Irwin, 1977). Of these, by far the most important is National Bulk Carriers, with its project on the Jari River in Amapá (Kalish, 1979). Purchased in 1967 by the American billionaire Daniel K. Ludwig for a reported $10 million, it totals 16,000 km². Some 1,000 km² have been planted with gmelina and pine trees, to feed a $275 million pulpmill that will shortly start to produce 750 t of paper pulp a day. The project's overall investment has now reached $740 million. Jarilandia also grows rice, raises cattle, and produces kaolin. Another 1,000 km² of plantations are already mapped out.

Forest Conversion

Of the 10 largest countries of the TMF biome, Brazil is the most difficult for which to determine how much forestland has been converted to alternative uses. This is especially regrettable in that the amount of forest being eliminated per year is almost certainly as much as in any two other countries combined. The situation is simplified, however, by the fact that most human intervention into the Amazonian forests is of an absolute kind: Timber harvesting, which may have a marginal or marked effect on the residual forest but still leaves a forest, is only a very minor factor in Amazonia (at any rate, to date). The main forms of intervention are smallholder colonization and cattle raising, both of which entail complete elimination of the original forest.

During the past few years, a number of figures have been publicized proposing that appreciable amounts of forest are being eliminated each year. While there is much variation among these figures, a body of ostensibly reputable opinion seems to suggest that as much as 260,000 km² of forest have been cleared during the recent past (generally taken to mean something like the last two decades). True, if one were to consider all the Amazonian forest that has existed within recorded memory, there could be some substance to a figure of this magnitude. (For example, the forest of the Bragantina zone at the easternmost end of Amazonia, an area of some 25,000 km², was settled by immigrant farmers around the turn of the century, and within the space of some three or four decades lost virtually all its forest cover, until all that now remains is grossly denuded landscape with exhausted soils.) Certain senior scientists, including the former head of Instituto Nacional de Pesquisas da Amazonia, Dr. Warwick E. Kerr, gives credence to a figure of 260,000 km², suggesting that at least one-tenth of the original forest cover has been eliminated.

It is difficult to comment on the validity of such assertions. Whereas bioclimatic data suggest that the original spread of the Amazonian forest was considerably greater than within the recent past (Sommer, 1976, reviews the arguments), it cannot be stated with assurance how much forest in fact existed at the turn of the century. Nor can one satisfactorily ascertain just how much forest now remains in all the areas in question, not just eastern Pará (for which good data are becoming available, see below), but for other fringe territories around the Amazonian forest zone. For purposes of this review, then, these figures are disregarded. They are not rejected: They are considered to be too insubstantiated to play a part in the assessment being attempted here.

Other figures suggest that only half as much forest has been eliminated—at any rate, during the recent past. For example, the main forestry agency, IBDF, asserts (according to several officials consulted in February 1979) that during the period 1966–1977 a total of 114,697 km² of forest were eliminated. This works out at an average of 10,427 km² per year, though of course, due to the accelerating rate of conversion during the 1970s, the annual amount must be larger in the late 1970s than in the mid-1960s. The agency charged with responsibility for Amazonia, SUDAM, states (according to several authorities consulted in February 1979) that during the period 1966–1975, a total of 115,000 km² were accounted for (45,000 through cattle raising, 35,000 through smallholder settlement and other agricultural colonization, 30,000 through highway construction, and 5,000 through timber harvesting); this makes an average of 12,777 km² per year. These two sets of figures are roughly comparable. Again, however, it is difficult to evaluate them, in the absence of additional objective assessments. The Brazilian agency that has spent several years on detailed mapping of Amazonia, RADAMBRASIL, is known to have completed collecting and collating data, and analyzing the results; but the agency is not yet in a position to disclose its findings and conclusions. When RADAMBRASIL can publish its comprehensive results, the situation will become much plainer, and much less open to argument.

Meantime, a documented survey has recently been completed by Brazil's National Institute for Space Research (INPE) (dos Santos and Novo, 1978; Sonnenburg, 1978; Tardin *et al.*, 1979). According to Landsat images taken from 1975 to 1978, over an investigation area of 552,000 km^2 in northeastern Pará (around 15 percent of Amazonia), more than 41,000 km^2, or 7.4 percent, have been completely converted from forest cover to alternative forms of use (in 2 of the 31 areas analyzed, 28 percent of the forest has been eliminated). True, the area under investigation is one that has been subject to exceptional amounts of colonization, settlement, and exploitation. But it is certainly not the only area to be subjected to development of both intensive and extensive kinds in recent years; much the same can be said of the southeast border zone of Pará, also of a significant sector of northern Mato Grosso, an appreciable fringe of Rondonia, and parts of Acre and Amapá (plus other patches in more central sectors of Amazonia, *e.g.*, along the highway stretch Maraba-Altamira-Itaituba, and in the *varzea* floodplains). Indeed, large tracts of forest have been eliminated along a broad swathe extending through the forest zone traversed by the Belém-Brasília Highway since its construction 15 years ago.

Tempting as it may be to try to produce a best judgment figure for total amount of forest cleared in Amazonia, and of the current clearing rate, this survey does not attempt any calculation of that sort, on the grounds that all such semi-arbitrary reckonings will shortly be overtaken by a comprehensive remote sensing assessment. The INPE is in the process of mapping the remainder of Amazonia, and should have results available, in the form of comprehensive documentary information, by early 1980. This will provide objective evidence that should leave little doubt about the status of this vast tract of the TMF biome—and should thus put an end to the contentious arguments that have characterized the debate about Amazonia during the past decade. Brazil was the first developing nation to establish a broad-scale remote sensing program, and it has now developed the largest capability, including a Landsat ground-receiving station. The Landsat findings will mark a major step forward in Brazil's efforts to conduct rational planning for its Amazonia forest resources.

In addition, through routine and systematic use of Landsat imagery, Brazil will be able to conduct ongoing monitoring of Amazonia. This will prove all the more pertinent to the extent that marginal conversion of the Amazonian forests could have more than marginal consequences. Even were forest conversion not to become extensive by, perhaps, the year 2000, elimination of large sectors of forest could affect remaining forests throughout the basin. This is because of the nature of hydrological systems that govern Amazonia's water regime. As revealed by recent research (Salati *et al.*, 1978), less than half of the region's rainfall drains away, via rivers with their 27,000 km² of surface area, into the Atlantic Ocean. The rest of the rainfall is returned to the atmosphere through evapotranspiration. At the same time, part of the rainfall derives from moisture circulating within the region, rather than from outside, *e.g.*, from the Atlantic. This means that the region serves as a source of much of its own moisture. The implications could be profound. When a portion of the forest is eliminated, the remainder could prove less capable of evapotranspiring as much moisture as was circulating through the ecosystem before. In turn, this could mean a steadily desiccating ecosystem. And so on, with each reduction of the forest expanse. According to government officials in Manaus, Belém, and Brasília (February 1979), Brazil envisages that eventually 400,000 km² of forest will be cleared for agriculture, and as much again for other purposes.

Thus a series of urgent questions is raised. At what stage could Amazonia's forest start to be transformed into a different, *i.e.*, drier, type of forest? Has the process already begun? If so, how far has it gone? Could it still be reversed? What could be the ecosystem-wide consequences of forest conversion on the scale envisaged by the Brazilian government? These are questions that the scientific community scarcely knows how to formulate as yet, let alone supply answers to. It is to the Brazilian government's credit that, while remaining committed to its ultimate policy of developing Amazonia, it is now restraining the formerly headlong pace of its programs to open up Amazonia. Through 10 years of often difficult experience, Brazil has learned that it must proceed cautiously if it is to achieve worthwhile development of its huge Amazonian territories. It is a measure of Brazil's new attitude toward Amazonia that the recently installed president , His Excellency Sr. Joao Baptista Figueiredo, has established a federal committee to propose to Congress a new conservation framework for the immense forestland resources of Amazonia. Another example of this attitude was His Excellency's June 5 (1979) decrees that create three new conservation units in Brazil, including a mammoth 22,000-km² national park of Pico da Neblino in Amazona state, extending from the Venezuelan border in the north to the Negro River in the south.

THE CARIBBEAN

The Caribbean Islands generally, while located in the TMF zone, possess very little forest anymore, due to long-standing pressure from their human populations (Howard, 1977; Whitmore, 1974). The only significant tracts are reputed to be some 16,000 km² in Cuba, 1,550 km² in Puerto Rico, 11,000 km² in the Dominican Republic, and 2,350 km² in Trinidad and Tobago. In virtually each of these cases, however, the remnant forests are severely disrupted or grossly degraded through unregulated exploitation of various sorts. From the standpoint of documenting primary moist forests, they can be virtually disregarded.

CENTRAL AMERICA

Since the five countries of Central America—Costa Rica, El Salvador, Guatemala, Honduras, and Nicaragua—plus Belize and Panama cover relatively small areas, 537,840 km² in total, it is convenient here to consider them all together. The region has featured extensive moist forests in the past, many of them wet forests, and some of them were unusually diverse, with rich stocks of species (D'Arcy, 1977). However, these forests have been widely exploited for timber, and, more significant still, forestlands have been taken for various forms of informal and planned agriculture. As a result, most parts of the region now have only remnant patches of forest. Since 1950 the area of man-established pasturelands and the number of beef cattle in Central America have more than doubled—an expansion that has occurred almost entirely at the expense of primary forests, of which two-thirds are now thought to have been cleared (Myers, 1979; Parsons, 1977).

A salient factor of present-day Central America is pressure from human populations (Denevan, 1976; Wasserstrom, 1978). In 1920, the region supported 4,890,000 persons; in 1979, there are almost 23 million; and in the year 2000, the projected number is likely to exceed 39 million. The average urbanization rate at present is around 30 percent, much higher than for most TMF countries of Africa and Southeast Asia, but considerably lower than for most of the countries of tropical Latin America, which means that large communities are rural inhabitants, dependent upon agriculture for their livelihood. Panama is an exception: Of its 1.9 million people, 40 percent live in Panama City and Colón and another 10 percent in other urban areas, so the population exerts less pressure on remaining forests than is the case in other countries of the region.

Belize

Belize's 22,965 km² are officially considered to contain about 20,000 km² of forestlands, though a large portion consists of open woodland and various forms of savannah. Moist forest is reported to account for no more than 16,300 km², of which only 12,200 km² support vigorous communities. Evergreen rainforest occurs in the southern, more mountainous part of the country, with over 4,000 mm of rainfall, though little remains in the coastal plain; this forest area has been extensively disrupted by cyclones as well as by human activity. Evergreen rainforest also occurs as mangrove and swamp forests, while in the north, on low-lying outcrops of limestone, occurs semi-deciduous rainforest, together with a species-rich old secondary forest in the region of abandoned Mayan cultivation (Whitmore, 1974). Generally speaking, the forests are considered to be extremely varied and rich in flora.

Timber exploitation affects some 10,000 km², extracting a highly selective harvest that nevertheless exerts a significant impact on the residual forest. To date, lack of forest-industry infrastructure has limited the volume of wood produced, and Belize has been importing timber from Mexico. The government intends to reverse this imbalance in its timber trade.

Belize supports a small human population, around 125,000 persons. At the same time, there is an abundance of arable land, permitting moderately intensive agriculture (the government considers that altogether 8,800 km² could support planned agriculture, part of it in the moist forest zone). As a consequence, the forests have hitherto been subjected to little exploitation pressure from formal and informal agriculture. By 1976, only 872 km² were under permanent cultivation for sugarcane, bananas, and citrus fruits, plus some pasture, while shifting cultivation is reputed to account for less than 200 km².

This all means that some 11,000 km² may still support good-quality moist forest, albeit subject to some disruption through light-impact timber harvesting.

Costa Rica

Of Costa Rica's 49,132 km², a 1967 inventory estimated the forest area to be 22,000 km², most of it evergreen or semi-evergreen rainforest, together with some deciduous and montane cloud forest (Persson, 1974). Subsequent investigations (Tosi, 1972) indicated that primary moist forest could be said to constitute 17,772 km², secondary moist forest 1,688 km², old degraded forest 2,304 km², and intermediate old, secondary forest 3,729 km², for a total of almost 25,000 km². Still more recent surveys (Cannon *et al.*, 1978; Dirección General Forestal de Costa Rica, 1977) suggest that the forested area could now amount to only some 16,000 km².

For many years, considerable tracts of forest, estimated at 300–500 km² per year, have been turned over to agriculture and other nonforestry land use. Prominent among these conversion purposes has been cattle raising. In 1950, Costa Rica's pastures covered 12.4 percent of the country, whereas they now account for around one-third of national territory (Parsons, 1976). In 1960, Costa Rica's cattle herds totalled slightly over 900,000, but they have now topped 2 million. During the 1960s, beef production expanded by 92 percent, but during the course of that decade, local consumption of beef declined by 26 percent, to a mere 8 kg per head per year, almost all the extra output being exported. Costa Rica now exports around 45 million kg/year, of which well over half goes to the United States, for a value of around $40 million (Central America as a whole exports an average of one-third of all beef produced, but Costa Rica exports two-thirds).

However, during the presidency of Daniel Oduber in the mid-1970s, a more systematic and rational strategy was adopted for the country's forests. A Natural Resources Institute was proposed to conduct ecologic evaluation studies of national territory, and to formulate a program for integrated land-use planning. The national parks network was expanded, until it contained a greater proportion of land than is the case for any other Latin American country. Under the new President, Rodrigo Carazo, this parks network is scheduled to be expanded still further, until it will amount to about 10 percent of national territory.

El Salvador

Of El Salvador's 21,393 km², only 2,600 km² can properly be classified as forest, much of which is degraded, and in some places grossly. This is hardly other than can be expected for the most densely populated nation in Latin America, supporting 4.4 million people at a density of over 200 persons per km². At least 4 million depend upon agriculture for their livelihood, and at least 80 percent of the populace requires charcoal for its fuel needs. Thus forests in El Salvador are largely a matter of history.

Guatemala

Of Guatemala's 108,889 km², 53,000 km², or almost 49 percent of the country, are reported to be forested (this brief account is based on the author's observations, 1976; Gómez. 1979; Hederström, 1977; Mittak, 1975, 1977; and recent governmental documentation). Of this forest extent, about 10,000 km² consist of temperate coniferous montane forests (LaBastille and Pool, 1978; Veblen, 1978), the rest being TMF. The main TMF areas are in the Department of Petén in the northeast, occupying one-third of national territory; even though less than half the land is considered arable, the government plans to colonize and develop large portions of this forest, particularly through a 9,000-km² project near the Mexican border scheduled for intensive agriculture. This initiative continues a decades-long trend to convert moist forests to agriculture and cattle raising. The Ministry of Agriculture believes that through establishment of corn, rice, and banana croplands, and of ranching enterprises, Petén's population can be increased several times over.

Apart from these brief remarks, one is inclined to agree with Persson (1974) that very little is known about forests in many parts of Guatemala.

Honduras

Of the country's 112,044 km², some 70,500 km² are reported, according to recent government documentation, to be forested. Rather more than 40,000 km² are classified as moist forests, mostly in the eastern sector of the country, where they make up part of the relict Mosquitia Forest, one of three major expanses of rainforest remaining in Middle America. (Certain estimates of the early 1970s, *e.g.*, Persson, 1974, put the proportion of TMF somewhat higher, albeit interspersed with open stands of Caribbean pine.)

The main factor in conversion of Honduras' moist forests in the past has been agricultural expansion, notably cattle raising. The Instituto Nacional Agrario has recently designated several moist forest areas for colonization and agricultural development.

Nicaragua

Of Nicaragua's 147,943 km², forestlands are officially designated to cover 64,000 km², much of which can be categorized as moist forest—around 50,000 km² in the early 1970s (Persson, 1974), now reduced to some 35,000 km² (United Nations Country Office in Nicaragua, personal communication, January 16, 1979). The remainder constitutes mainly montane coniferous forest.

Although Nicaragua is considered to feature the largest tract of TMF remaining in Central America, this is only a small portion of what is reputed to have existed half a century ago. It is being eliminated at a rate of at least 400 km² per year (conceivably twice as fast), partly due to shifting cultivation and partly due to settlement agriculture.

The principal cause for the recent regression of moist forest is the encroachment of man-established pasture, often preceded by shifting cultivation (slash-and-burn agriculture), widely practiced by a large proportion of the population. In an attempt to modernize the country's agricultural sector, the Instituto Agrario, in conjunction with the Instituto de Fomento Nacional, is trying to introduce formal planned agriculture into extensive parts of the eastern region, possibly including part of the Mosquitia Forest. In addition, timber exploitation has extensively disrupted primary forests for around half a century, and especially during the past two decades.

Panama

Of Panama's 75,474 km², a total of 40,816 km² are officially classified as forests. Of this area, 38,873 km² may be categorized as lowland rainforest, and 1,736 km² as moist montane forest. But at least 10,000 km² of these forestlands are reputed to have been seriously disrupted through slash-and-burn agriculture. For example, the tributary watersheds surrounding the Canal, originally covered with dense rainforest, and as recently as 1952 still 85 percent forested, have lost much of their forest cover in the past two decades, both to cultivation and stock raising (Agency for International Development, 1978; Wadsworth, 1978). The largest remaining tract of lowland evergreen rainforest is found in Darien province, an unusually diverse and species-rich area. How long the Darien forests will survive is questionable in view of proposals to complete the last link of the PanAmerican Highway.

COLOMBIA

Of Colombia's 1,138,000 km², forestlands are officially designated as covering 678,000 km², or 60 percent of national territory. Not all these "forestlands," however, are forested. Since World War II, at least 200,000 km² of forest are believed to have been eliminated through human activity, mostly in the highland zone running down the center of the country and in the Uraba area in northwestern Colombia. More recently, a fair amount of lowland forest has been cleared, notably at the foot of the eastern Cordillera and bordering onto Amazonia: Since the mid-1960s, some 16,000 km^2 of forest in the Caquetá and Putumayo territories have been given over to settlement agriculture and stock raising, while a further 45,000 km^2 of these lowland forests are in the process of being cleared or are scheduled for clearing. Official forest-lands even include some 10,000 km^2 characterized as *vegetación deserticia* and another 10,000 km^2 as "eroded zones." Thus "natural forests," *i.e.*, forests little disturbed by man, are now estimated to occupy only 364,000 km^2, or 32 percent of national territory (Table 11). (This review is based on the author's visit, 1979; and on Ayala, 1978; Canadian International Development Agency, 1977; CONIF, 1979; Delgado and Vallejo, 1977; Dodson and Gentry, 1978; Eden and Andrade, in press; Florez and Rendon, 1977, 1978; Gentry, 1977, 1979; Kirby, 1976, 1977; Proyecto Radargrametrico (PRORADAM), 1975; Tosi, 1976; World Bank, 1975.)

TABLE 11   Colombia: Recent Estimates of Forest Area (km^2)

Year of Estimate	Agency Conducting Estimate	Estimated Total Forest Area	Estimated Forest Area in Amazonia
1966	Instituto Geográfico, Agustin Codazzi	646,000	n.a.[a]
1972	INDERENA (Instituto de Desarrollo de los Recursos Naturales Renovables)	512,000	386,000
1975	FAO/BIRF	468,000	349,000
1976	INDERENA-Canada (CIDA)	463,000	349,000
1977	CONIF (Corporacion Nacional de Investigación y Fomento Forestal)	394,000	270,000

[a] Not available.

NOTE: The discrepancies between the 1977 CONIF data and the earlier figures stem not so much from rapid man-caused depletion of forests, as from new methods of mapping, notably side-looking radar under Proyecto Radargrametrico del Amazonas (PRORADAM). Moreover, PRORADAM may not have included all savannah areas in Amazonia, nor the recent colonization incursions, thus producing a lower figure for forest cover as compared with earlier estimates.

SOURCE: Florez and Rendon, 1978; CONIF, personal communication, 1979.

Natural forests include two main regions: the Pacific region, extending along the Pacific coast and into contiguous highland areas, comprising some 57,200 km², or 4.6 percent of the country; and the Amazonian region and environs, of lowland evergreen rainforest, covering some 309,000 km², or 27.2 percent.

Pacific Region

The Pacific region is officially estimated, according to a recent survey, to comprise 57,250 km² of forests (Table 12). The region is defined as lying between the Pacific coast and the height-of-land boundary formed by the western Cordillera, and by the borders with Panama and Ecuador. It is an exceptionally wet zone, some parts of it receiving well over 10,000 mm of rainfall per year. Although this Choco region, as it is known, is one of the richest floristic areas on earth, it is one of the most poorly known, and could even rank as the least botanically known area of South America (Dodson and Gentry, 1978; Gentry, 1977). Much of the region can be categorized as lowland evergreen rainforest, encompassing the greater part of the Pacific coast rainforest that extends from Panama to Ecuador, and covering the coastal plain on the western slopes of the Andes (with montane rainforest on the higher slopes of the Cordillera). The region contains several acknowledged centers of species diversity, some of which possibly coincide with the so-called Pleistocene refugia (Gentry, 1979; Prance, in press).

Although some 77 percent of these forests can be considered, in terms of exploitable timber, commercial forests or potentially commercial forests, 84 percent of them can still be considered unexploited. Because of the extremely damp climate, plus infertile and poorly drained soils, agriculture, mostly of subsistence type, is difficult at best, and is mainly confined to 1-km strips along the main rivers. This in part explains why over half of the population of 600,000 live in urban communities. Moreover, road construction and other forms of infrastructural development are not readily pursued. Thus a large part of the region remains under primary forest. Given the need for Colombia's economy to exploit the country's timber resources, however, and because their inaccessibility ensures that it will be many years before Amazonia's forests can make a significant contribution, the Pacific region can be expected to undergo expanding exploitation for timber. Already a considerable area has been extensively disrupted, if not destroyed outright, at the southern end of the Choco, and where the northern extension borders Panama at the Darien Gap (Gentry, 1979).

TABLE 12   Colombia: Forests of Pacific Region (km²)

Forest Type	Total (and %)		Exploited or Converted to Other Uses	Exploited Areas	Unexploited Areas
Commercial or potentially commercial					
Low hills (mixed-species forests on undulating terrain, largest potentially exploitable reserve of wood in region)	21,781	(53.0)	1,743	412	19,626
High hills (similar to low hills forests, but with low wood volume and on highly erodable terrain, so unlikely to be exploited in foreseeable future)	8,251	(20.0)	30	81	8,140
Guandal (mainly freshwater swamp forests, principal source of commercial timber)	7,985	(19.5)	3,348	1,091	3,546
Mature mangrove	2,419	(5.9)	2,419	—	—
Nato (transition forests between guandal and mangrove)	669	(1.6)	277	32	360
SUBTOTAL	41,105	(100.0)	7,817	1,616	31,672
Noncommercial					
Mountains	14,588	(90.4)	22	—	14,566
Swamps, lakes, and water courses	1,077	(6.7)	—	—	1,077
Young mangrove	394	(2.4)	—	—	394
Brush	86	(0.5)	—	—	86
SUBTOTAL	16,145	(100.0)	22	—	16,123
GRAND TOTAL	57,250		7,839	1,616	47,795

SOURCE: Canadian International Development Agency, 1977.

Amazonia

The Oriente sector of Colombia, *i.e.*, the Orinoco and Amazon basins, constitutes well over half the country. Yet it supports less than 5 percent of the population. Therefore, given the problems of rural-urban migration related to population pressures in upland farming areas, especially unemployment, the government has encouraged colonization of Amazonia, where few vested interests would be upset.

Shortly after the end of World War II, initial measures were undertaken to attract settlers, especially in a narrow belt of plains at the foot of the eastern Cordillera on the fringe of the largely unexplored lowland rainforest of Amazonia. The activity centered on two areas, Caquetá (13,950 km^2) and Putumayo (11,540 km^2). In 1934, these two areas supported 26,590 people; by 1951, the total had increased almost 2.4 times to 63,387; by 1964, by a further 2½ times, to 160,200; and by 1975, by almost another 2 times to 403,000. During the period 1951–1974, the average annual growth rate for Caquetá was 6.6 percent, and for Putumayo 5.2 percent. Of the present populace in these two areas, over 90 percent are nonindigenous, by contrast with less than one-third nonindigenous in the rest of Amazonia, which contains only 51,310 people (CONIF, 1978; Eden and Chesney, 1977; Espadas, 1975; Florez and Rendon, 1977, 1978; Kirby, 1976, 1977; Proyecto Radargrametrico, 1975; World Bank, 1975).

By early 1979, the annual growth rate for the two areas had reached 15,000 persons. With an average family size of six persons, this means a total of 2,500 families. Being mostly landless peasants from the Cordillera, with a background confined largely to growing coffee and similar highland crops, they have very little idea of how to respond to lowland forest environments with 2,000–4,000 mm of rainfall per year. So the settlement strategy has focused on supplying a large plot of land to each colonist family. According to the World Bank, which has provided almost half the 1971–1978 funding for the $56 million settlement program, each colonist now receives a plot that generally ranges from 40–85 ha (a holding of less than 50 ha is considered only marginally capable of returning an adequate living). Between one-tenth and one-sixth of the holdings are given over to crop growing, between one-third and one-half are used for pasture, and the rest are left unexploited. Despite low stocking rates, the emphasis is increasingly on cattle raising, with an average number of cattle per family ranging from 19 in Putumayo to 29 in Caquetá (in 1974, Caquetá had 625,000 head of cattle, of which 29,000 were consumed locally and 42,000 sold out of the region). Through a process of consolidation on the part of a few successful ranchers, some 600 holdings now amount to 500–1,000 ha each; one notable enterprise, Larandia, formerly covered 44,000 ha with 25,000 head of cattle before it was divided into six separate ranches.

The influx of new settlers each year is believed to be accounting for some 1,500–2,000 km^2 of forest. Despite the vast amounts of timber felled—at least 3.5 million m³ per year, according to early-1979 estimates—less than 1 percent is sawn and sold.

During the last few years, official enthusiasm for this type of settlement has declined. This has been primarily due to the rapid decline in productivity of agricultural lands—a not unexpected repercussion in territories with low-fertility soils and high annual rainfall. In fact, many small-scale cattle ranchers have gone bankrupt after only 5–10 years of operation. The minimum stocking rate is now considered one head of cattle to 2 ha, and the minimum holding some 300 ha to 60–100 head, allowing for the sale of a few animals each year to supply a basic cash income. Despite these constraints, a leading government agency, Instituto Colombiano de Reforma Agraria (INCORA), continues to express support for cattle ranching and related forms of agricultural settlement in the low-lying forestlands of Amazonia. By contrast, another government agency, Instituto de Desarrollo de los Recursos Naturales Renovables (INDERENA), has become much more cautious about the entire prospect of exploiting Amazonia through these broad-scale, extensive, and essentially wasteful methods.

As of early 1979, the government was doing less to promote migration into Amazonia. With apparent support of the President, it is formulating a change of policy as regards settlement, and it is immediately slowing down plans to build roads and establish supporting infrastructures. With regard to the longer-term future, however, the government is plainly committed to some form of eventual development for Amazonia. Whether the emphasis will be on agriculture or timber exploitation is not yet clear. Experience is demonstrating that the region is generally too wet, and features soils of too low fertility, for conventional forms of agriculture. As for timber exploitation, with the constraints of market preferences and harvesting technology, the lowland rainforest is too heterogeneous to make lumbering anything but difficult at best. Moreover, the rivers of Amazonia flow away from the country's main markets, making extraction of timber a less promising prospect than in other such rainforests.

The future course of events depends, of course, on the planning that becomes possible when the government obtains basic data concerning its forest resources in Amazonia. Through radar-mosaic surveys conducted during the 1970s, the government discovered that in forestlands exploited to date, colonization and timber harvesting have been far more extensive than previously supposed. Thus there is now a premium on detailed mapping of remaining forests. A major survey and inventory project, Proyecto Radargrametrico de Amazonas, has been under way since the mid-1970s. It is to present a comprehensive report, with details of such conditions as forest types, wood volumes, and soil distributions, by early 1980. This survey project will later be integrated with a Landsat remote sensing program that is now getting under way.

Of Ecuador's 299,976 km², some 180,000 km², or 60 percent, are classified as forested (Persson, 1974; Putney, 1976; Sourdat and Costode, 1977). Of particular importance are the Amazonian forests, covering around 87,000 km², and the coastal wet forests, 27,000 km² comprising some 58 percent of the country's forests. Of the Amazonian sector, by far the greatest portion is covered with upland moist forest, mostly evergreen rainforest, on slopes down from the treeline on the eastern side of the Andes to the lowland plains. This is one of the wettest parts of the whole Amazonian basin, with no seasonal variation in rainfall. Floristically it is very rich (though extremely poorly known), and includes the large Napo center of diversity. The coastal forests comprise both lowland and montane evergreen rainforest, extending as high as the treeline on the western slope of the Andes. Comprising the southern end of the Pacific coast region rainforest extending from Colombia, they are likewise very diverse (Gentry, 1978, 1979; Dodson and Gentry, 1978; Grubb *et al.*, 1963; Sourdat and Costode, 1977). Indeed, Ecuador as a whole has an extremely rich flora (with by far the greatest diversity to be found in the forests): The country perhaps features as many as 20,000 plant species, compared with an estimated 20,000 for all of Central America including southern Mexico, and 25,000–30,000 for all of Brazilian Amazonia. Moreover, the flora contains a very definite endemic element, being especially rich in epiphytes.

Amazonia

The Amazonian forests remain largely undisturbed, due to the lack of roads and poor river communications that have restricted human incursions. Nevertheless, between 1950 and 1962 the population of the Oriente region grew 1.7 times to 79,000, followed by a further 2.1-times growth by 1974 to 168,000 (Kirby, 1976). Following the discovery of oil in the late 1960s there has been some intensive road-building activity, accompanied by increasing settlement: "The pace of (forest) destruction is rapidly and continually accelerating" (Gentry, 1978).

Thus the population growth rate has expanded markedly during the 1970s. This applies especially to the Napo area, which in 1974 included 38 percent of the rural population of Amazonia; featuring good soils, the Napo Forest is being rapidly converted to oil-palm plantations. Most of the new immigrants are "spontaneous settlers," *i.e.*, subsistence peasants who have found themselves landless elsewhere, and who now seek to make a living from the "empty lands" of Amazonia through small-scale crop growing (under the Land Colonization Laws, any land which is undisturbed forest is, by definition, unproductive, and thus becomes subject to expropriation for distribution to landless farmers). In addition, a limited number of immigrants engage in extensive forms of agriculture, notably cattle ranching; in Napo, as much as 81 percent of agricultural lands are under pasture, many in 30–50-ha parcels, while occasional holdings are several times larger, such as those of 1,000 ha near Aguarico.

Coastal Forests

As for the coastal forests, they represent

. . . the country's fastest-disappearing habitats, . . . opened up within the last decade by road construction. . . . In the last five or six years formerly extensive wet forest vegetation has been converted to almost solid banana and oil palm plantations. The coastal lowland wet forest probably contains more acutely threatened plant species than any other part of Ecuador . . . and possibly even all South America (Gentry, 1977).

Before the area was penetrated by the first road in 1960, it was almost completely covered with undisturbed primary forest; but within 10 years the wet forest had virtually disappeared except for a few small patches, one of which was converted into the Rio Palenque Science Center (containing more than 800 plant species in 87 ha of natural forest, many of them endemic—probably the highest recorded plant diversity in the world) (Dodson and Gentry, 1978; Gentry, 1979).

In conclusion, it is apparent that Ecuador's moist forests, and especially its extraordinarily diverse and species-rich rainforests, are being rapidly converted away from their undisturbed status as primary forests. No quantitative information is available concerning total areas involved, much less the different ecotypes in question. Nor are any projections available to indicate detailed trends for the next one or two decades. However, a reasonable prognosis, on the basis of information from authoritative observers, cannot rule out the prospect that Ecuador's forests could well undergo progressive disruption and impoverishment within the years immediately ahead.

FRENCH GUIANA

French Guiana, 97,369 km², lies, like Suriname, mostly on the Guyana Shield with its center of diversity. The populace of less than 100,000 is almost entirely concentrated along the coastal belt. Forest cover is estimated to total 86,460 km² (Marchand, 1973; Persson, 1974), but no details, whether qualitative or quantitative, are available concerning the vegetation types, except that the predominant ecotype is lowland evergreen rainforest, probably with some heath forest and possibly some lower montane rainforest in the southwest. In addition, there are a few hundred square kilometers of mangrove forest, and a few small patches of swamp forest.

Exploitation of the forests and forestlands, for whatever purpose, appears to be negligible; indeed, for the greater part of the country, it is almost certainly nonexistent. This situation appears likely to persist for the foreseeable future.

GUYANA

Guyana's approximately 215,000 km² are extensively covered with evergreen rainforest except for an 80-km wide coastal zone that supports 90 percent of the population of 826,000 people.

The most widespread ecotype is lowland evergreen rainforest (interdigitated with various forms of heath forest), estimated to cover some 134,000 km². In the southern part of the country, there are several extensive tracts of montane rainforest, estimated to cover 47,500 km². In addition, there are some patches of swamp and marsh forest, estimated to cover 5,300 km². These statistics derive from inventories and reconnaissance surveys carried out in the early 1970s, but conversion of primary forest is proceeding so slowly that one can reasonably accept the figures as valid in 1979. (This brief review is based on Fanshawe, 1952; Persson, 1974; Conservator of Forests in Georgetown, data obtained from aerial-photography surveys and authoritative on-ground investigations which can be considered to be "adequately reliable," *i.e.*, accurate within 10 percent, 1979.)

Although timber exploitation constitutes the main form of land use in accessible forest areas, it is confined to less than one-third of the country's total forested extent. Logging is highly selective, with one species producing more than 50 percent of lumber extracted by volume, and six species comprising more than 75 percent. Average annual timber output for 1973–1977 has been around 220,000 m³, causing marginal disruption for less than 100 km² of forest each year.

The coastal-zone populace looks to the interior forests for its supplies of firewood and charcoal. Harvesting is mostly conducted on a planned and systematic basis by a few commercial operators, rather than through random gathering on the part of rural inhabitants. The impact amounts to marginal disruption for less than 100 km² of forest each year.

Shifting cultivation occurs in limited parts of the western highlands, notably in the Pakaraima Mountains, and in the southern sector of the country. It is mainly practiced by Amerindians who make up no more than 5 percent of the nation's populace. No estimates are available concerning the amount of forest affected, but the consequence is likely to be small or very small. Planned agriculture and cattle ranching are concentrated along the narrow coastal belt, in riverine areas, and in savannah zones, so forests are little affected. An oil-palm project in the northwestern sector will entail clearing of a little over 40 km² of forest by 1983; this apart, no large-scale plantation projects are envisaged. A hydroelectric scheme at Mazaruni near the Venezuela border could, if completed, flood about 2,600 km², but the project has been stalled for several years.

All in all, there seems little prospect that Guyana's primary forests will be much modified within the foreseeable future.

MEXICO

Of Mexico's 1,963,133 km², forests, both tropical and temperate, account, according to a National Forestry Inventory in 1977, for some 400,000 km², or 22 percent of the country. Since the forest cover is closely associated with topography, moist forests, estimated to cover 110,000 km², are found notably in the southern part of the country—though except for a few patches in the extreme southeast, these moist forests can be considered subtropical rather than tropical. Montane forests on the Cordillera consist of open stands of pine, oak, and juniper species. (This survey is based on Gardono et al., 1975; Gómez-Pompa, 1978; Inventario Nacional Forestal, 1977; Mata et al., 1971; Persson, 1974; Rodriguez-Bejerano, 1978; Rzedowski, 1978; Soto et al., 1979; Vovides and Gómez-Pompa, 1977.)

The only remaining substantial tropical evergreen forest is the Lacandon Forest near Mexico's southern border—especially significant in that it forms one of the three large remaining lowland rainforests in all of Middle America. Covering some 13,000 km², it has been extensively disturbed through shifting cultivation, timber harvesting, and cattle raising. Two smaller patches of tropical rainforest are found at the

Isthmus of Tehuantepec, totalling some 2,000–3,000 km², and at Las Tuxtlas in Veracruz province, only a few thousand hectares.

These remnants of TMF are undergoing rapid conversion. The principal cause lies with government-sponsored colonization programs, notably for planned agriculture and especially for coffee plantations and cattle ranches. Programs of this sort are under way in parts of Veracruz and Chiapas, while there are plans to create additional settlements in the states of Quintana Roo and Campeche. As for subsistence agriculture and other forms of "spontaneous farming" in forestlands, colonization by otherwise landless peasants has been taking place throughout Chiapas for several decades; as much as 25 percent of the Lacandon Forest near the Guatemala border is believed to have been eliminated through this cause. Furthermore, a new project for 13,000 km² of this forest will entail immediate cultivation of 6,000 km²; with a government investment of $4 million, the project is intended to supply employment to 25,000 Lacandon Indians.

However, over 26,000 km² of the Lacandon Forest have been declared a forest reserve, of which the 3,300-km² Montes Azules have been set aside as a UNESCO biosphere reserve.

Regrettably, detailed quantitative information is not readily available for Mexico's TMF. The country recognizes the need for hard data on which to base its forest planning policies, and a remote sensing and resource mapping program is expected to produce much statistical detail by late 1980 if not earlier (Soto *et al.*, 1979).

PERU

Of Peru's 1,285,215 km², some 775,000 km², or 60 percent of the country, are believed to contain forests. Of these forests, around 650,000 km² are considered to be evergreen rainforest, the great bulk of it in Amazonia. In the extreme northwest of Peru, close to the Ecuador border, occurs a tiny patch of Pacific coast rainforest, as a small southern extension of the exceptionally wet rainforest that reaches northward as far as Panama. (This review is based on M. J. Dourojeanni, personal communication, Director-General of Forests and Wildlife, October 1978–February 1979; Dourojeanni, 1976, 1979; Durham, 1977, 1979; Gentry, 1977; Malleux, 1975.)

The territorial entity that is legally designated as Amazonia, covering 785,400 km², comprises a lowland area of 696,000 km², and an upland zone (600–4,000-m elevation) of 89,000 km². At least 80 percent of the region is considered to be covered with evergreen rainforest—an ecotype that is here wet throughout the year, except for a slightly seasonal variation in the south. The region contains several centers of species diversity, which may coincide with certain of the so-called Pleistocene refugia.

The principal factor in conversion of the Amazonian forests is agricultural settlement. According to a 1940 census, Amazonia then contained 406,820 people (6.1 percent of the national total), of whom 326,091 were rural inhabitants (Table 13). By 1972, these figures had increased to 1,307,675 (9.3 percent), and 926,266. According to demographic and socioeconomic projections, Amazonia by the end of the century is likely to contain some 5 million people (18.9 percent), of whom 2,500,000 will be rural inhabitants (Dourojeanni, 1979). In 1937, the area of cropland in the Amazonia forests was estimated at 1,081 km², or 7 percent of the total cultivated area of Peru; by 1968, the figure had quadrupled to 4,290 km², or 20 percent—the increase accounting for half the increase in Peru's total cultivated areas (Durham, 1977, 1979). In one locality the rural population increased from 10,543 in 1940 to 62,111 in 1972 (for an annual rate of increase approaching 6 percent), while the amount of cultivated land increased from 32 km² in 1943 to 439 km² in 1974.

Various forms of forest farming, and especially shifting cultivation, are believed to have eliminated sizable tracts of rainforest on the eastern slopes of the Andes during the period 1945–1975 (Dourojeanni, 1979). Although no more than 10,000 km² of forestlands are cultivated annually, it is thought that agriculture has accounted for some 45,000 km² of rainforest in total. Cattle raising is estimated to have accounted for a further 6,000 km², which means that agriculture of all forms can be said to have eliminated some 51,000 km² of rainforest to date, or 6.3 percent of Amazonia's total forest extent.

It is important to understand the impulse behind the growing spread of agriculture in Amazonia forestlands. According to Durham (1979), who has made extensive studies of the advance of the "settlement

TABLE 13   Peruvian Amazonia: Population Growth

Year	Amazonia Population	Percentage of National Total	Rural Population
1940	406,820	6.1	326,091
1961	874,942	8.5	656,974
1972	1,307,675	9.3	926,266
2000 (projected)	5,000,000	18.9	2,500,000

SOURCE: Dourojeanni, 1979; Durham, 1977.

frontier" in the forested lowlands, the critical factor is not only that migrants overflowing from the Andes find themselves being pushed into frontier forestlands in search of land. They are rather pulled by the prospect of raising tropical fruits and beef to meet market demand from Lima and other major cities of Peru west of the Andes, and of raising cash crops, notably coffee and coca (*Erythroxylon coca*), to meet market demand from countries overseas. In other words, most deforestation is not attributable to invasions of subsistence farmers from overcrowded highlands; rather, it is due to inducements of commercial enterprises far beyond Amazonia, fostered in part by the Peruvian government and in part by communities still further afield.

However, these trends may be stabilizing, as a result of experience with irrigation projects in the coastal desert region of the country, which are yielding better agricultural returns than pioneer agriculture in the Amazonian rainforest (Terborgh, personal communication, 1979). Moreover, petroleum exploration has been less productive in Peru than in neighboring Ecuador, with the result that there has been comparatively little road building; and the road-building program has been recently curtailed due to the chronic financial plight of the government. However, as Gentry (1977) remarks, "destruction along the road from Tingo Maria to Pucallpa and the new Carretera Marginal along the base of the Andes (which will soon be completed along the entire length of the Huallaga Valley) indicate that the same irreversible forces are operating." At the same time, the government is still inclined to regard parts of its Amazonian territory as a potential salvation for its population and food problem: On the basis of recent agroforestry breakthroughs near Uramiguas, it seems possible that highly weathered and acid soils of the lowland forest can readily yield more rice, corn, and soybeans, among other crops, than can lands cleared by bulldozers, which strip tropical soils of their topsoil (Bandy *et al.*, 1978).

What amounts of forests are now being cleared, and what is the prospect for the end of the century? It is difficult to obtain substantive data for a region that is so remote from the rest of the country and characterized by poor communications. Nevertheless, some preliminary calculations have been attempted (Dourojeanni, 1979) in order to indicate the nature and scale of the exploitation patterns that may well lie ahead for Amazonia. The total area under effective agricultural use and under rotation is now estimated to be 13,200 km^2 or thereabouts, while as much as 37,380 km^2 of land have been abandoned as unfit for further use. In addition, and supposing that each family of eight persons is clearing an average of 1 ha of new land per year, an additional 2,250 km^2 are accounted for each year. These figures add up to a total of

52,830 km² (to be compared with a figure of 51,000 km² earlier proposed for cultivation and ranching together, and arrived at through a different calculation). The prognosis for the year 2000 is that the number of rural families will have grown from the present 225,000 to 312,500, and that they will be clearing 1.5 ha per family per year, for a total of 4,680 km². The entire area under effective use and under rotation by that stage is projected to have reached 30,240 km² or thereabouts, and the area abandoned and with little further use, 89,760 km². This all means that the accumulative area cleared will have reached roughly 120,000 km².

As for timber exploitation, small-scale logging and sawmilling, causing no more than marginal disruption to the residual forest, were affecting some 4,540 km² by the late 1960s (Dourojeanni, 1979). By 1978, the amount of forest affected had grown to 11,000 km² per year. In addition, some heavy commercial logging has commenced during the second half of the 1970s, leaving a markedly modified forest of around 30 km² per year (Dourojeanni, 1979). The total amount of forest now affected by logging is estimated to have reached some 70,000 km². By the end of the century, the amount affected per year is projected to be 20,000 km², and the accumulative total some 300,000 km².

True, these calculations, like those for the impact of agriculture, are no more than informed estimates (designated by Dourojeanni, Director-General of Forestry, as "adequately reliable," *i.e.*, accurate within 10 percent), while those for the end of the century are advanced only as a very preliminary rough attempt to recognize the scope and intensity of human activities that are likely to affect Amazonia's forests during the next two decades. These projections indicate that as much as 420,000 km² of forestlands could well bear the mark of human intervention by the end of the century. This will amount to some 54 percent of the Amazonian region and almost 65 percent of the present rainforest.

All the more apposite and urgent, then, are current plans on the part of the Directorate-General of Forestry to maintain at least 20 percent of Amazonia in pristine form, set aside as parks and reserves (Dourojeanni, 1979). All the more timely, too, are the government's efforts to assess its natural resource stocks in Amazonia through a remote sensing program under the National Office for the Evaluation of Natural Resources. Information from this resource survey, in quantitative detail, should start to become available during 1980.

SURINAME

Suriname, approximately 162,000 km², lies mainly on the Guyana Shield with its center of diversity. Almost 90 percent of the population of 510,000 lives in the capital and chief port Paramaribo, while other human settlements are concentrated along the coastal plain. The remainder of the country, at least 85 percent of national territory, is covered with uninhabited and undisturbed primary forest—an estimated 133,520 km² of evergreen rainforest (both lowland and upland), some 9,790 km² of swamp and marsh forest, and some small patches of mangrove forest (Persson, 1974; Suriname Forest Service, personal communication, 1979).

Timber concessionaires hold harvesting rights in some 20,000 km² of accessible forests close to the coastline. Selective logging removes about 10 percent of the stand, without serious damage to the residual forest. No more than 300 km² are affected per year, a rate that is not expected to increase for the next several years. Given that there is little pressure from agricultural communities on forestlands—indeed the bulk of the populace displays little inclination for agriculture—there is little likelihood that, for some time to come, the country's forests will be converted to nonforestry uses, such as agricultural settlements or cash-crop plantations, at a rate much beyond the present 20 km² or so per year.

Suriname is exceptional in having taken major measures to safeguard its primary forests. A network of parks and reserves protects examples of all major ecosystems, and totals more than 50,000 km², almost one-third of national territory and one-third of the forest estate (Mittermeier and Milton, 1976).

In summary, there appears to be every prospect that Suriname's extensive primary forests will remain little changed for many years.

VENEZUELA

Of Venezuela's 916,490 km², it was estimated in the early 1970s that some 352,310 km² could still be considered to constitute primary rainforest (Hamilton, 1976; Hamilton *et al.*, 1976; Medina *et al.*, 1977; Persson, 1974; Steyermark, 1977). Of this rainforest extent, some 167,000 km² could be classified as evergreen rainforest, 94,000 km² as deciduous rainforest, and 20,000 km² (mostly in the south) as montane rainforest.

Of the overall total, some 314,400 km², or 89 percent, are located south of the Orinoco River, in the state of Bolivar and in Amazonas Territory. North of the Orinoco River, around 73,930 km² are believed to have been formerly covered with moist forest, mostly rainforest, but now only about 30 percent of the original total remains (33 percent disappeared during the period 1950–1975 alone). Logging has been going on for decades, with a significant sawmill industry. In addition, much forest has been converted to crop growing and livestock grazing. If present exploitation trends persist (and they are likely to accelerate), within another two decades this northern forest area could be reduced to only about 14,000 km² or even less.

As mentioned, the great bulk of primary moist forests in Venezuela lies south of the Orinoco River, where, with the exception of some agricultural clearing along the border between Amazonas Territory and Colombia, human influence seems to have been marginal at most. Of the nation's population of almost 13.5 million, 85 percent live in urban communities, especially along the coastal belt. This means that, unlike most other countries of the Amazon basin, there are few landless peasants seeking "empty lands" in forest territories for subsistence agriculture. Thus one can realistically accept a recent summary view to the effect that "south of the Orinoco River, large areas of primary rainforest still exist, particularly in Amazonas Territory" (Hamilton, 1976).

A program to develop the south was launched in 1968, and in 1972 an army-built road to Brazil was completed, but there has been little agricultural settlement or timber exploitation. In 1975 the government imposed a ban on the main lumbering areas of the state of Bolivar (though a little illegal timber cutting has continued). In the main, the Commission for the Development of the South (CODESUR) seems to have proceeded cautiously, and the Ministry of the Environment has advocated that at least 60 percent of the forest extent be left undisturbed. How far this approach will be maintained by the new government, installed in March 1979, is not clear. In early 1979, there were indications that beef interests might seek to open parts of these southern forests. Moreover, Venezuela is finding that its development revenues, notably its oil earnings, have been overspent, so there is growing incentive to exploit the forests and to bring the country's wood-products trade into surplus (forests south of the Orinoco have been producing only around 66,000 m³ per year, virtually all from the state of Bolivar).

Venezeula's rainforests are thought to contain several centers of species diversity, certain of which may coincide with so-called Pleistocene refugia. Beyond this, and the summary statements given above, one is obliged to agree with Persson (1974) that little is known about the nature and extent of Venezuelan forests. To meet this lack of information, the government has instituted a remote sensing survey, including both Landsat and side-looking radar, to conduct a resource inventory of 175,750 km² of forestlands by 1981.

10 Regional Review: Tropical Africa

Tropical Africa is reputed to contain some 1,500,000–1,675,000 km² of tropical moist forests (TMF). Of this total, some 70,000–88,000 are believed to occur in West Africa, 20,000–23,300 in East Africa, plus 15,000 in Madagascar, and 1,450,000–1,550,000 in Central Africa (very roughly 900,000–1,000,000 in Zaire alone).

These figures must be viewed, by comparison with the other two main TMF regions, as crude reckonings. Tropical Africa appears to have much less, and much less reliable, information available than is the case for Southeast Asia and many parts of tropical Latin America.

Furthermore tropical Africa appears to contain a much smaller proportion of rainforest of much poorer quality than the other two regions (while far richer than temperate-zone forests) (Meggers et al., 1973). However, Africa's moist forests feature several centers of diversity and high species endemism (Hamilton, 1976; Prance, in press).

These various characteristics are dealt with in more detail in the country profiles that follow.

CAMEROON

Of the Federal Republic of Cameroon's 475,258 km², much of the smaller southern part is still covered with moist forest, almost all of evergreen ecotype. In particular the southwest, where mountains rise to over 4,000 m, is exceptionally wet, with certain localities receiving

151

10,000 mm of rain per year. (This summary is based on the author's observations during the 1970s; Persson, 1975, 1977.)

It is apparent that large areas of moist forest have been disrupted, if not entirely eliminated, through human activities, notably timber exploitation and shifting cultivation. Regrettably no reliable estimates are available for the areas involved: A limited forestry inventory was conducted in 1967, but none since that time. In the main, one is inclined to agree with Persson (1975): "The estimates of how much forest really remains are quite unreliable." However, for the sake of establishing a benchmark, however preliminary and approximate, of the present situation, a recent figure supplied by the Department of Forestry suggests that the amount of primary forest remaining could be as little as 175,000 km² and conceivably much less; UNESCO (UN Educational, Scientific, and Cultural Organization) (1978) estimates as little as 130,000 km².

The main form of forest exploitation is timber harvesting. During the second half of the 1970s, Cameroon has been producing around 1.3 million m³ of logs per year, and the government plans to increase this to 2.5 million m³ as soon as possible. Logging is widespread in the coastal zone, extending inland as far as Sangmelima, Yaoundé, and Bertoua. The greater the distance from the coast, the greater the difficulty in extracting timber, except for the southeastern sector where logs can be transported by river through the neighboring People's Republic of the Congo. A recent extension of the Trans-Cameroon Railway will bring several new forest tracts within reach, though a large area in the east, difficult of access and little exploited to date, may well remain beyond the reach of timber harvesters for some years to come. Logged areas are now thought to total as much as 85,000 km², and at least an additional 60,000 km² have been given out as timber concessions. A notable recent initiative is the project near Edea for utilizing mixed hardwoods in order to manufacture paper pulp; the initial objective is to process 500,000 m³ of wood per year, yielding 122,000 t of pulp, all of which will be exported to Europe.

Apart from these few remarks, very little knowledge seems to be available concerning Cameroon's forests. Similarly, next to nothing has been published concerning plans for conservation and exploitation of the forest resource, except for a preliminary announcement of a full-scale inventory of forest cover that is in early stages of planning. This lack of information is the more regrettable, since certain of Cameroon's rainforests, especially those bordering Gabon, could well feature the richest flora in Africa (Letouzey, 1976; Richards, 1963). The area has been postulated as a center of diversity, and part of a presumed Pleistocene refugia (Grubb, in press; Hamilton, 1976; Kingdon, 1971).

CONGO

Of the People's Republic of Congo's 342,635 km², forests are reputed to account for around 100,000 km² (UNESCO, 1978). Since these forests lie within Africa's equatorial zone, they can reasonably be categorized as moist forests, with 30,000 km² ranking as evergreen forests and the rest deciduous forests. Most of them are located in the central and northern parts of the country, with a few patches closer to the Atlantic seaboard (Persson, 1975, 1977).

With only 1.6 million people, population pressure on the forests is slight. Indeed, the country possesses over 20 ha of forest per head of rural populace. This means that if the entire rural population were engaged in shifting cultivation within forestlands, rotational periods of fallow would be long enough to allow forest ecosystems to recover from temporary exploitation. Nor do the agricultural needs of the country seem likely to present a threat to forests for some long time to come.

As for timber exploitation, the country's peak output was 2.5 million m³ in 1974, a remarkably low total considering the size of the forest resource. An explanation lies in the remote and inaccessible location of the northern forests, almost half of which are inundated for much of the year. Thus, although the southern patches of forest make up only about one-fifth of the entire forest estate, almost all log output comes from this small proportion. As a result, however, the southern forests are being rapidly depleted of their best stocks of hardwoods, but since exploitation hitherto has been highly selective, a second harvest may soon become available.

Apart from this summary, very little information is available concerning Congo's forests. This is particularly unfortunate since the western portion of the northern forests is considered one of the most diverse and species-rich areas in the Zaire basin forests. No details are available concerning possible forthcoming forest surveys, vegetation mapping projects, or resource inventories. At the same time, it must be said that, for the reasons cited above, the great bulk of Congo's primary forests seem likely to remain little disturbed for many years.

GABON

Gabon, 268,000 km², lies entirely within the equatorial climatic zone. On the Atlantic coast there is some 2,000–4,000 mm of rainfall per year, diminishing in the east to about 1,800 mm, while the dry season ranges from 7 to 14 weeks. Virtually the entire country is forested, except for some patches of savannah woodland and grassland along the southeast border. Although no recent precise figures are available, the country is believed to possess at least 205,000 km² of moist forest, most of it lowland evergreen forest, with, in the drier areas, various intermediate subtypes between evergreen and semi-deciduous forests. The latter may constitute some 60,000 km² in the eastern part of the country; evergreen rainforest is probably limited to some 25,000 km² near the coast; and the remainder can be characterized as evergreen moist forest. (This review is based on the author's observations, 1975; Catinot, 1978; Persson, 1975, 1977.)

Because of its extensive oil, uranium, and manganese deposits, and a GNP that has already reached $2,600 for each of the country's 650,000 citizens, Gabon perceives little incentive to exploit its forestry resources beyond the present moderate level, which already earns $100 per head per year for each member of the populace. In 1975, commercial timber concessions amounted to 80,750 km², the great bulk in the semi-deciduous forests. With a peak log output in 1973 of almost 3.5 million m³, the amount of newly logged forest each year is thought to be limited to roughly 3,000 km². Moreover, since as little timber is extracted as 10 m³/ha, the impact on the residual forest is light. Until the early 1970s, not many forest areas were accessible to timber exploiters, since there were very few roads, and the river network did not lend itself to transportation of logs to coastal ports; but the new Libreville-Belinga Railway is making accessible extensive forests of the interior.

Gabon's population of only 700,000 is generally concentrated in the coastal plain, especially Libreville and other coastal cities. Population pressure on the interior is negligible, and there has been virtually no agricultural disturbance of the forests. In fact, Gabon possesses 43 ha of forest per head of its total populace, and 55 ha per head of its rural populace—some 10 times higher than for almost all other countries of the TMF biome. A little shifting cultivation is appearing in the north and south, but it is very limited in extent and impact.

A new $280 million papermill is planned as a leading source of paper pulp in Africa, and the tropics' largest installation for processing mixed hardwoods. To produce 700 t of bleached sulphate pulp per day, the mill requires around 1 million m³ of wood per year. To supply these requirements, some 500 km² of forests will be clear-cut over a period of 30 years. To compensate, some 25–30 km² of forest plantations are scheduled to be established each year.

This favorable analysis of Gabon's forest estate suggests that it is reasonable to envisage little change for many years. This is especially encouraging in view of the center of diversity astride the Gabon-Cameroon border, which has an exceptional number of endemic plant species and a major concentration of endemic mammal species, particularly primates (Bigalke, 1968; Kingdon, 1971; Richards, 1973).

GHANA

Of Ghana's 238,220 km², the moist forest zone is estimated to encompass somewhere between 80,000 and 100,000 km². The precise figure for this zone is of little consequence, since most of Ghana's moist forests have been severely depleted, if not eliminated altogether. Remaining moist forests are almost entirely confined to forest reserves, which, according to the Conservator of Forests in Accra, now total 19,864 km². Some small patches of moist forest still persist outside the reserves, estimated at around 500 km², these patches being all that remain of unreserved forests totalling 3,500 km² in 1972 and 15,000 km² in 1954 (according to Annual Reports of the Forestry Department). In short, roughly half of Ghana's forests have been eliminated during the past 25 years. According to a recent World Bank estimate, forest stocks outside the reserves may become incapable of producing more than negligible amounts of timber by 1982; and the areas of moist forest under properly reserved status amount to no more than 16,000 km². (This brief review draws on the author's observations throughout 1975; Persson, 1975, 1977; Conservator of Forests, personal communication, 1979.)

Evergreen moist forest is limited to the southwestern corner of the country, covering a mere 1,700 km². Elsewhere moist forest ecotypes comprise various forms of semi-deciduous and deciduous forests, according to the rainfall gradient, which spans 1,800–3,000 mm with a dry season of 2–5 months. From a bio-ecological as well as a commercial standpoint, the forests are generally of poor quality.

The main factor accounting for the regression of Ghana's moist forests during the past several decades has been shifting cultivation. Ghana's populace of over 11 million tends to be concentrated in the southern part of the country, *i.e.*, in the moist forest zone. The fallow period allowed by shifting cultivators has steadily declined from an average of around 20 years at the end of World War II, to 10 years or less by the early 1970s, and more recently to as little as 3 years in certain localities. This trend means that shifting cultivators now exploit forest environments with an intensity that does not allow local ecosystems to recover: The amount of forest that shifting cultivators have been accounting for each year is estimated to have been as high as 5,000 km² (Persson, 1975, 1977). As a consequence, "informal farmers" have caused much of the former moist forest cover to be steadily eliminated; and by the late 1970s, shifting cultivators were penetrating ever more deeply into forest reserves. But due to lack of reliable information, it is not possible to say how far shifting cultivation is overexploiting forest reserves.

In summary, it appears likely that what little undisturbed moist forest as still remains in Ghana may shortly be eliminated. In terms of West Africa's moist forests overall, Ghana's forests are, ecologically speaking, among the most species-poor.

IVORY COAST

Of Ivory Coast's 330,149 km², roughly half are located in the TMF zone of West Africa. Not all of this area, however, is forested; in fact, only about one-third at most can be said to be still covered with moist forest, much of it disrupted if not degraded. In extensive areas, a large proportion of the forest has been reduced to a mosaic of remnant 10-ha patches surrounded by various forms of agricultural settlement. Thus there is good reason to credit recent assertions, including estimates by the World Bank, that primary moist forest may now be reduced to as little as 30,000 km² or even less. (This review is based on the author's observations during the 1970s; Bernhard-Reversat et al., 1978; Kernan, 1967; Lanly, 1969; Persson, 1975, 1977; Schmithüsen, 1977; and information from the Ministry of Planning in Abidjan.)

In the coastal plain and in the southern lowlands, with rainfall above 1,800 mm per year and two short dry seasons, the predominant formation is evergreen moist forest. Further inland, as the topography becomes steadily more elevated and the climate becomes marked by a single lengthy dry season, the moist forest gives way to open types of forests, and eventually to savannah woodlands.

According to bioclimatic data, moist forests may once have covered as much as 150,000 km² or almost half the country (Aubreville, 1947; Lanly, 1969; Sommer, 1976). By shortly after the end of World War II, however, moist forests covered only about one-half of the bioclimatic zone. In 1966, the country's first comprehensive forest inventory, conducted through aerial photography by the Development Resources Corporation of New York, revealed only 89,979 km² of relatively undisturbed primary forest, plus 57,010 km² of severely degraded or secondary forest; the survey also revealed that during the 1960s there had been an estimated rate of forest regression of some 3,000 km² per year (Lanly, 1969; Schmithüsen, 1977). In 1974, an additional survey showed that no more than 54,000 km² of primary forest remained, plus perhaps another 32,000 km² of secondary forest (Persson, 1975, 1977).

This drastic reduction in forest area has occurred primarily in central and southern parts of the country, which in 1966 contained well over three-quarters of the Ivory Coast's closed moist forests (Table 14). The decline has been especially severe in eastern zones, which, during the period 1966–1974, lost two-thirds of their 30,000 km² of closed forest.

There are two basic reasons for the rapid regression of the Ivory Coast's moist forests: timber exploitation and agricultural expansion.

Timber Exploitation

Until the late 1950s, many commercially valuable tracts of moist forest remained beyond the reach of timber harvesters, because communications in the country's interior were poor. After the Ivory Coast became independent, however, it embarked on a successful program of economic expansion and technological advancement. As a consequence, there are now 25,000 km of all-weather roads in the moist forest zone, while a modern seaport on the western coast handles log exports in bulk—two developments that have fostered the opening of previously unexploited forestlands. In addition, rapid harvesting has also been encouraged by the forestlands' favorable terrain and well-drained soils. In response to burgeoning demand on European markets for special hardwoods from the tropics, the Ivory Coast's log exports rose from 1.1 million m³ in 1960 to 3.5 million in 1973, over one-third of all tropical Africa's timber exports, which placed the country fourth among all tropical exporters of hardwoods after the "big three" countries of Southeast Asia. The 1973 exports brought in 26 percent of the total foreign-exchange earnings, worth more than coffee and cocoa together.

Timber extraction tends to be highly selective. Of 400 tree species available, only 25 serve commercial purposes. The average rate of harvest is only 7–10 m³ per ha. This extensive mode of exploitation requires large areas of new forest to be opened each year, as much as 4,000 km² during the period 1966–1974 (Schmithüsen, 1977) and possibly as much as 5,000 km² per year during the late 1970s. Given the amount of primary forest remaining, it is clear that this growing rate of exploitation would, if simply projected, lead to the final elimination of exploitable forests within a very short time, some reputable observers suggest as early as 1985. Afforestation currently amounts to only 30 km² per year and is scheduled to be expanded to 100 km² per year, but obviously the latter rate is grossly incapable of making even a dent in the problem of deforestation.

Agricultural Expansion

Still more important as a cause of conversion of the Ivory Coast's moist forests is the expansion of agriculture, especially small-scale cultivation on the part of various sorts of forest farmers. As commercial loggers open primary forests with timber tracks, large numbers of sub-

TABLE 14 Ivory Coast: Decline of Closed Forest, 1966–1974 (km²)

Region	Total Area	Closed Forest, 1966	Closed Forest, 1974	Amount Lost, 1966–1974	Percentage Loss[a]
Northwest	21,320	7,460	6,500	960	12.9
Northeast	30,060	13,730	5,500	8,230	59.9
Centernorth	36,120	20,390	9,000	11,390	55.9
Centersouth	17,300	12,090	9,500	2,590	21.4
Southeast	25,550	16,520	5,200	11,320	68.5
Southwest	25,820	19,600	18,300	1,300	6.6
TOTAL	156,170	89,790	54,000	35,790	39.9

SOURCE: Lanly, 1969; Persson, 1975, 1977; Schmithüsen, 1977.

NOTE: Of the 54,000 km² of closed forest reputedly remaining in 1974, a considerable part, probably over half, is degraded forest, much of it reduced to 10-ha relicts surrounded by various forms of indiscriminate agriculture. Moreover, it is estimated that at least 4,000 km² of closed forest are eliminated each year by cultivators.

[a] Determined by dividing amount lost, 1966–1974, by closed forest, 1966, ×100.

sistence cultivators are enabled to penetrate deep into forest territories that have hitherto been closed to them. This trend has been exacerbated during the past decade by the Sahel droughts, which have tended to cause waves of impoverished peasants to move steadily from drier savannah zones in the north toward moister forested areas in the south. Clearing away the residual forest that has been left by commercial loggers, these small-scale cultivators soon cause the moist forests to be far more depleted than the timber harvesters did. In the process, they account for large amounts of wood: During the period 1966–1974, timber harvesting extracted some 41 million m³ of merchantable timber, but forest farmers are estimated to have burned or otherwise disposed of some 186 million m³ of wood of all kinds.

According to field investigations, it can be said that roughly for every 5 m³ of logs removed by a timber exploiter, 1 ha of residual forest will be eliminated through follow-on cultivators (Lanly, 1969; Sommer, 1976). Now that most forestlands outside forest reserves have been logged and farmed, cultivators are encroaching onto the reserves themselves, in some places affecting as much as 20 percent of the reserved forest estate.

In summary, the Ivory Coast is notable for the manner in which, during the course of only two decades, it has allowed its capital stock of moist forests to be exploited on a once-and-for-all basis, apparently disregarding (at least in practical terms) any considerations of sustained-yield exploitation of both forest resources and forestlands. This is all the more regrettable in that the southwestern section of the country features part of the center of diversity straddling the border between Liberia and the Ivory Coast, and possibly coinciding with the so-called Upper Guinea Pleistocene Refuge, a forest area that is exceptionally rich in endemic species of both plants and animals, notably mammals (Bigalke, 1968; Grubb, in press; Hamilton, 1976; Kingdon, 1971; Myers, in press b).

KENYA

Of Kenya's 582,421 km², a 1977–1978 survey has revealed that only 16,702 km² can be considered forested, of which primary moist forest (seasonally moist, hence deciduous) is now believed to make up only 10,521 km². (This report is based on the author's 21 years' residence in Kenya; Migongo, 1978; Owino *et al.*, 1979; Republic of Kenya, 1979.) Since these data are derived not only from recent forest department records, but from Landsat imagery and aerial photography backed up by ground-truth checks, they can all be considered to be adequately reliable, *i.e.*, accurate within 10 percent, and they would probably be considered correct within 3 percent were it not for the fact that they do not take account of the encroachment of illegal settlers and cultivators, and of the activities of charcoal burners and illegal timber fellers.

Forest regression is believed to have been especially marked during the past 20 years, primarily as a result of expanding need for land by the largely agricultural populace. Regrettably no accurate benchmark statistics are available for forest cover in the past. However, reputable observers with many decades of residence in Kenya assert that before World War II the country's forest cover could have been 3 and possibly 4 times as large as now, while bioclimatic patterns suggest that two centuries ago there could have been twice as much again.

Among notable forest areas, the Kakamega Forest, located at 1,500-m altitude in western Kenya, is the easternmost relict of the equatorial forests that stretch across the Zaire basin. It thus contains variations of species that, being on the extreme fringe of their range, are adapted to environments different from their parent stocks. Officially stated to cover 230 km², this forest now amounts to little over 100 km², and is being steadily destroyed by timber cutters, charcoal burners, and development planners who wish to replace the primary forest remnants with exotic-tree plantations. At present rates of loss (which are likely to accelerate), this forest will be entirely eliminated shortly after the turn of the century. Nearby is the Nandi Forest, which in 1963 covered 1,636 km² and has been reduced by 1976 to 1,074 km². At present rates of loss, this forest too will disappear within another 25 years.

A single lowland moist forest is worth brief mention, the Arabuko-Sekoke Forest on Kenya's coast, comprising moist deciduous forest with some drier variations. A trifling fraction of what was once a forest extending for hundreds of kilometers along East Africa's coast, it has been reduced to 360 km². It is the only known habitat of three bird and at least one mammal species. In addition, the forest almost certainly contains an appreciable number of endemic reptiles, insects, other creatures, and plants. It is being destroyed for the same reasons as the inland forests, and at the present rate of clearing, it may well not survive much beyond the end of the century.

LIBERIA

Liberia's 11,094 km² lie almost entirely within the moist forest zone of West Africa. Rainfall ranges from 2,000 to 4,000 mm per year, with two short dry seasons for most of the country and a single 4-month dry season in the northern section. In earlier times, moist forest was presumably the natural vegetation for at least 100,000 km² of the country. But due to the impact of shifting cultivation (see below), much if not most of the country's primary forests have been transformed into various types of degraded secondary forest, or have been cleared away altogether. Of the remaining forests, roughly half, located in the southern sector of the country, can be categorized as evergreen rainforest, and the other half as deciduous forest. (This summary is based on the author's observations during the 1970s; Persson, 1975, 1977.)

So widespread has been human modification of Liberia's original forests, that estimates in the early 1970s indicated that as little as 25,000 km² of primary forest remain (of these relicts, some 16,000 km² have been established as forest reserves in which logging is permitted but settlements are not, the latter rule being difficult to enforce). In addition, there are some 23,000 km² of "broken forest" in which shifting cultivation has long been widespread. In fact, shifting cultivation is the dominant form of agriculture practiced in Liberia. It is very difficult to obtain reliable information for the numbers of people and the areas of land involved. All that reasonably can be stated is that large areas that were formerly forest have now been converted to rotational bush fallow and permanent scrubland. While sparsely populated localities feature rotation rates of 15–25 years, the rotation in areas closer to the coast occurs every 2–4 years. Recent estimates by the World Bank suggest that some 300 km² of primary forest are converted to degraded forest, or transformed into bushland, by shifting cultivation each year. In addition, large-scale plantations are planned for 1,400 km² of primary forest (Sommer, 1976).

As for logging, timber concessions cover some 16,550 km². Log output of around 2 million m³ per year is reckoned to account for some 2,000 km² of primary forest each year.

These two factors—shifting cultivation and commercial logging—appear likely to bring an end to all of Liberia's primary forests within another 10 years at most. This is all the more regrettable because the eastern portion of these forests encompasses part of a center of diversity straddling the border between Liberia and the Ivory Coast.

In view of its declining forest estate, Liberia has determined to conduct a detailed forest survey. With the support of the Food and Agriculture Organization of the United Nations, the Forestry Development Authority has initiated a country-wide inventory of forest resources, through aerial-photography/Landsat sensing and geodetic/ground-truth surveys. In addition, the Ministry of Agriculture is undertaking a program to identify forest soils for their agricultural potential, with particular regard to cash-crop plantations, small-scale mixed cultivation, and cattle ranching. These various projects have only recently begun, so results will not be available until about 1980.

MADAGASCAR

Of Madagascar's 587,562 km², only the eastern coastal/montane zone receives sufficient annual rainfall—2,500 mm, distributed throughout the year—to support moist forest. (This brief review is based on the author's observations, 1976; Bernardi, 1974; Chauvet, 1972; Koechlin, 1972; LeRoy, 1978; Persson, 1975, 1977; Rauh, 1979.)

The eastern moist forest is strikingly heterogeneous. It harbors many species-rich communities. It features an exceptionally high level of endemism, reputedly 89 percent. (Of more than 10,000 flowering plant species known in Madagascar, over 80 percent are endemic; this flora could represent only a small proportion of a much higher number of taxa that could once have existed in Madagascar before nearly 80 percent of the primary vegetation was destroyed.) While the eastern moist forest may once have extended for as much as 62,000 km², and possibly far more, it has now been reduced, as a consequence of shifting cultivation, to only 26,000 km² at most. Moreover, at least half of this relict has been disrupted and impoverished through shifting cultivation, which, having steadily grown more extensive and intensive during the past several decades, is currently reckoned to be accounting for 2,000–3,000 km² per year.

Beyond this brief summary statement, little can be said about Madagascar, even in approximate terms—the data are just not available. All that can fairly be asserted at present is that a tract of Africa's moist forests, that some observers consider to be among the richest of all TMF, has already been mostly reduced from primary forest to various forms of degenerate secondary forest, savannah woodland, and scrub; and little hope remains that the remnant patches of primary forest will survive much beyond 1985.

NIGERIA

Of Nigeria's 924,000 km², a 200,000-km² belt along the southern part of the country, where rainfall ranges from 2,000 to 3,750 mm per year, may be said to lie within the TMF zone. Yet, so extensively have forests been cleared in the past that surveys in the early 1970s revealed that moist forests have been reduced to less than 45,000 km² (Persson, 1975, 1977). According to the Federal Department of Forestry in Lagos, there now remain only 25,495 km² of moist forests that are worth classifying as forest reserves, of which no more than 16,000 km² can be considered sufficiently stocked to warrant further timber exploitation, and of which 1,281 km² have been converted into forest plantations. In addition, there are around another 25,000 km² of nonreserved forest. The forest reserves are believed to contain roughly half the wood volume of the entire country, while the nonreserved forests have been severely disrupted and impoverished. Of the moist forests, only a small portion, in the southwest and central-south sectors of the country, can be categorized as evergreen rainforest. (This brief review is based on visits to the country during the 1970s; Lawton, 1978; Onochie, 1975, 1979; Onweluzo, 1979; Persson, 1975, 1977.)

The main source of forest conversion is shifting cultivation. As is not unexpected in a country with more than 80 million people (and a population density in the moister, more fertile areas of over 200 persons per km²), forest farming of one type and another has been widely practiced for many decades. Certainly most of the lowland forests have been cleared at some time for cultivation, as evidenced by fragments of pottery and pieces of charcoal in moist forest soils (Lawton, 1978). According to experienced observers (*e.g.*, Persson, 1975, 1977), at least 70,000 km² of open woodland may have been closed moist forest as little as half a century ago, before it became degraded through the excessive exploitation of shifting cultivators with their ever growing numbers. In many parts of the country, rotation periods are now thought to have become as short as 4 years or less, allowing forest ecosystems virtually no chance to recover. Although even a rough grasp of shifting cultivation's impact is obviated by gross lack of reliable data, there seems little doubt, in the view of experienced authorities, that it is the key factor in the decline of Nigeria's forests.

A related problem lies with timber exploitation. Logging has been going on for most of the present century, and many unreserved forests have been exploited to such an extent that the proportion of wood volume remaining is now estimated to be as low as 30 percent. In 1966, Nigeria exported 500,000 m³ of timber, in 1970, 200,000 m³, and in 1976, 93,000 m³—since which time all exports have been banned. Most of the forests in forest reserves have been assigned to commercial concessionaires, and present exploitation patterns indicate that forests will have been exhausted of commercial timber by 1990 at the latest and possibly as early as 1985. Even were the exploitation of forest reserves shifted to a sustained-yield system, the reserves could supply only 2 million m³ of timber per year, whereas, by 1995 domestic demand for industrial wood is projected to have reached 11.7 million m³. This means that unless Nigeria can greatly expand its plantation program forthwith, it will need to import large amounts of timber from other parts of tropical Africa within the near future, thus intensifying exploitation pressures in the countries concerned.

The government recognizes that, in order to formulate a comprehensive conservation strategy for its remnant forests, it must prepare detailed vegetation maps on which to base land-use capability analysis. To this end, the Federal Department of Forestry has recently completed a 2-year aerial-photography survey, and is now utilizing Landsat imagery in conjunction with on-site investigations. The survey's results are expected to become available by early 1980.

SIERRA LEONE

Sierra Leone's 71,712 km² lie almost entirely within the moist forest zone of West Africa. So far as can be determined—and this is no more than a very approximate assessment—as much as 50,000 km² may still have featured little-disturbed moist forest as recently as the end of World War II. It is a measure of the pervasive impact of human activities that the amount of primary moist forest now believed to remain is officially stated to be no more than 2,900 km². Permanent forest reserves total some 3,000 km², insufficient to supply domestic need. (This summary review is based on two visits, 1972, 1975; Persson, 1975, 1977.) No experienced reliable observer believes other than that virtually the entire forest extent has been subject, at some stage or other, to shifting cultivation and related forms of indiscriminate forest farming. Similarly mangrove forests formerly extended along the entire coastline, but have now virtually vanished, due to overexploitation for firewood and building poles. During 1975–1976, a Food and Agriculture Organization of the United Nations/UN Development Program survey covered the entire country through aerial photography. This initiative should result in the release of vegetation maps by 1980.

TANZANIA

Of Tanzania's 943,072 km², moist forest is believed to comprise no more than 9,400 km², located almost entirely in the northern part of the country. They consist of a few relict montane tracts, in, e.g., the Usambara, the Pare, and the Uluguru mountains. These isolated remnants harbor many endemic species, together with a degree of subspecific differentiation without parallel elsewhere in Africa (Carcasson, 1964; Moreau, 1966; Turner, 1977). The Usambara Forest, where a great proportion of identified species are endemic, is reputed to have lost 70 percent of its forest cover within the last 20 years; the other montane forests in northern Tanzania have suffered similarly, most reduced to fragments that are undergoing rapid attrition. ·

UGANDA

Uganda's 243,317 km² are reputed to contain roughly 7,500 km² of moist forest, mainly in the southwestern portion of the country where they represent a partial spillover of the extensive center of diversity in eastern Zaire (for example, less than 200 km² of the Semliki Forest features 380 bird species [Kingdon, 1973]). In view of recent events in Uganda, very little is known about the present status of its moist forests, except that they have been undergoing various degrees of human disruption for many years, as is to be expected for one of the most densely populated countries of equatorial Africa.

ZAIRE

Zaire's 2,344,928 km² encompass a major portion of the Zaire (Congo) basin. The whole of the central and northern region receives around 2,000 mm of rainfall, sometimes much more, distributed throughout the year, and the natural vegetation is moist lowland forest, some limited sectors of which can be characterized as evergreen rainforest. (This summary is based on the author's observations, 1972–1979; Food and Agriculture Organization of the United Nations/World Bank, 1978; Persson, 1975, 1977; Synnott, 1977.)

Various figures have been proposed for the extent of Zaire's moist forests. While some estimates are as high as 1,100,000 km², many propose some 900,000 km² and UNESCO (UN Educational, Scientific, and Cultural Organization) (1978) suggests only 750,000 km². It proves exceedingly difficult to ascertain which estimate is more likely—if indeed the actual situation falls within the range cited. Of all countries of tropical Africa, Zaire is exceptionally lacking in adequate documentation (some 26 inquiries dispatched as part of the present survey elicited only one substantive response). This is especially untoward since, if the country is considered to possess the better part of 1 million km² of moist forests, this means it features over half of all moist forests in tropical Africa, and probably around one-tenth of the entire TMF biome. Thus it is important in principle to attempt as informed and reasonable an estimate as possible of the forest extent in Zaire. Bioclimatic data indicate that the figures given probably represent a "reasonable educated estimate"; and, for want of anything better (a point which is stressed), they are accepted here for purposes of this survey.

The question then arises, how much of this forest extent can be considered as primary forest? Again, no assessments, however approximate and preliminary, are available. One must depend upon the meager data base available, derived from the few agency assessments as have been conducted and from reports of reliable field researchers who have worked extensively in Zaire's forest zones. A 1974–1976 Canadian International Development Agency (CIDA) survey of 50,000 km^2 in the central part of the country has been followed by a review carried out by Italconsult on the basis of satellite coverage of 91,400 km^2 in western Zaire; and the country has concluded an agreement with the U.S. National Aeronautics and Space Administration for a comprehensive survey within the next few years.

Zaire's population of around 27.5 million is mostly rural, depending for livelihood on underdeveloped agriculture that consists mainly of shifting cultivation. According to crude calculations, this forest-farmer community could well be clearing 20,000 km^2 of forest per year. However, since Zaire possesses over 6 ha of forest per head of the rural population, it is probable that rotation fallow periods are still long enough to allow forest ecosystems to recover. Nevertheless, intermittent investigations reveal that large areas of primary moist forest are interspersed with patches of secondary forest of various ages. Unfortunately, no statistical details are available concerning the amounts of these categories.

As for timber exploitation, lumbering is confined to areas close to the few communications that exist, mainly river networks. By the mid-1970s, log production reached 0.5 million m^3 per year, but has been declining since that stage. Log exports during the 1970s have averaged more than 30,000 m^3 per year, a mere 2 percent of Gabon's.

The vast central portion of the Zaire basin, lying almost entirely within Zaire, features vegetation that is generally akin to that of the western and eastern sectors of the basin; yet it does not harbor many of the animal species that are widespread elsewhere, and it reveals little endemism (Hall, 1978; Hall and Moreau, 1970). Especially in the zone south of the Zaire River, which, although covered in forest today, is the site of Kalahari sands that imply desert conditions in the recent past (Moreau, 1966), the fauna is markedly species-poor. However, a forest area in the northeast contains the largest number of mammalian species in tropical-forest Africa, 15 percent of them being restricted to this zone (Bigalke, 1968; Kingdon, 1971). Generally speaking, this extensive area is more ecologically varied than almost all the remainder of the basin, and it has been postulated as one of the so-called Pleistocene refuges (Grubb, in press; Hamilton, 1976; Livingstone, 1979; Kingdon, 1971; Myers, in press a).

A salient feature of Zaire is its large network of protected areas, totalling 78,000 km² to date. Unfortunately a large proportion of this protected area comprises a single huge park, the Salonga Park, which, being located in the center of the country, serves to protect the least desirable of Zaire's lowland moist forests. Toward the eastern border, the 10,800-km² Maiko Park probably does more to safeguard Zaire's main center of species diversity and endemism. President Mobutu has repeatedly declared that he will increase his country's system of protected areas to reach 350,000 km², or 15 percent of the country; but none of these additional areas has yet been set aside, and there is no information on how many will be located in the moist forest zone, and particularly in the northeastern center of diversity. Were these ambitious conservation plans put into effect, it could mark a notable advance in terms of safeguarding a substantial amount of tropical Africa's moist forests.

Meantime, disruptive pressures of population growth and economic expansion do not exert much impact on the great bulk of Zaire's forests. At least, that is the situation to date; but, in view of the bankruptcy of the national economy, there could be efforts in the near future to extract a greater harvest from the timber resource. As a prognosis for the foreseeable future, however, one can expect little change in a situation that is, from a conservation standpoint, favorable.

These few evaluatory comments are advanced very tentatively, merely as a gesture of broad qualitative judgment concerning the present status and conservation outlook of this large sector of the TMF biome. While survival prospects can be considered hopeful, it should be borne in mind that, bio-ecologically speaking, these lowland moist forests of the Zaire basin are far from matching the biotic diversity of Latin America or Southeast Asia (Meggers *et al.*, 1972; Whitmore, 1975).

11 Summation

There is a single dominant conclusion to the survey: The TMF biome is undergoing conversion of extensive sectors.

A second major conclusion is that conversion trends and patterns are highly differentiated. Certain sectors of the TMF biome are undergoing widespread conversion at rapid rates, other sectors are experiencing moderate conversion at intermediate rates, while still other areas are encountering little change. Furthermore, the situation in the future is likely to remain highly differentiated, possibly in a manner that does not represent a simple extrapolation of the present situation.

DIFFERENTIATED CONVERSION RATES

Appreciable parts of the biome are undergoing conversion faster than many had supposed, whereas certain limited areas are probably undergoing little change.

Thus it is important to recognize that elimination of TMF is not a phenomenon common to all parts of the biome: Virtually all lowland forests of the Philippines and peninsular Malaysia seem likely to become logged over by 1990 at the latest, possibly much earlier. Much the same applies to most parts of West Africa. Little could remain of Central America's moist forests within another 10 years, probably less. Almost all of Indonesia's lowland forests have been scheduled for timber exploitation by the year 2000, and at least half by 1990. Extensive areas of Amazonia in Colombia and Peru could be claimed for

168

cattle ranching and various forms of cultivator settlement by the end of the century; and something similar is true for much of the eastern sector of Brazil's Amazonia.

By contrast, Central Africa is sparsely inhabited and has abundant mineral resources. This reduces the incentive to liquidate forest capital in order to supply funding for various forms of economic development. Hence there could well remain large expanses of little-disturbed forest by the end of the century. Similarly, the western portion of Brazil's Amazonia, because of its remoteness and perhumid climate, could undergo only moderate change.

In short, the overall outcome is likely to be extremely patchy, both in terms of geographic areas and degree of conversion (ranging from marginal disruption to outright elimination).

Areas Undergoing Broad-Scale Conversion at Rapid Rates

1. Most of Australia's lowland tropical forests, both rainforests and seasonal forests, due to timber exploitation and planned agriculture; could be little left by 1990 if not earlier.

2. Most of Bangladesh's forests, both lowland and upland, predominantly rainforests, due to timber exploitation, forest farming, and population pressure; could be little left by 1990 if not earlier.

3. Much of India's forests, predominantly seasonal forests, mainly upland, due to forest farming and population pressure; could be little left by 1990.

4. Much if not most of Indonesia's lowland forest, predominantly rainforests, due to timber exploitation, forest farming, and transmigration programs; could be little left in Sumatra and Sulawesi by 1990, in Kalimantan and most of the smaller islands by 1995, and in Irian Jaya by the year 2000.

5. Much of Sumatra's and Sabah's lowland forests, almost all rainforests, due to timber exploitation; could be little left by the year 2000 if not earlier.

6. Most of peninsular Malaysia's lowland forests, almost all rainforests, due to timber exploitation and planned agriculture; could be little left by 1990 if not earlier.

7. Much if not most of Melanesia's lowland forests, due to timber exploitation and planned agriculture; could be little left by 1990.

8. Most of the Philippines' lowland forests, predominantly rainforests, because of timber exploitation and forest farming; could be little left by 1990 if not earlier.

9. Much if not most of Sri Lanka's forests, predominantly rain-

forests, mostly upland, due to timber exploitation and forest farming; could be little left by 1990.

10. Much if not most of Thailand's forests, almost all seasonal forests, both lowland and upland, due to timber exploitation (especially illegal felling) and forest farming; could be little left by 1990 if not earlier.

11. Much of Vietnam's forests, almost all seasonal forests, both lowland and upland, especially in the south, due to forest farming, timber exploitation, and immigration from the north; could be little left by 1990.

12. Parts of Brazil's eastern and southern sectors of Amazonia, lowland rainforests, notably in Pará, Mato Grosso, and Rondonia; due to cattle raising, colonist settlement, and forest farming; appreciable tracts could be converted by 1990.

13. Most if not virtually all of Brazil's Atlantic coast strip of moist forest, due to timber exploitation and cash-crop agriculture, notably sugarcane plantations; could be little left by 1990 if not a good deal earlier.

14. Much if not most of Central America's forests, notably rainforests, both lowland and upland, due to forest farming, cattle raising, and timber exploitation; could be little left by 1990 if not earlier.

15. Parts of Colombia's lowland rainforests on the borders of Amazonia, especially in Caquetá and Putumayo, due to colonist settlement and cattle raising; extensive tracts could be converted by 1990.

16. Much of Ecuador's Pacific coast forests, mostly very wet and very rich rainforests, both lowland and upland, due to plantation agriculture and some timber exploitation; could be widely converted by 1990.

17. Much if not most of Madagascar's forests, especially rainforests, both lowland and upland, due to forest farming and timber exploitation; could be little left by 1990 if not earlier.

18. Much if not most of East Africa's relict montane forests, especially in northern Tanzania, mostly seasonal forests, due to timber exploitation, firewood cutting, and forest farming; could be little left by 1990.

19. Much if not most of West Africa's forests, mainly seasonal forests, due to timber exploitation and forest farming; could be little left by 1990 if not earlier.

Areas Undergoing Moderate Conversion at Intermediate Rates

These areas cannot be so readily listed as those under *Areas Undergoing Broadscale Conversion at Rapid Rates,* since less is known about their present status and future prospects. The listing is deliberately conservative.

1. Parts of Burma's lowland forests, almost all seasonal, due to forest farming and some timber exploitation; appreciable areas could be converted by the year 2000 if not earlier.

2. Much of Papua New Guinea's forests, mostly seasonal, both lowland and upland, due to timber exploitation and forest farming; extensive areas could be converted by the year 2000 if not earlier.

3. Parts of Brazil's Amazonia forests, lowland rainforests, notably in Amapá, Acre, sections of the TransAmazonia Highway system and of the *varzea* floodplains, and areas selected for timber exploitation, *e.g.*, Tapajos River area; due to colonist settlement, forest farming, cattle raising, and timber exploitation; appreciable tracts could be converted by 1990.

4. Parts of Colombia's Pacific coast forests, very wet and very rich rainforests, both lowland and upland, due to timber exploitation; extensive sectors could become converted by 1990.

5. Much of Ecuador's Amazonia forests, almost all rainforests, both lowland and upland, due to colonist settlement, forest farming, some planned agriculture, and also oil exploitation; appreciable areas could be converted by 1990, and much more by the year 2000.

6. Much of Peru's Amazonia forests, almost all rainforests, both lowland and upland, due to colonist settlement, forest farming, and some planned agriculture; appreciable areas could be converted by 1990, and much more by the year 2000.

7. Parts of Cameroon's forests, both seasonal and rainforests, both lowland and upland, due to timber exploitation and forest farming; extensive areas could be converted by 1990.

Areas Apparently Undergoing Little Change

Like *Areas Undergoing Moderate Conversion*, these areas cannot be so readily listed as those under *Areas Rapidly Undergoing Broadscale Conversion*, since less is known about their present status and future prospects. The listing is deliberately conservative, especially as concerns the long term.

1. Much of Brazil's western Amazonia, lowland rainforests, generally wetter and richer than eastern Amazonia; except for some timber extraction in limited areas, and some cultivation of *varzea* floodplains, exploitation of this huge zone could prove difficult in view of its unusually wet climate and distance from markets; it is reasonable to

anticipate—so far as can be ascertained, and the point is stressed—that much of this vast tract of lowland rainforest could remain little changed for some time, possibly until the year 2000.

2. Much of the forests of French Guiana, Guyana, and Suriname, almost all rainforests, both lowland and upland; timber exploitation, at present very limited, may expand, but, because population pressures are low, there is little likelihood of widespread colonist settlement and forest farming. So it is reasonable to anticipate—with caveat as under Brazil above—that large areas may remain little changed for a good while to come, possibly until the year 2000.

3. Much of the Zaire basin, comprising Congo, Gabon, and Zaire; some rainforest in Gabon, remainder mainly seasonal, almost entirely lowland; population pressures are low, and there are abundant mineral resources on which to base national economic development; timber exploitation, primarily limited to northern Congo and to Gabon, could expand; but in the main, it is reasonable to anticipate—with caveat as under Brazil above—that large areas may remain little changed for a good while to come, possibly until the year 2000.

In sum, the situation is highly differentiated, between and within the three main regions, as well as within some individual countries.

With respect to future trends, it seems plain that human population growth and economic aspirations, already factors of importance, will exert progressive pressures on TMF until their impact by the year 2000 could represent a colossal change from the present position. At the same time, it is necessary to bear in mind that exploitation patterns can change. It would be a mistake to suppose that the future will amount to a simple extrapolation of the present situation. Some exploitation trends could reveal a geometric rather than an arithmetic progression, while others could decline in significance or even fade away as they are supplanted by innovative forms of exploitation. Such discontinuities could arise as shifts in consumer demand in the developed world for special hardwoods from the tropics and in both developed- and developing-world demand for paper pulp from mixed hardwoods from the tropics. Some of these future possibilities are considered in Chapters 4–7.

PROBLEMS OF DOCUMENTATION

In view of the overall decline of the TMF biome, the establishment of as much documentation as possible of actual rates of forest regression in as many countries as possible is urgent, especially in the 16 countries that comprise 70–75 percent of the biome and in the 10 countries that have most of the richest type of TMF, *viz.*, lowland rainforest. Intensive surveys should be instituted for select localities that are known to be likely sites of exceptional ecological values such as centers of species diversity, and that are known to be undergoing unusually rapid attrition of their forest cover.

Because of the often large areas involved, and the usually impenetrable nature of TMF, most countries of the biome do not possess documentary evidence concerning their forests that amounts to much better than "informed estimates." True, these estimates are far better than nothing; they enable us to recognize the nature and scale of the challenge confronting those who wish to determine optimal ways to safeguard the biome for long-term sustainable uses of diverse kinds (including preservation of selected localities). The great bulk of statistics, however, cannot be construed to represent other than "best judgment assessments," and many of them are in effect "guesstimates."

For example, certain countries publish figures that are outdated, on the grounds that they do not yet possess adequate survey capabilities to offer anything more worthwhile. Indonesia continues to state that its forest cover amounts to 1,220,000 km². This figure is at least 20 years old, and does not take into account the widespread logging, shifting cultivation, and transmigration programs that during the past two decades have accounted for large areas of undisturbed forest, possibly as much as one-third of the entire extent. This discrepancy is all the more significant in that Indonesia could well encompass almost one-tenth of the entire TMF biome.

In addition, certain countries do not distinguish in their statistical records between actual forest cover and "forestlands," the latter term being used to mean something like "public lands not alienated for certain specific purposes." As a result, official forestlands in for instance the Philippines include sizable and long-established human communities, even urban settlements.

Thus it is essential to recognize that many published estimates of forest cover are of doubtful validity. This reservation applies especially to the ways in which these estimates are frequently used. For example, Zaire's forest cover is often stated to be around 1 million km², or more than 10 percent of the entire TMF biome. Yet the most recent and far-ranging appraisal of Africa's forests emphasizes that its best estimate for Zaire, based on 1972 information, derives from poorly known data with an accuracy level of plus or minus 40 percent. When Zaire is considered in conjunction with Indonesia (whose information gaps have been mentioned) and Brazil (whose statistical surveys have yet to be published), we find that as much as 5 million km², or well over half the entire biome, have yet to be documented in substantive fashion.

In these circumstances, estimates of conversion rates for most areas should be estimated with great caution. In view of the widely variable categories of "information" that must be used in such surveys, a concise, overall statement of the present status of TMF is simply not possible. The same applies, only more so, for extrapolations for the future.

This report should be read, therefore, with these critical constraints constantly in mind. While compiling the report, the author has been careful to avoid "bogus accuracy." Rather, he has frequently sought to describe the situation in many countries with what might be termed "precise imprecision."

COMPREHENSIVE AND SYSTEMATIC SURVEYS

Within the past 2 years or so, a number of countries have published results of comprehensive and systematic surveys, accomplished in the main through remote sensing techniques. These reports provide substantive and authoritative data for forest cover.

The two main countries in question are the Philippines and Thailand. The first of these features predominantly evergreen rainforest, the second almost entirely monsoonal deciduous forest. Thus a useful comparison can be drawn between two major distinctive forest ecotypes.

Each of these two countries finds that its forest cover is in fact far less than had been supposed as recently as the early 1970s. The Philippines now possesses only 38 percent forest cover as compared with former estimates of 57 percent, while Thailand now possesses only 25 percent as compared with 48 percent. Moreover, the forests of Thailand's eastern region, comprising over 15,000 km² in 1972, have been regressing at a rate of over 5 percent per year.

Several other countries, including a number of large ones and notably Brazil and Indonesia, have recently instituted comprehensive remote sensing programs for their forest resources. They should be able to publish systematized results within the next 1–2 years. An interim report for northeastern Pará in Brazil's eastern Amazonia reveals that an area of 35,612 km² has lost 28 percent of its forest cover within only 5 years. These remote sensing programs will greatly assist in achieving detailed evaluation of very extensive expanses of TMF.

POPULATION PRESSURE, ESPECIALLY FROM FOREST FARMERS

The largest factor in conversion of TMF lies with forest farmers of various sorts. Often known as shifting cultivators, these farmers are becoming less able to practice the forms of rotational agriculture that formerly constituted sustainable use of forest territories. Due to increase in their numbers, they now make intensive as well as extensive use of forest environments, with the effect that local ecosystems cannot recover fast enough. In addition, these traditional farmers are now being joined by large communities of subsistence peasants, who, due to lack of land elsewhere, are moving into forests where they adopt a slash-and-burn style of agriculture that leaves little possibility of forest regeneration.

These forest farmers have been estimated in the mid-1970s to total at least 140 million persons, or roughly 20 million families. If each family clears 1 ha each year, this means they are accounting for some 200,000 km² of forest each year. True, a good number of these farmers exploit secondary forests; and in some sectors of primary forest, *e.g.*, in Zaire, population densities may still be low enough to permit sustainable use of the forest with prospect to eventual regeneration of primary vegetation. But a number of recent studies suggest that forest farmers are converting at least 100,000 km² of primary forest to permanent cultivation each year.

In short, this factor could well be accounting for over 1 percent of the biome each year. When other factors are included in the reckoning— timber harvesting, planned agriculture, cattle raising—it is easy to give credence to long-established estimates from the Food and Agriculture Organization (FAO) of the United Nations and other agencies to the effect that well over 100,000 km² of TMF are being eliminated each year. Indeed it is possible to believe that the rough estimate of 20 ha disappearing per minute, equivalent to more than 105,000 km² per year, could be significantly low. A nearer estimate could lie with the figure advanced by the Director-General of FAO at the Eighth World Forestry Congress in October 1978: 40 ha per minute, equivalent to over 210,000 km² per year.

Moreover, population growth rates in many countries of the TMF biome are among the highest on earth. Unless economic development proceeds faster than hitherto (providing opportunities for alternative forms of earning a living), it is possible that a large proportion of the population increase in these countries will cause the numbers of forest farmers to grow disproportionately. In other words, while overall population growth in the countries in question may result in total numbers increasing by around two-thirds by the year 2000, the number of forest farmers could at least double and conceivably could expand much more. These calculations are crude to a degree: They are advanced merely as a measure of population pressures that could overtake TMF during the next two decades.

EXCEPTIONALLY ENDANGERED AREAS

Certain sectors of the biome feature unusually rich forest ecosystems. These include localities with centers of species diversity and high levels of endemism. In a number of instances, these exceptionally rich forest tracts are experiencing exceptionally rapid conversion. They thus merit priority. Examples include northwestern and eastern parts of peninsular Malaysia, northwestern Borneo, the coastal forests of Brazil in and adjacent to the states of Bahia and Espíritu Santo, the Pacific coast rainforest of Ecuador and Colombia with its perhumid climate and uniquely rich flora, Madagascar, Sri Lanka, New Caledonia, and the so-called Pleistocene refugia of southwestern Ivory Coast.

References

Aiken, S. R., and M. R. Moss. 1975. Man's impact on the tropical rainforest of peninsular Malaysia. Biol. Conserv. 8(3):213–229.

Agency for International Development. 1978. Panama Project Paper: Watershed Management. AID/LAC/010. Agency for International Development, Washington, D.C.

Aksornkoae, S. 1978. Structure of Mangrove Forests in Thailand. Faculty of Forestry, Kasetsart University, Bangkok, Thailand. 19 pp., mimeo.

Aldred, A. H. 1976. Measurement of Tropical Trees on Large-Scale Aerial Photographs. Information Report FMR-X-86. Forest Management Institute, Ottawa, Ontario, Canada.

Alim, A., and S. A. Imam. 1978. Shifting cultivators of Chittagong Hill tracts district of Bangladesh. Forest News 2(2):3–5.

Alvim, P. de T. 1977. The balance between conservation and utilization in the humid tropics with special reference to Amazonian Brazil. Pp. 347–352 in G. T. Prance and T. S. Elias (eds.) Extinction is Forever. New York Botanical Garden, Bronx, New York.

Arnold, J. E. M. 1979. Wood energy and rural communities. Nat. Res. Forum 3:229–252.

Arnold, J. E. M., and J. Jongma. 1978. Fuelwood and charcoal in developing countries. Unasylva 29(118):2–9.

Ashton, P. S. 1964. Ecological studies in the mixed dipterocarp forests of Brunei State. Oxford Forestry Memoirs No. 25:1–75.

Ashton, P. S., and M. Ashton. 1976. The Classification and Mapping of Southeast Asian Ecosystems. Transactions of Fourth Aberdeen-Hull Symposium on Malesian Ecology, Miscellaneous Series No. 17, Department of Geography, University of Hull, United Kingdom. 103 pp.

Ashton, P. S. 1977. A contribution of rain forest research to evolutionary theory. Ann. Mo. Bot. Gard. 64(4):694–705.

Asian Development Bank. 1976. The Forest Economy of Papua New Guinea. Asian Development Bank, Manila, Philippines.

Asmoro, P., K. Darmoyuwono, J. Rais, and Z. D. Kalensky. 1978. Integrated Resource

Mapping by Multistage and Multisensor Remote Sensing in Indonesia. National Coordination Agency for Surveys and Mapping (BAKOSURTANAL), Jakarta, Indonesia.

Aubreville, A. M. A. 1947. The disappearance of the tropical forests of Africa. Unasylva 1(1):5–11.

Australian Conservation Foundation. 1975. Forestry Policy. Australian Conservation Foundation, Sydney, Australia.

Ayala, J. C. T. 1978. Amazonia 2000. INDERENA, Bogotá, Colombia.

Backer, M., and K. Openshaw. 1972. Timber Trends Study in Thailand. Project Working Document FO: DP/THA/69/017. Food and Agriculture Organization, Rome, Italy.

Baker, H. G. 1970. Evolution in the tropics. Biotropica 2(2):101–111.

Baltaxe, R., and J. Lanly. 1975. The UNEP/FAO Pilot Project on Tropical Forest Cover Monitoring. Forestry Division, Food and Agriculture Organization, Rome, Italy.

Bandy, D., H. Villachica, P. A. Sanchez, and J. J. Nicholaides. 1978. Continuous cropping in the Amazon jungle. Paper presented at American Society of Agronomy Annual Meeting.

Baur, G. 1964. The Ecological Basis of Rainforest Management. Forestry Commission of New South Wales, Sydney, Australia.

Beard, J. S. 1955. The classification of tropical American vegetation types. Ecology 36:89–100.

Bene, J. G., H. W. Beall, and A. Cote. 1977. Trees, Food and People. International Development Research Centre, Ottawa, Canada.

Benetahuan, L. I. 1974. Proceedings of LILI-NAS Workshop on Natural Resources, Jakarta, September 11–16. National Academy of Sciences, Washington, D.C.

Bernardi, L. 1974. Problèmes de conservation de la nature dans les îles de l'Ocean Indien, 1: Meditiation à propos de Madagascar. Saussurea 5:37–47.

Bernard-Reversat, F., C. Hottel, and G. Lemee. 1978. Structure and functioning of evergreen rain forest ecosystems of the Ivory Coast. Pp. 557–574 in Tropical Forest Ecosystems. Natural Resources Research XIV, UNESCO, Paris, France.

Berry, M. J., and W. J. Howard. 1973. Fiji Forest Inventory (3 vol.) Land Resource Study No. 12. Land Resources Division, Overseas Development Administration, Tolworth, United Kingdom.

Berutti, P. A. 1978. Desenvolvimento da Amazônia Inpoe Uma Politica Global e Unica, Que Se Sobreponha as Divergencias Setoriais. Instituto Brasileiro de Desenvolvimento Florestal, Brasília, Brazil.

Bethel, J. S., and K. J. Turnbull. 1974. Studies of the inland forests of South Vietnam and the effects of herbicides upon those forests. One of a series of volumes of working papers published as Part B of The Effects of Herbicides in South Vietnam. National Academy of Sciences, Washington, D.C. 277 pp.

Beukenkamp, R. L. 1975. Amazonia: Part 1, Brazilian settlers drawn to new area. Foreign Agric. 13(37):8–9, 16; and Part 2, Preference for family farms noted in Amazonia settlement. Foreign Agric. 13(38):6–7.

Bigalke, R. C. 1968. Evolution of mammals on southern continents: The contemporary mammal fauna of Africa. Q. Rev. Biol. 43:265–300.

Bina, R. T., R. Jara, B. de Jesus, and E. Lorenzo. 1978. Mangrove Inventory of the Philippines Using the Landsat Multispectral Data and the Image 100 System. Natural Resources Management Center, Quezon City, Philippines. 9 pp., mimeo.

Boonkird, S. 1978. A modified forest village system for reforestation in eastern and southern Thailand. Forest News 2(2):32–33.

Boonyobhas, C., and Klankamsorn, B. 1976. Application of ERTS-1 Imagery in Forestry. Technical Report 760130. National Research Council of Thailand, Bangkok, Thailand.

Braun, H. 1974. Shifting Cultivation in Africa. Report of the FAO/SIDA/ARCN Regional

Seminar of Shifting Cultivation and Soil Conservation in Africa. Food and Agriculture Organization, Rome, Italy.

Brenan, J. P. M. 1978. Some aspects of the phytogeography of tropical Africa. Ann. Mo. Bot. Gard. 65:437–478.

British Overseas Development Administration. 1970. Fiji Forest Inventory. Land Resources Division, Directorate of Overseas Surveys, Overseas Development Administration, London, United Kingdom.

Bruce, R. W. 1976. Production and Distribution of Amazon Timber. FAO/UNDP/IBDF FO:DP/BRA/71/545, Field Document No. 21, Brasília, Brazil.

Bruneau, M., and T. LeToan. 1978. An interpretation of northern Thailand swiddening and multiple cropping systems using multidata Landsat images and computer compatible tapes. *In* Proceedings of 12th International Symposium on Remote Sensing of the Environment, Manila, Philippines, 1978, Vol. 1. Environmental Research Institute of Michigan, Ann Arbor, Michigan.

Brünig, E. F. 1977. The tropical rain forests—A wasted asset or an essential biospheric resource? Ambio 6(4):187–191.

Bryers, P., and S. Goulds. 1978. Bolivia's junta welcomes racists. New Statesman July 28th, 1978:110. London, United Kingdom.

Budowski, G. 1978. Agro-Forestry: A Bibliography. Centro Agronómico Tropical de Investigación y Enseñanza (CATIE), Turrialba, Costa Rica.

Budowski, G. 1977. Agro-Forestry in the Humid Tropics. Tropical Agricultural Research and Training Centre (CATIE), Turrialba, Costa Rica.

Bureau of Forest Development (Philippines). 1977. 1977 Philippine Forestry Statistics. Bureau of Forest Development, Quezon City, Philippines.

Burgess, P. F. 1973. The impact of commercial forestry on the hill forests of the Malay Peninsula. BioIndonesia 1:17–23.

Canadian International Development Agency. 1977. Forestry in the Pacific Region of Colombia. CIDA, Ottawa, Canada.

Cannon, T. K., R. A. Ellefsen, K. B. Craib, and J. Crespo. 1978. The application of remote sensing techniques to foreign vegetation surveys in tropical areas and urban fringe land-use problems in Costa Rica. Pp. 2081–2090 *in* Proceedings of 12th International Symposium on Remote Sensing of the Environment, Manila, Philippines, 1978, Vol. III. Center for Remote Sensing Information and Analysis, Environmental Research Institute of Michigan, Ann Arbor, Michigan.

Carcasson, R. H. 1964. A preliminary survey of the zoo-geography of African butterflies. E. Afr. Wildl. J. 2:122–157.

Castro, C. P. 1978. Shifting cultivation in the Philippines. Forest News 2(2):20–21.

Catinot, R. 1978. The forest ecosystems of Gabon: An overview. Pp. 575–579 *in* Tropical Forest Ecosystems. Natural Resources Research XIV, UNESCO, Paris, France.

Chaiyapechara, S. 1978. Hill tribes of Thailand. Forest News 2(2):22–24.

Chambers, M. J. G., and S. A. Sobur. 1977. Problems in Assessing the Rates and Processes of Coastal Changes in the Province of South Sumatra. PSESL/Research Report/003. Bogor Agricultural University, Bogor, Indonesia. 21 pp., mimeo.

Champion, H. G., and S. K. Feth. 1968. Revised Survey of the Forest Types of India. Manager of Government Publications, New Delhi, India.

Chandrasekharan, C. 1976. Forestry Situation in Malaysia. Food and Agriculture Regional Office, Bangkok, Thailand.

Chandrasekharan, C. 1977. Country Forestry Report: Indonesia. Food and Agriculture Organization Regional Office, Bangkok, Thailand.

Chandrasekharan, C. (ed.) 1978. Shifting cultivation. Forest News 2(2):1–25.

Chauvet, B. 1972. The forests of Madagascar. Pp. 191–200 *in* R. Battistini and G. Richard-

Vindard (eds.) Biogeography and Ecology in Madagascar. W. Junk, The Hague, Netherlands.

Choudhury, M. U., et al. 1978. A Landsat inventory of the agriculture and forest resources in Bangladesh. In Proceedings of 12th International Symposium on Remote Sensing of the Environment, Manila, Philippines, 1978. Environmental Research Institute of Michigan, Ann Arbor, Michigan.

Chudnoff, M. 1976. Any-tree harvest for industrial processing in the humid tropics. Import/Export Wood Purch. News 2(4):6–8.

Chunkao, K., N. Thangtham, P. Dhaamanonda, and S. Boonyawat. 1976. Watershed Management Research on Mountainous Lands: Ten-Year Report 1966–1976. Faculty of Forestry, Kasetsart University, Bangkok, Thailand. 22 pp., mimeo.

Clarke, W. C. 1976. Maintenance of agriculture and human habitats within the tropical forest ecosystem. Hum. Ecol. 4:247–259.

Cliff, E. P. 1966. Long-Range Forest Policy for South Vietnam. U.S. Department of Agriculture, Washington, D.C.

Combe, J., and G. Budowski. 1978. Classification des Techniques Agro-Forestieres. Tropical Agricultural Research and Training Center (CATIE), Turrialba, Costa Rica.

Combe, J. 1979. Sistemas Agro-Forestales en America Tropical. Tropical Agricultural Research and Training Center (CATIE), Turrialba, Costa Rica.

Conklin, H. C. 1963. The Study of Shifting Cultivation. Pan American Union, Washington, D.C.

Corporación Nacional de Investigación y Fomento Forestal. 1979. Mapa de Areas de Vocación Forestal. Agropecuaria, y de Uso Multiple de Colombia. Corporación Nacional de Investigación y Fomento Forestal (CONIF), Bogotá, Colombia.

Cox, V. 1977. Brazil: The Amazon gable. Dev. Digest 15(1):82–86.

Crocombe, R., and R. Hide. 1971. New Guinea: Unity in Diversity. Pp. 292–333 in R. Crocombe (ed.) Land Tenure in the Pacific. Oxford University Press, London.

Cruz, J. 1973. Nature conservation in Sri Lanka. Biol. Conserv. 5:199–208.

Daniel, J. G., and A. Kulasingam. 1974. Problems arising from large-scale forest clearing for agricultural use. Malays. Forester 37(3):152–160.

Danjoy, W. A., and F. G. Sadowski. 1978. Use of Landsat in the study of forest classification in the tropical jungle. Paper presented at the 12th International Symposium on Remote Sensing of the Environment, April 20–27, 1978, Manila, Philippines.

D'Arcy, W. G. 1977. Endangered landscapes in Panama and Central America: The threat to plant species. Pp. 89–104 in G. T. Prance and T. S. Elias (eds.) Extinction is Forever. New York Botanical Garden, Bronx, New York.

Davis, S. H. 1977. Victims of the Miracle: Development and the Indians of Brazil. Cambridge University Press, New York.

Delgado, A. F., and D. R. Vallejo. 1977. El Potencial Forestal de Colombia. Corporación Nacional de Investigación y Fomento Forestal (CONIF), Bogotá, Colombia.

Denevan, W. M. (ed.) 1976. The Native Populations of the Americas in 1492. University of Wisconsin Press, Madison, Wisconsin.

Denevan, W. M. 1977. The causes and consequences of shifting cultivation in relation to tropical forest survival. Paper presented to International Congress of Latin-American Geographers, Paipa, Colombia, August 3–9, 1977. Department of Geography, University of Wisconsin, Madison, Wisconsin. 16 pp., mimeo.

Denevan, W. M. 1978. The causes and consequences of shifting cultivation in relation to tropical forests survival. In W. M. Denevan (ed.) The Role of Geographical Research in Latin America. Conference of Latin American Geographers, Publication No. 7. Muncie, Indiana.

Department of Forestry (of Bangladesh). 1978. Country Report for Eighth World Forestry Congress, Jakarta, October 1978. Department of Forestry, Dacca, Bangladesh.

Department of Forestry of Sri Lanka. 1978. Forestry Statistics 1978. Colombo, Sri Lanka.

Diamond, J. M. 1976. A Proposed Natural Reserve System for Papua New Guinea. Wildlife Branch, Department of Natural Resources, Konedobu, Papua New Guinea. 20 pp., typescript.

Diamond, J. M., and M. N. Raga. 1977. The Lowland Avifauna of the Fly River Region. Wildlife Publication 77/11. Department of Natural Resources, Konedobu, Papua New Guinea.

Diamond, J. M. 1978. A Proposed Natural Reserve System for Papua New Guinea. University of California Medical Center, Los Angeles, California. 20 pp., mimeo.

Diaz, C. P. 1976. Industrial Forest Plantations: An Economic-Oriented Approach to Reforestation in the Philippines. Forest Research Institute, Laguna, Philippines.

Dickenson, J. C. III. 1972. Alternatives to monoculture in the humid tropics of Latin America. Prof. Geogr. 24:217–222.

Dillman, R. D. 1978. Nationwide Forestry Applications Program. U.S. Forest Service and National Aeronautics and Space Administration, Houston, Texas.

Dirección General Forestal de Costa Rica. 1977. Cobertura de Bosques de Costa Rica. Ministerio de Agricultura y Ganadería, San José, Costa Rica.

Dobzhansky, T. 1970. Genetics of the Evolutionary Process. Columbia University Press, New York.

Dodson, C. H., and A. H. Gentry. 1978. Flora of the Rio Palenque Science Center. Selbyana 4(1–6):i.

Douglas, I. 1975. Pressures on Australian rain forests. Environ. Conservation 2:109–119.

Douglas, J. S., and R. A. de J. Hart. 1976. Forest Farming. Watkins Publishers, London, United Kingdom.

Dourojeanni, M. J. 1975. Conservation strategies for tropical rain forests with special reference to national parks and equivalent reserves. *In* Proceedings of IUCN Thirteenth Technical Meeting, Kinshasa, Zaire, International Union for Conservation of Nature and Natural Resources, Morges, Switzerland.

Dourojeanni, M. J. 1976. Una nueva estrategia para el desarrollo de la Amazonia Peruana. Revista Forestal del Perú 6(1–2):41–58.

Dourojeanni, M. J. 1979. Desarrollo Rural Integral en la Amazonia Peruana, con Especial Referencia a las Actividades Forestales, 5–23 March 1979, Oaxtepec, México. Department of Forest Management, Universidad Nacional Agraria, Lima, Peru. 29 pp., typescript.

Draper, S. 1975. Forestry in Rural Development. Rural Development Working Paper No. 2. The World Bank, Washington, D.C.

Dung, N. 1975. Forest Resources: Scenario for the Year 2000. PREPF Phase I Report III: 26–35. Institute for Population, Resources, Environment and the Philippines Future, Manila, Philippines.

Durham, K. F. 1977. Expansion of agricultural settlement in the Peruvian rainforest: The role of the market and the role of the state. Paper presented to Joint Meeting of the Latin American Studies Association and the African Studies Association, November 2–5, 1977, Houston, Texas. Department of Biology, Stanford University, Stanford, California.

Durham, K. F. 1979. The Forest Frontier: Environment and Development in Eastern Peru. Ph.D. Dissertation. Department of Political Science, University of Michigan, Ann Arbor, Michigan.

Dwyer Mission. 1966. Recommendations for the Development of the Forest Resources of South Vietnam, U.S. Agency for International Development, Saigon.

Economics Commission for Asia and the Far East. 1975. Report of the Study Mission on Hardwood Resources in the Philippines, Indonesia and Malaysia. Asian Industrial Development Council, Bangkok, Thailand.

Economic Commission for Europe. 1976. European Timber Trends and Prospects, 1950–2000. Timber Bulletin for Europe Suppl. 3 Vol. 29. Economic Commission for Europe, Geneva, Switzerland.

Eden, M. J., and L. Chesney. 1977. Uso Preliminar de Imagenes Landsat para el Estudio de la Vegetación en el Territorio Federal Amazonas de Venezuela. Oficiana para los Estudios Especiales en la Región Sur de Venezuela (CODESUR), Caracas, Venezuela.

Eden, M. J., and A. Andrade (in press). Report of June-September 1977 Expedition to Araracuara in the Middle Caquetá Basin in Eastern Colombia. Bedford College, London, United Kingdom, and Department of Anthropology, University of Los Andes, Bogotá, Colombia.

Ekström, T. 1976. Tropical Africa in the World Paper Economy. Institut för Skogsekonomi, Stockholm, Sweden.

Erfurth, T. 1976. Toward the wider use of tropical wood products. Unasylva (112 and 113):119–126.

Espadas, O. T. 1975. Projecto de colonización rural del Caquetá (etapa 2) Colombia. In O. T. Espadas (ed.) Casos y Ejercicios sobre Projectos Agrícolas. The World Bank, Washington, D.C.

Ewel, J., and L. Conde. 1976. Potential ecological impact of increased intensity of tropical forest utilization. Forest Products Laboratory, Madison, Wisconsin.

Falesi, I. C. 1974. Soils in the Brazilian Amazon. Pp. 201–220 in C. Wagley (ed.) Man in the Amazon. University of Florida Press, Gainesville, Florida.

Fanshawe, D. B. 1952. The Vegetation of British Guiana: A Preliminary Review. Institute Paper No. 29, Imperial Forestry Institute, Oxford, United Kingdom.

Farnworth, E. G., and F. G. Golley (ed.) 1974. Fragile Ecosystems: Evaluation of Research and Application in the Neotropics. Springer-Verlag, New York. 258 pp.

Flamm, B. R., and J. H. Cravens. 1971. Effects of War Damage on the Forest Resources of South Vietnam. J. For. 69(11):784–789.

Florez, A. D., and D. V. Rendon. 1977. La Colonización y Protección del Recurso Forestal. Corporación Nacional de Investigación y Fomento Forestal, Bogotá, Colombia.

Florez, A. D., and D. V. Rendon. 1978a. La Colonización y Protección del Recurso Forestal. Memoria del Mapa de Areas de Vocación Forestal, Agropecuaria, y de Uso Multiple de Colombia. Corporación Nacional de Investigación y Fomento Forestal (CONIF), Bogotá, Colombia.

Food and Agriculture Organization. 1974. Report on the Regional Seminar on Shifting Cultivation and Soil Conservation in Africa, 2–21 July 1973. University of Ibadan, Nigeria. FAO/SIDA/TF 109. Food and Agriculture Organization, Rome, Italy.

Food and Agriculture Organization. 1976. Forest Resources in Asia and the Far East. Food and Agriculture Organization, Rome, Italy.

Food and Agriculture Organization. 1978. 1977 Yearbook of Forest Products. Food and Agriculture Organization, Rome, Italy.

Food and Agriculture Organization and World Bank. 1978. Forestry Sector in Zaire. (2 vol.) 57/78 ZAI:15. Food and Agriculture Organization, Rome, Italy.

Forest Department of Sarawak. 1976. Proceedings of Sixth Malaysian Forestry Conference, 1976 (2 vol.). Forest Department, Kuching, Sarawak.

Fox, J. E. D. 1972. The Natural Vegetation of Sabah and a Natural Regeneration of the Dipterocarp Forests. Ph.D. Thesis, University of North Wales, Bangor, United Kingdom.

Garduno, H., R. Garcia-Lagos, and F. Garcia-Simo. 1975. Present and Potential Landuse Mapping in Mexico. Pp. 1823–1829 *in* Proceedings of NASA Earth Resources Survey Symposium, Volume I-C: 1823–1839. National Aeronautics and Space Administration, Houston, Texas.

Gentry, A. H. 1977. Endangered plant species and habitats of Ecuador and Amazonian Peru. Pp. 136–149 *in* G. T. Prance and T. S. Elias (eds.) Extinction is Forever. New York Botanical Garden, Bronx, New York.

Gentry, A. 1979. Extinction and conservation of plant species in tropical America: A phytogeographical perspective. Pp. 115–121 *in* I. Hedberg (ed.) Systematic Botany, Plant Utilization and Biosphere Conservation. Almqvist and Wiksell, Uppsala, Sweden.

Golley, F. B., and E. Medina (eds.) 1975. Tropical Ecological Systems. Springer-Verlag, New York. 398 pp.

Gómez, I. P. 1979. Cubierta Arbórea de Guatemala. Universidad de San Carlos, Guatemala.

Gómez-Pompa, A. 1978. Ecología de la Vegetación de Veracruz. Compañía Editorial Continental S. A., Mexico.

Good, R. d'O. 1974. The Geography of the Flowering Plants, Fourth Edition. Longman, London, United Kingdom.

Goodland, R. J. A., and H. S. Irwin. 1975. Amazon Jungle: Green Hell to Red Desert? Elsevier Scientific Publishing Company, New York. 155 pp.

Government of Burma. 1977. Five-Year Development Programme 1977/78–1981/82, Rangoon, Burma.

Government of Burma. 1979. Forestry Situation. Department of Forestry, Rangoon, Burma.

Government of Fiji. 1977. The Forest Economy of Fiji 1976. Government of Fiji, Suva, Fiji.

Government of Malaysia. 1975. Third Malaysia Development Plan 1976–1980, Government Printer, Kuala Lumpur, Malaysia.

Government of Malaysia. 1978. Availability of Forest Resources in Peninsular Malaysia. Department of Forestry, Kuala Lumpur, Malaysia.

Government of Papua New Guinea. 1977. Compendium of Statistics. Office of Forests, Boroko, Papua New Guinea.

Government of Papua New Guinea. 1978. Facts and Figures. Economics Branch, Office of Forests, Boroko, Papua New Guinea.

Greenland, D. J. 1975. Bringing the Green Revolution to the shifting cultivator. Science 190:841–844.

Greenland, D. J., and R. Herrera. 1977. Shifting cultivation and other agricultural practices. *In* Patterns of Use of Tropical Forest Ecosystems. Soil Sciences Department, University of Reading, United Kingdom.

Gregersen, H. N., and A. Contreras. 1975. U.S. Investment in the Forest-Based Sector in Latin America. Johns Hopkins University Press, Baltimore, Maryland.

Grigg, D. B. 1974. The Agricultural Systems of the World—An Evolutionary Approach. Cambridge University Press, London, United Kingdom.

Grinell, H. R. 1975. A Study of Agri-Silviculture Potential in West Africa. International Development Research Centre, Ottawa, Canada.

Grubb, P. J., J. R. Lloyd, T. D. Pennington, and T. C. Whitmore. 1963. A comparison of montane and lowland rain forest in Ecuador, I: The forest structure, physiognomy and floristics. J. Ecol. 51:567–601.

Guiness, P. (ed.) 1977. Transmigrants in South Kalimantan and South Sulawesi. Report Series No. 15. Population Institute, Gadjah Mada University. Yogyakarta, Indonesia.

Haantjens, H. A. 1975. Papua New Guinea: An example of conservation opportunity in the humid tropics. Search 6:477–484.

Hadi, S., and R. S. Suparto (eds.) 1977. Proceedings of Symposium on the Long-Term Effects of Logging in South-East Asia. Regional Centre for Tropical Biology (BIOTROP), Bogor, Indonesia.

Hall, B. P., and R. E. Moreau. 1970. An Atlas of Speciation in African Passerine Birds. British Museum of Natural History, London, United Kingdom.

Hall, B. P. 1978. An Atlas of Speciation in African Non-Passerine Birds. British Museum of Natural History, London, United Kingdom.

Hamilton, A. C. 1976. The significance of patterns of distribution shown by forest plants and animals in tropical Africa for the reconstruction of Upper Pleistocene and palaeoenvironments: A review. Pp. 63–97 in E. M. Van Zinderen Bakker (ed.) Palaeoecology of Africa, the Surrounding Islands and Antarctica. Balkema Press, Cape Town, South Africa.

Hamilton, L. S. 1976. Tropical Rainforest Use and Preservation: A Study of Problems and Practices in Venezuela. Sierra Club Special Publication. International Series No. 4. Office of International Environment Affairs, Sierra Club, New York.

Hamilton, L. S., J. Steyermark. J. P. Veillon, and E. Mondolfi. 1976. Conservación de los Bosques Húmedos de Venezuela. Sierra Club-Consejo de Bienestar Rural, Caracas, Venezuela.

Hammond, H. L. 1977. Remote sensing: Brazil explores its Amazon wilderness. Science 196:513–515.

Hansell, J. R. F., and J. R. D. Wall. 1976. Land Resources of the Solomon Islands. Land Resource Study No. 18. Land Resources Division, Overseas Development Administration, Tolworth, United Kingdom.

Hanson, A. J. (in press). Transmigration for Marginal Land Development. In G. Hansen (ed.) Agricultural and Rural Change in Indonesia.

Hanson, A. J., and J. Koesoebiono. 1979. Settling coastal swamplands in Sumatra: A case study for integrated resource management. Pp. 121–178 in C. MacAndrews and S. L. Sien (eds.) Developing Economies and the Environment, The Southeast Asian Experience. McGraw-Hill International Book Company, Singapore.

Hauck, F. W. 1974. Shifting Cultivation and Soil Conservation in Africa. Soils Bulletin No. 24. Food and Agriculture Organization, Rome, Italy.

Hecht, S. B. 1980. Some Environmental Effects of Converting Tropical Rainforest to Pasture in Eastern Amazonia. Unpublished Ph.D. Dissertation, Department of Geography, University of California, Berkeley.

Hederström, T. 1977. Guatemala, Análisis de la Situación y Futura del Sector Forestal. FAO Document GUA/72/006. Food and Agriculture Organization, Guatemala.

Hildebrant, G., and H. J. Boehnel (eds.) 1979. Proceedings of International Symposium on Remote Sensing for Observation and Inventory of Earth Resources and the Endangered Environment, July 2–8, 1978, Freiburg, West Germany (3 vol.). International Society for Photogrammetry, University of Freiburg, West Germany.

Holdridge, L. R. 1967. Life Zone Ecology (revised edition). Tropical Science Center, San Jose, Costa Rica.

Holdridge, L. R., W. C. Grenke, W. H. Hathaway, T. Liang, and J. A. Tosi. 1971. Forest Environments in Tropical Life Zones. Pergamon Press, New York.

Hopkins, M. S., J. Kikkawa, A. W. Graham, J. G. Tracy, and L. J. Webb. 1977. An ecological basis for management of rain forests. Pp. 57–66 *in* R. Munroe and N. C. Stevens (eds.) The Border Ranges. Royal Society of Queensland, Brisbane, Australia.

Howard, R. 1977. Conservation and the endangered species of plants in the Caribbean Islands. Pp. 105–114 *in* G. T. Prance and T. S. Elias (eds.) Extinction is Forever. New York Botanical Garden, Bronx, New York.

Hoyle, M. A. 1978. Forestry and conservation in the Solomon Islands and the New Hebrides. Tigerpaper 5(2):21–24.

Hunting Technical Services, Ltd. 1969. Land Capability Survey for Government of the State of Brunei (3 vol.) Borehamwood, United Kingdom.

Inansothy, S. 1975. Changes of Vegetation and Soil Properties After Logging of Natural Forests. BIOTROP Internal Report. Regional Centre for Tropical Biology (BIOTROP), Bogor, Indonesia.

Indonesia Government. 1975. Forestry National Plan 1975–2000. Directorate General of Forestry, Jakarta, Indonesia.

Indonesia Government. 1978. Forestry Development in Indonesia. Directorate General of Forestry, Jakarta, Indonesia.

International Union for Conservation of Nature and Natural Resources. 1979. Categories, objectives and criteria for protected areas. Annex to General Assembly Paper G. A. 78/24. *In* Proceedings of IUCN Fourteenth Technical Meeting (forthcoming). International Union for Conservation of Nature and Natural Resources, Morges, Switzerland.

Inventario Nacional Forestal. 1977. Estadísticas del Recurso Forestal de la República Mexicana. SARH SFF Publication No. 42, Mexico City, México.

Irwin, H. S. 1977. Coming to terms with the rain forests. Garden 1(2):29–33.

Jahn, E. G., and S. B. Preston. 1976. Timber: More effective utilization. Science 191:757–761.

Jamil, H. B. A. 1978. Primitive economic formations in peninsular Malaysia. Forest News 2(2):14–16.

Janzen, D. H. 1973. Tropical agroecosystems. Science 182:1212–1219.

Japan Economic Research Center. 1976. A Five-Year Forecast of the Japanese Economy. 1976–1980. Japan Economic Research Center, Tokyo, Japan.

Johnson, N. E. 1976. Biological opportunities and risks associated with fast-growing plantations in the tropics. J. For. 74(7):206–211.

Johnson, N. E. 1977. The tropics—Century 21 wood supply? Weyerhauser Lecture Ser.: 20–34. Weyerhauser, Inc., Tacoma, Washington.

Kalensky, Z. D., K. Darmoyuwono, T. F. Potts, and T. Michino (in press). Thematic map of Lombok Island from Landsat computer compatible tapes. Paper presented at 12th International Symposium on Remote Sensing of the Environment, April 20–26, 1978, Manila, Philippines. Environmental Research Institute of Michigan, Ann Arbor, Michigan.

Kalish, J. 1979. Jari. Pulp Pap. Int. January 1979: 37–52.

Kanamori, H., S. Sekiguchi, Y. Murota, and Y. Yamanoue. 1975. Future of the Japanese Economy and its Primary Commodities Requirements. Japan Economic Research Center, Paper No. 26. Tokyo, Japan.

Karlberg, S. 1976. Draft Paper on Timber/Kenaf Farming. Committee for Coordination of Investigations of the Lower Mekong Basin, Bangkok, Thailand.

Kartawinata, K. 1975. The exploitation of natural forests and natural areas development. BioIndonesia 1:17–23.

Kartawinata, K., and A. Amawidjaja. 1974. Coordinated Study of Lowland Forests of Indonesia. Regional Center for Tropical Biology (BIOTROP) and Faculty of Forestry, Bogor Agricultural University, Bogor, Indonesia.

Keays, J. L. 1974. Full-tree and complete-tree utilization for pulp and paper. For. Prod. J. 24(11):13–16.

Keil, C. 1977. Forestry Projects for Rural Community Development. Rural Development Division, The World Bank, Washington, D.C.

Kernan, H. S. 1967. Notes on the Ivory Coast. Yale Forestry School News, Yale University, New Haven, Connecticut.

Kernan, H. S. 1968. Preliminary Report on Forestry in Vietnam. Working Paper No. 17. Joint Development Group, Saigon, South Vietnam. 108 pp., mimeo.

King, K. F. S. 1968. Agri-Silviculture. University of Ibadan, Nigeria.

King, K. F. S., and T. Chandler. 1978. Wasted Lands. International Centre for Research in Agroforestry, Nairobi, Kenya.

Kingdon, J. 1971. East African Mammals: An Atlas of Evolution in Africa (vol. 1). Academic Press, London, United Kingdom.

Kingdon, J. 1973. Endemic mammals and birds of western Uganda. Uganda J. 37:1–7.

Kirby, J. M. 1976. Agricultural land use and settlement of Amazonia. Pac. Viewpoint 17(2):105–132.

Klankamsorn, B. 1978. Use of satellite imagery to assess forest deterioration in Eastern Thailand. Pp. 1299–1306 in Proceedings of 12th International Symposium on Remote Sensing of the Environment, Manila, Philippines, 1978 (vol. II). Environmental Research Institute of Michigan, Ann Arbor, Michigan.

Kleinpenning, J. M. G. 1975. The Integration and Colonization of the Brazilian Portion of the Amazon Basin. Institute of Geography and Planning, Nijmedgen, Holland.

Koechlin, J. 1972. Flora and vegetation of Madagascar. Pp. 145–190 in R. Battistini and G. Richard-Vindard (eds.) Biogeography and Ecology in Madagascar. W. Junk, The Hague, Netherlands.

Kunstadter, P., E. C. Chapman, and S. Sabhasri (eds.) 1978. Farmers in the Forest: Economic Development and Marginal Agriculture in Northern Thailand. University Press of Hawaii, Honolulu, Hawaii.

LaBastille, A., and D. J. Pool. 1978. On the need for a system of cloud-forest parks in Middle America and the Caribbean. Environ. Conservation 5(3):183–190.

Lachowski, H. M., and D. L. Dietrich. 1978. Forest Inventory of the Philippines Using Satellite Imagery. General Electric Company, Beltsville, Maryland. 10 pp., mimeo.

Lachowski, H. M., D. L. Dietrich, R. M. Umali, E. A. Aquino, and V. A. Basa. 1978. Landsat-Assisted Forest Inventory of the Philippine Islands. NRMC Research Monograph No. 4. Natural Resources Management Center, Ministry of Natural Resources, Manila, Philippines.

Lamb, D. 1977. Conservation and management of tropical rain forests: A dilemma of development in Papua New Guinea. Environ. Conservation 4:121–129.

Lamb, D. 1980. Some ecological and social consequences of logging rain forests in Papua New Guinea. In J. I. Furtado (ed.) Proceedings of Fifth International Symposium of Tropical Ecology, International Society for Tropical Ecology, Kuala Lumpur, Malaysia, April 1979.

Lanly, J. P. 1969. La régression de la forêt dense en Côte d'Ivoire. Bois For. Trop. 127:45–59.

Lanly, J. P., and J. Clement. 1979. Present and Future Forest and Plantation Areas in the Tropics. FO:MISC/79/1. Food and Agriculture Organization, Rome, Italy.

Lawton, R. M. 1978. The management and regeneration of some Nigerian high forest ecosystems. Pp. 580–588 in Tropical Forest Ecosystems. Natural Resources Research XIV, UNESCO, Paris, France.

Lekagul, B., and J. McNeely. 1978. Mammals of Thailand. Association for Conservation of Wildlife, Bangkok, Thailand.

Lekagul, B., and J. McNeely. 1978. Thailand launches extensive reforestation program. Tigerpaper 5(1):9–13.

Lembke, C. 1970. Forestry in the British Solomon Islands. Aust. Timber J. 36:46–48.

Lembke, C. 1971. Forestry in Fiji. Aust. Timber J. 37:57–61.

Lembke, C. 1974. New era for Papua New Guinea forest industries. Aust. For. Ind. J. 40:6–31.

LeRoy, J. F. 1978. Composition, origin and affinities of the Madagascar vascular flora. Ann. Mo. Bot. Gard. 65:535–589.

Letouzey, R. 1976. Flore du Cameroun. Boissierra (Geneva) 24:571–573.

Lewis, W. H., and M.P.F. Elvin-Lewis. 1977. Medical Botany. John Wiley, New York.

Lowe-McConnell, R. H. (ed.) 1969. Speciation in Tropical Environments. Academic Press, New York.

Lugod, G. C. 1975. Crops to raise and not cut the trees. Canopy 1(3):8–10.

Malleux, J. 1975. Mapa Forestal del Perú. Universidad Nacional Agraria, Lima, Peru. 161 pp., plus maps.

Marchand, H. 1973. Development of the forests of French Guiana: Pipe dream or reasonable aim? Rev. Forestal Fr. 25:201–214.

Marshall, A. G. 1973. A start to nature conservation in the New Hebrides. Biol. Conservation 5(1):67–69.

Mata, G. F., J. J. Lopez, X. M. Sanchez, F. M. Ruiz, and F. T. Tacaki. 1971. Tipos de Vegetación de la República Mexicana. Subsecretaria de Planeación. Dirección General de Estudios, Dirección de Agrolegio, México.

May, R. M. 1975. The tropical rainforest. Nature 257:737–738.

McIntosh, D. H. 1973. New Horizons: Forestry in Papua New Guinea. Jacaranda Press, Brisbane, Australia.

McNeely, J. A. 1977. Is there a future for the Thai forests? Conserv. News, September 1977:1–5.

Medina, E., R. Herrera, C. Jordan, and H. Klinge. 1977. Man and the Amazon rain forest. Nat. Resour. 13(3):4–6.

Meggers, B. J. 1973. Some problems of cultural adaptations in Amazonia, with emphasis on the pre-European period. Pp. 311–320 in B. J. Meggers, E. S. Ayensu, and W. D. Duckworth (eds.) Tropical Forest Ecosystems in Africa and South America: A Comparative Review. Smithsonian Institution Press, Washington, D.C.

Meijer, W. 1970. Regeneration of tropical lowland forest in Sabah, Malaysia, 40 years after logging. Malay Forester 32:204–229.

Meijer, W. 1973. Devastation and regeneration of lowland dipterocarp forests in Southeast Asia. BioScience 23(9):528–533.

Meijer, W. 1975. Indonesian Forests and Land Use Planning. University of Kentucky Bookstore, Lexington, Kentucky.

Mekong Committee. 1978. Agriculture in the Lower Mekong Basin. Committee for Coordination of Investigations of the Lower Mekong Basin, Bangkok, Thailand.

Migongo, E. 1978. An Inventory of Kenya Forests—A Conservationist's Viewpoint. Report to Forest Working Group of the East African Wildlife Society. Nairobi, Kenya. 4 pp., mimeo.

Miller, L. D., K. Nualchawee, and C. Tom. 1978. Analysis of the Dynamics of Shifting Cultivation in the Tropical Forests of Northern Thailand, Using Landscape Modeling and Classification of Landsat Imager. National Aeronautics and Space Administration, Technical Memorandum 79545. Goddard Space Flight Center, Greenbelt, Maryland.

Miller, L. D., and D. L. Williams. 1979. Monitoring forest canopy alteration around the world with digital analysis of Landsat imagery. *In* Proceedings of ISP/IUFRO International Symposium of Remote Sensing Observation and Inventory of Earth Resources and the Endangered Environment. University of Freiburg, West Germany.

Mittak, W. L. 1975. Estimación de la Deforestación y la Reforestación Necesaria. Working Document No. 10, UNDP/FAO/GUA/72/006. Office of Food and Agriculture Organization, Guatemala.

Mittak, W. L. 1977. Estudios para la Reforestación Nacional. Working Document No. 25, FO:DP/GUA/72/006. Food and Agriculture Organization, Guatemala.

Mittermeier, R. A., and K. Milton. 1976. General jackpot: Suriname's nature parks can do wonders for a wildlife list. Animal Kingdom 79(6):26–31.

Morain, S. A., and B. Klankamsorn. 1978. Forest mapping and inventory techniques through visual analysis of Landsat imagery: Examples from Thailand. Pp. 417–426 in Proceedings of 12th International Symposium on Remote Sensing of the Environment, Manila, Philippines, 1978 (vol. I). Environmental Research Institute of Michigan, Ann Arbor, Michigan.

Moran, E. F. 1976. Agricultural Development and the Trans-Amazon Highway. Latin American Studies Working Papers, University of Indiana, Bloomington, Indiana.

Moreau, R. E. 1966. The Bird Faunas of Africa and Its Islands. Academic Press, London, United Kingdom.

Mori, S. A., and L. A. M. Silva. 1979. The herbarium of the Centro de Pesquisas and Cacau at Itabuna, Brazil. Brittonia 31(2):177–196.

Mungkorndid, S. 1978. Population Data in Communities Practicing Shifting Cultivation in Thailand. Institute of Population Studies, Chulalongkorn University, Bangkok, Thailand.

Mungkorndid, S., and K. Eadkeo. 1978. Forestry in Thailand. Occasional Paper, Faculty of Forestry, Kasetsart University, Bangkok, Thailand.

Mustaffa, S. 1978. Indonesia steps up transmigration. Populi 5(3):7–13.

Muthoo, M. K., A. C. do Prado, H. L. Potma, S. Kengen, and M. R. A. Alpande. 1977. Situação Florestal Brasileira. FAO/UNDP/IBDF, Instituto Brasileiro de Desenvolvimento Florestal, Brasília, Brazil.

Muthoo, M. K. 1978. Forestry Development and Research in Brazil: National Forest Policy Planning and Development. UNDA/FAO/IBDF. FO:BRA/76/027 Technical Report No. 9, Brasília, Brazil.

Myers, N. 1976. An expanded approach to the problem of disappearing species. Science 193:198–202.

Myers, N. 1979. The Sinking Ark. Pergamon Press, Oxford and New York.

Myers, N. (in press a). Conservation of forest animal and plant genetic resources in tropical rainforests. In Proceedings of Eighth World Forestry Congress, Jakarta 16–28 October 1978. Food and Agriculture Organization, Rome, Italy.

Myers, N. (in press b). Forest refugia and conservation in Africa—with some appraisal of survival prospects for tropical moist forests throughout the biome. In G. T. Prance (ed.) Proceedings of Symposium on the Biological Model for Diversification in Tropical Lowland Forests. Columbia University Press, New York.

National Academy of Sciences. 1974. The Effects of Herbicides in South Vietnam. National Academy of Sciences, Washington, D.C.

National Research Council of Thailand. 1976. Thailand's Forest Resources and Management. Division of Research, Bangkok, Thailand.

Nations, J. D., and R. B. Nigh. 1978. Cattle, cash, food and forest: The destruction of the American tropics and the Lacandon Maya alternative. Culture Agric. 6:1–5.

Neilsen, U., and A. H. Aldred. 1978. New developments for tropical surveys prove successful. Paper presented to International ISR/IUFRO Symposium on Remote Sensing for Observation and Inventory of Earth Resources and the Endangered Environment, July 2–8, 1978, Freiburg, West Germany. Canadian Forestry Service, Ottawa, Canada.

Nor, S. M., and H. T. Tang. 1973. Some aspects of the utilization and conservation of the forest resources of West Malaysia. Pp. 103–111 *in* Proceedings of Symposium on Biological Research and National Development, Malayan Nature Journal, Kuala Lumpur, Malaysia.

Nualchawee, K., and L. D. Miller. 1978. Spatial Land-Use Inventory, Modeling and Projection for Northern Thailand, with Inputs from Existing Maps, Airphotos and Landsat Imagery. Technical Report. Goddard Space Flight Center, Greenbelt, Maryland.

Nuttonson, M. Y. 1963. The Physical Environment and Agriculture of Vietnam, Laos, and Cambodia. American Institute of Crop Ecology, Washington, D.C.

Nyyssonen, A. 1978. Forestry Development and Research in Brazil: Inventories for Amazonian Forestry Development. Food and Agriculture Organization DP/BRA/76/027 Technical Report No. 8, UNDP/FAO/IBDF, Brasília, Brazil.

Omakupt, M. 1978. Land use inventory of North Thailand using Landsat imagery. Pp. 2297–2306 *in* Proceedings of 12th International Symposium on Remote Sensing of the Environment, Manila, Philippines, 1978 (vol I). Environmental Research Institute of Michigan, Ann Arbor, Michigan.

Onochie, C. F. A. 1975. Proposals for a Programme of Conservation of Natural Vegetation in Nigeria: Report on the Establishment of Strict Natural Reserves. Federal Department of Forestry Research, Ibadan, Nigeria.

Onochie, C. F. A. 1979. Remarks in Proceedings of Workshop on State of Knowledge of the Nigerian Rainforest Ecosystem, 24–26 January 1979, University of Ibadan, Nigeria. National Committee for Man and the Biosphere Programme, UNESCO, Lagos, Nigeria.

Onweluzo, B. S. K. 1979. Forestry in Nigeria. J. Forestry July 1979:431–433.

Opler, P. A., H. G. Baker, and G. W. Frankie. 1977. Recovery of tropical lowland forest ecosystems. Pp. 379–421 *in* J. Cairns and K. Dickson (eds.) Recovery and Management of Damaged Ecosystems: University of Virginia Press, Charlottesville.

Oram, A. K. 1971. Policy Proposals for the Licensing and Exploitation of Fiji's Natural Forests. Report, Office of Conservator of Forestry, Fiji.

Orians, G. H., and E. W. Pfeiffer. 1970. Ecological effects of the war in Vietnam. Science 168:544–554.

Orlando, U. Q., J. A. Tosi, and L. R. Holdridge. 1975. Memoria Explicitiva y Mapa Ecológico de Bolivia. Ministerio de Asuntos Campasinos y Agropecuarios, La Paz, Bolivia.

Osbourn, D. F. 1975. Beef production from improved pastures in the tropics. World Rev. Anim. Prod. 11(4):23–31.

Overgaard, J. 1975. Logging in the Indigenous Forests of Fiji. Food and Agriculture Organization, Rome, Italy.

Owen, N. G. 1971. The rice industry of mainland Southeast Asia 1850–1914. J. Siam Soc. 59(2):75–143.

Owino, F., A. W. Diamond, and N. Ochanda. 1979. Report on Forest Working Group—March 1979. Forest Working Group of East African Wildlife Society, Nairobi, Kenya. 12 pp., mimeo.

Paijams, K. 1975. Map and Explanatory Notes to the Vegetation of Papua New Guinea. Land Research Series No. 35. Commonwealth Scientific and Industrial Research Organization, Melbourne, Australia.

Paijams, K. (ed.) 1976. New Guinea Vegetation. Australian National University Press, Canberra, Australia.

Palmer, J. R. 1977. Forestry in Brazil—Amazonia. Commonw. For. Rev. 56(2):115–130.
Pandolfo, C. 1978. A Floresta Amazônica Brasileira. Superintendência do Desenvolvimento da Amazônia, Departamento de Recursos Naturais. Ministerio do Interior, Brasília, Brazil.
Parsons, J. J. 1976. Forest to pasture: Development or destruction? Revista Biol. Tropical 24(Supp.1):121–138.
Pearson, D., and A. Pryor. 1978. Environment North-South: An Economic Interpretation. Wiley-Interscience, New York.
Persson, R. 1974. World Forest Resources: Review of the World's Forest Resources in the Early 1970s. Research Notes No. 17. Department of Forest Survey, Royal College of Forestry, Stockholm, Sweden.
Persson, R. 1975. Forest Resources of Africa, Part I: Country Descriptions. Department of Forest Survey, Research Notes No. 18. Royal College of Forestry, Stockholm, Sweden.
Persson, R. 1977. Forest Resources of Africa, Part II: Regional Analysis. Department of Forest Survey, Research Notes No. 22. Royal College of Forestry, Stockholm, Sweden.
Pettinger, L. R. 1978. A Selected Bibliography: Remote Sensing Applications for Tropical and Subtropical Vegetation Analysis. U.S. Geological Survey, Sioux Falls, South Dakota.
Pires, J. M. 1978. The forest ecosystems of the Brasilian Amazon: Description, functioning and research needs. Pp. 607–627 in Tropical Forest Ecosystems. Natural Resources Research XIV. UNESCO, Paris, France.
Pollisco, F. S. 1975. Reforestation and silvicultural techniques for the regeneration of Philippines forests. Canopy (monthly publication of the Forest Research Institute, Philippines) 1(6):1–6.
Population Center Foundation. 1978. Images from the Future: The Philippines in the Year 2000. Population Center Foundation, Manila, Philippines.
Potma, H. L. 1976. Brazil: A Statistical Digest of the Forestry Situation. Instituto Brasileiro de Desenvolvimento Florestal. Research Note No. 12. Brasília, Brazil.
Prance, G. T. 1977. The phytogeographic subdivisions of Amazonia and their influence on the selection of biological reserves. Pp. 195–213 in G. T. Prance and T. S. Elias (eds.) Extinction is Forever. New York Botanical Garden, Bronx, New York.
Prance, G. T. 1978. The origin and evolution of the Amazon flora. Interciencia 3(4):207–222.
Prance, G. T. (ed.) (in press). Proceedings of Symposium on the Biological Model for Diversification in Tropical Lowland Forests. Columbia University Press, New York.
Pringle, S. L. 1976. Tropical moist forests in world demand, supply and trade. Unasylva 28(112 and 113):106–118.
Pringle, S. L. 1977. The future availability of world pulp. A world picture. Unasylva 29:18–25.
Pringle, S. L. 1978a. The Outlook for Forest Products Demand and Supply. Progress Report on an FAO/Industry Study, presented to the Eighth World Forestry Congress, Jakarta, October 1978. Food and Agriculture Organization, Rome, Italy.
Pringle, S. L. 1978b. Quantity and quality of the tropical forests. Paper presented at Conference on Improved Utilization of Tropical Forests, Forest Products Institute, Madison, Wisconsin, May 1978. Food and Agriculture Organization, Rome, Italy.
Proyecto Radargramétrico de Amazonas. 1975. Plan Para la Evaluación Preliminar de los Recursos Naturales de la Amazonia Colombiano. Proyecto Radargramétrico de Amazonas y Instituto Geográfico Agustín Codazzi, Bogotá, Colombia.

Proyecto INDERENA-Canada. 1976. Informe sobre el Recurso Forestal y las Industrias Forestales de la Costa Pacífica Colombiana. 1976. Canadian International Development Agency, Bogotá, Colombia.

Putney, A. 1976. Estrategia Preliminar para la Conservación de Areas Silvestres Sobresaliento del Ecuador. UNDP/FAO/ECU/71/527. Food and Agriculture Organization, Quito, Ecuador.

Rahman, R. A. 1976. The Economic Viability of the Malaysian Timber Industry—An Overview. Staff Paper No. 2. Department of Economics, Universiti Pertanian Malaysia, Kuala Lumpur, Malaysia.

Rao, K. R. 1978. Country report: India. *In* Proceedings of 12th International Symposium on Remote Sensing of the Environment, Manila, Philippines, 1978. Environmental Research Institute of Michigan, Ann Arbor, Michigan.

Rauh, W. 1979. Problems of biological conservation in Madagascar. Pp. 405–421 *in* D. Bramwell (ed.) Plants and Islands. Academic Press, New York.

Raup, D. M., S. J. Gould, T. J. M. Schopf, and D. S. Simberloff. 1973. Stochastic models of phylogeny and the evolution of diversity. J. Geol. 81(5):525–542.

Raven, P. H. 1976. Ethics and attitudes. Pp. 155–179 *in* J. B. Simmons *et al.* (eds.) Conservation of Threatened Plants. Plenum Press, New York.

Raven, P. H., B. Berlin, and D. E. Breedlove. 1971. The origins of taxonomy. Science 174:1210–1213.

Reis, M. S. 1978. Uma Definição Técnico-Policia para O Aproveitamento Racional dos Recursos Florestal, Instituto Brasileiro de Desenvolvimento Florestal, Brasília, Brazil.

Republic of Kenya. 1979. Development Plan 1979–83. Government Printer, Nairobi, Kenya.

Revilla, A. V. 1976. A Critical Evaluation of N. Dung's Forest Resources: Scenario for the Year 2000. PREPF Research Note No. 53. Population, Resources, Environment, and the Philippines Future, Manila, Philippines.

Richards, P. W. 1952. The Tropical Rain Forest. Cambridge University Press, London.

Richards, P. W. 1963. Ecological notes on West African vegetation: II. J. Ecol. 51: 123–149.

Richards, P. W. 1973. The tropical rain forest. Sci. Am. 229(6):58–68.

Richardson, S. D. 1978. Foresters and the Faustian bargain. Pp. 156–161 *in* Proceedings of Conference on Improved Utilization of Tropical Forests, May 21–26, 1978, Madison, Wisconsin. U.S. Forest Service Forest, Products Laboratory, Madison, Wisconsin.

Rodriguez-Bejerano, D. 1978. Applications of Landsat and Skylab Imagery in Mexico: Detection of Erosion and Forest Damage. School of Natural Resources, University of Michigan, Ann Arbor, Michigan. 13 pp., mimeo.

Rollett, B. 1962. Forest Inventory of East Mekong (Cambodia). Report to the Government of Cambodia. FAO No. 1500. Food and Agriculture Organization, Rome, Italy.

Roque, C. R. 1978. Remote Sensing Program of the Philippines. Natural Resources Management Center, Department of Natural Resources, Quezon City, Philippines. 3 pp., mimeo.

Rosende, E. 1977. The TransAmazon Highway. Dev. Digest 15(1):76–81.

Routley, R., and V. Routley. 1973. The Fight for the Forests. Research School of Social Sciences, Australian National University, Canberra.

Routley, R., and V. Routley. 1977. Destructive Forestry in Australia and Melanesia. Pp. 347–397 *in* J. H. Winslow (ed.) The Melanesian Environment.

Rudolph, V. J., J. W. Simoes, and L. M. James. 1978. Forestry in Brazil: An awakening giant. J. Forestry, December 1978: 784–786.

Ruthenberg, H. 1976. Farming Systems in the Tropics (revised edition). Oxford University Press, London, United Kingdom.

Ryan, P. A. (ed.) 1972. Encyclopaedia of Papua New Guinea. Melbourne University Press, Melbourne, Australia.

Rzedowski, J. 1978. Vegetación de México. Linusa, Mexico City, México.

Sabhasri, S., P. Cheosakul, B. Indrambarya, and S. Vibulsresth. 1978. Thailand national remote sensing program: past, present and future. Paper presented to 12th International Symposium on Remote Sensing of the Environment, Manila, Philippines, 1978. Environmental Research Institute of Michigan, Ann Arbor, Michigan.

Sadikin, D. 1978. The Utilization of Tropical Hardwood from Indonesia. Development Studies Centre III: 14. Australian National University, Canberra, Australia.

Sadowski, F. G. 1978. The promises of remote sensing for forestry in developing countries. Paper presented to Symposium on the Use of Remote Sensing by Satellites for Agricultural Development in Latin America. Inter-American Development Bank, Washington, D.C.

Salati, E., et al. 1978. Recycling of Water in the Amazon Basin: An Isotopic Study. Division of Environmental Science, Center of Nuclear Energy and Agriculture, Piracicaba, Brazil.

Samapuddhi, K. 1975. Thailand's forest villages. Unasylva 27(107):20–24.

Sanchez, P. A. 1976. Properties and Management of Soils in the Tropics. John Wiley, New York.

Sanchez, P. A., and S. W. Buol. 1975. Soils of the tropics and the world food crisis. Science 188:598–603.

dos Santos, A. P., and E. M. L. de M. Movo. 1978. Deforestation Planning for Cattle Grazing in Amazon Basin Using Landsat Data. Report No. INPE-1225-PE/126. National Institute for Space Research (INPE), São Jose dos Campos, Brazil.

Sayn-Wittgenstein, L. 1978. New development in tropical forest inventories. Pp. 1187–1198 in Proceedings of 12th International Symposium on Remote Sensing of the Environment, Manila, Philippines, 1978 (vol. I). Environmental Research Institute of Michigan, Ann Arbor, Michigan.

Sayn-Wittgenstein, L., R. de Mild, and C. J. Inglis. 1978. Identification of Tropical Trees on Aerial Photographs. Information Report FMR-X-113. Forest Management Institute, Ottawa, Canada.

Schimper, A. F. W. 1903. Plant-Geography Upon a Physiological Basis. Oxford University Press, Oxford, United Kingdom.

Schmid, M. 1978. The Melanesian forest ecosystems. Pp. 654–683 in Tropical Forest Ecosystems. Natural Resources Research XIV UNESCO, Paris, France.

Schmithüsen, F. 1976. Forest utilization contracts on public land in the tropics. Unasylva 28(112–113):52–73.

Schmithüsen, F. 1977. Forstpolitische Ueberlegungen zur Tropenwaldnutzung in der Elfenbeinküste. Schweiz. Z. Forstwes. 128:69–82.

Schmithüsen, F. 1978. Contratos de Utilizacão Florestal com Referência Especial a Amazônia Brasileira. Instituto Brasileiro de Desenvolvimento Florestal, UNDP and FAO, Brasília, Brazil. 35 pp.

Schulte, W. (in press). Report on Population Data in Slash-and-Burn Forestry Communities in Asia. Population Programme of Economic and Social Policy Division, Food and Agriculture Organization, Rome, Italy.

Seavoy, R. E. 1973. The transition to continuous rice cultivation in Kalimantan. Ann. Assoc. Am. Geogr. 63:218–225.

Serrão, E. A. S., I. C. Falesi, J. B. da Veiga, and J. F. T. Neto. 1978. Productividade de pastagems cultivadas em solos de baixa fertilidad das areas de floresta do trópico húmido Brasileiro. Paper presented at Seminar on Producción y Utilización de Forrajes en Suelos Ácidos e Infertiles del Trópico, April 16–22, 1978. International Centre for Tropical Agriculture, Cali, Colombia.

Shimokawa, E. 1977. Japan's dependence upon wood chips pulp. Unasylva 29:26–27.

Siegenthaler, U., and H. Oeschger. 1978. Predicting future atmospheric carbon dioxide levels. Science 199:188–195.

Singh, M. M. (ed.) 1973. Proceedings of Symposium on National Utilization of Land Resources in Malaya, April 20–21, 1973. Malaysian Society of Soil Science, Kuala Lumpur, Malaysia.

Smit, G. S. 1978. Shifting cultivation in tropical rainforests detected from aerial photographs. Q. J. Int. Inst. Aerial Survey Earth Sci. 4:603–633.

Smitinand, T. 1977. Vegetation and Groundcover of Thailand. Faculty of Forestry, Kasetsart University, Bangkok, Thailand. 15 pp.

Smith, N. J. 1976. The TransAmazon Highway: A Cultural and Ecological Analysis of Settlement in the Humid Tropics. Ph.D. Dissertation, University of California, Berkeley, California.

Smith, N. J. M. 1978. Agricultural productivity along Brazil's TransAmazon highway. Agro-Ecosystems 4:415–432.

Sobur, A. S., et al. 1977. Remote Sensing Applications in the South East Sumatra Coastal Environment. PSPSL/Research Report/002. Bogor Agricultural University, Bogor, Indonesia. 29 pp., mimeo.

Soepadmo, E., and K. G. Singh (eds.) 1973. Proceedings of Symposium on Biological Resources and National Development. Malayan Nature Society, Kuala Lumpur, Malaysia.

Sommer, A. 1976. Attempt at an assessment of the world's tropical moist forests. Unasylva 28(112 and 113):5–24.

Sonnenburg, C. R. 1978. Overview of Brazilian Remote Sensing Activities. Report Nos. INPE-1323-NTE/126. National Institute for Space Research (INPE), São Jose dos Campos, Brazil.

Soto, M. F. Lozano, C. Mejia, J. A. Diez, and M. Medina. 1979. Mapping tropical vegetation zones in the state of Veracruz, Mexico. In Proceedings of 12th International Symposium on Remote Sensing of the Environment, Manila, Philippines, 1978. Environmental Research Institute of Michigan, Ann Arbor, Michigan.

Sourdat, M., and E. Costode. 1977. Reconocimiento Morfográfico y Edafológico de la Amazonia Ecuatoriana Zona Nor-Oriental. Ministerio de Agricultura y Ganadería, Quito, Ecuador.

Southeast Asia Development Advisory Group. 1973. Some Environmental Considerations for the Mekong Basin Project. Southeast Asia Development Advisory Group (SEADAG), Washington, D.C.

Spears, John S. 1978. Wood as an Energy Source: The Situation in the Developing World. Forestry Division, The World Bank, Washington, D.C.

Specht, R. L., E. M. Roe, and V. Boughton (eds.) Conservation of Major Plant Communities in Australia and Papua New Guinea. Aust. J. Bot., Suppl. 7.

Spencer, J. E. 1966. Shifting Cultivation in Southeast Asia. University of California Press, San Francisco, California.

Sternberg, H. O'R. 1973. Development and conservation. Erdkude 27(4):253–265.

Sternberg, H. O'R. 1975. The Amazon River of Brazil. Steiner Verlag, Wiesbaden, West Germany.

Steyermark, J. 1977. Future outlook for threatened and endangered species in Venezuela. Pp. 128–135 in G. T. Prance and T. S. Elias (eds.) Extinction is Forever. New York Botanical Garden, Bronx, New York.

deStiegueir, J. E. 1978. Forestry applications of NASA remote sensing programs. J. Forestry 76(4):208–211.

Stocker, J. C., D. A. Gilmour, and D. S. Cassells. 1977. The Future of our Northern Rain Forests in the Face of Economic and Political Reality. Proceedings of Conference of Institute of Foresters of Australia, Adelaide, Australia.

Stockholm International Peace Research Institute. 1976. Ecological Consequences of the Second Indochina War. Almquist and Wiksell, Stockholm, Sweden.

Stolz, R. 1977. Diagnóstico del Sector Forestal. Misión Forestal Alemana, La Paz, Bolivia.

Strahler, A. H., T. L. Logan, and N. A. Bryant. 1978. Improving forest cover classification accuracy from Landsat by incorporating topographic information. Paper presented at the 12th International Symposium on Remote Sensing of the Environment, April 20–26, 1978, Manila, Philippines.

Sukwong, S., et al. 1975. Status report on floristic and forestry aspects of mangrove forests in Thailand. Paper for National Seminar on Mangrove Ecosystems in Thailand. College of Forestry, Kasetsart University, Bangkok, Thailand. 37 pp.

Sumitro, A. 1976. Foreign Investment in the Forest-Based Sector of Indonesia: Increasing its Contribution to Indonesian Development. Faculty of Forestry, University of Gadjah Mada, Yogyakarta, Indonesia.

Suparto, R. S., et al. 1978. Proceedings of Symposium on the Long-Term Effects of Logging in South-East Asia. Regional Centre for Tropical Biology (BIOTROP), Bogor, Indonesia.

Swanson, C. W. 1975. Reforestation in the Republic of Vietnam. J. For. 73(6): 367–371.

Synnott, T. J. 1977. Monitoring Tropical Forests: A Review with Special Reference to Africa. MARC Report No. 5. The Monitoring and Assessment Research Centre (MARC), Chelsea College, University of London, London, England. 45 pp.

Tagudar, E. T. 1976. Development and management of industrial plantations inside the paper industries corporation of the Philippines. For. Hand. 1:47–49.

Tagudar, E. T. 1978. Agro-forestry as practised in the paper industries corporation of the Philippines. For. News 2(1):24–26.

Tardin, A. T., et al. 1979. Levantamento de Áreas de Desmatamento na Amazônia Legal Através de Imagens do Satelite Landsat. Report No. INDE-1411-NTE/142. National Institute for Space Research (INDE), Sao Jose dos Campos, Brazil.

Thomson, V., and R. Adloff. 1971. The French Pacific Islands: French Polynesia and New Caledonia. University Press, Berkeley, California.

Tinal, U., and J. L. Balenewan. 1974. A Study of Mechanical Logging Damage After Selective Cutting in the Lowland Dipterocarp Forest of East Kalimantan. Regional Centre for Tropical Biology (BIOTROP), Bogor, Indonesia.

Tosi, J. A. 1972. Los Recursos Forestales de Costa Rica. Tropical Science Center, San Jose, Costa Rica, 16 pp., mimeo.

Tosi, J. Jr. 1976. Bases Ecológicas para la Clasificación y Levantamiento del Mapa de Tipos de Bosques en Colombia. INDERENA/UNDP/FAO. Bogotá, Colombia.

Trevett, J. W. 1978. Vegetation mapping of Nigeria from radar. In Proceedings of 12th International Symposium on Remote Sensing of the Environment, Manila, Philippines, 1978. Environmental Research Institute of Michigan, Ann Arbor, Michigan.

Tsurumi, T. 1976. The Japanese are Coming: The Multinational Spread of Japanese Firms. Japan Economic Research Center, Tokyo, Japan.

Turner, D. A. 1977. Status and distribution of the East African endemic species. Scopus 1(1):2–11.

UNESCO. 1974. Report of International Working Group on Project I: Ecological Effects of

Increasing Human Activities on Tropical and Sub-Tropical Forest Ecosystems. Man and the Biosphere Report Series No. 16. UNESCO, Paris, France.

UNESCO, 1978. Tropical Forest Ecosystems: A State-of-Knowledge Report. Natural Resources Research XIV. UNESCO, Paris, France.

UNDP/UNIDO. 1977. Prospects for Additional Utilization of Forest Resources in Laos. United Nations Development Program (UNDP). Vientiane, Laos.

U.S. Department of Agriculture. 1978. Livestock Statistics in Selected Countries 1960–75; and World Livestock Numbers, Red Meat Production, Consumption and Trade 1974–78. *Foreign Agriculture Circular* FLM 9–78 and 10–78. U.S. Department of Agriculture, Washington, D.C.

U.S. Forest Service. 1978. Forest Statistics of the United States 1977. U.S. Forest Service, Washington, D.C., and Agency for International Development. 1978. Proceedings of the Conference on Improved Utilization of Tropical Forests, May 21–26, Madison, Wisconsin.

Valera, R. B. 1974. Industrial forest plantation. Philipp. For. 7(1 and 2):15-16.

Van Nao, T. 1978. Agrisilviculture: Joint production of food and wood. *In* Proceedings of Eighth World Forestry Congress, Jakarta, October 1978. Food and Agriculture Organization, Rome, Italy.

van Steenis, C. G. 1950. The delimitation of Malaysia and its main plant geographical divisions. Flora Malesiana Ser. I(1):70–75.

Veblen, T. T. 1978. Guatemalan conifers. Unasylva 29(118):25–30.

Vibulsresth, S,, C. Ketruangrote, and M. Sriplung. 1975. Distribution of Mangrove Forest as Revealed by the Earth Resource Technology Satellite Imagery. National Research Council and Applied Scientific Research Corporation of Thailand, Office of the Prime Minister, Bangkok, Thailand. 77 pp.

Vovides, A. P., and A. Gómez-Pompa. 1977. The problems of threatened and endangered plant species in Mexico. Pp. 77–88 *in* G.T. Prance and T. S. Elias (eds.) Extinction is Forever. New York Botanical Garden, Bronx, New York.

Wacharakitti, S., and L. D. Miller. 1975. Remote Sensing of Tropical Forests, with Emphasis on Landuse Planning: A Literature Review and Bibliography. Faculty of Forestry, Kasetsart University, Bangkok, Thailand.

Wacharakitti, S., and S. A. Morain. 1978. Procedures for land-use analysis in developing countries: Examples from Southeast Asia. Pp. 587–595 *in* Proceedings of 12th International Symposium on Remote Sensing of the Environment, Manila, Philippines, 1978 (vol. I). Environmental Research Institute of Michigan, Ann Arbor, Michigan.

Wacharakitti, S., 1978. The assessment of forest areas from Landsat imagery. Paper presented in Forestry Meeting, Royal Forest Department, Bangkok, Thailand, November 6–14 1978.

Wadsworth, F. H. 1978. Deforestation—Death to the Panama Canal. Pp. 22–24 *in* Proceedings of the U.S. Strategy Conference on Tropical Deforestation, June 12–14, 1978, Washington, D.C. U.S. Department of State and U.S. Agency for International Development, Washington, D.C.

Wasserstrom, R. 1978. Population growth and economic development in Chiapas: 1524–1975. Hum. Ecol. 6(2):127–143.

Watters, R. F. 1971. Shifting Cultivation in Latin America. Food and Agriculture Organization, Rome, Italy.

Webb, J. L. 1968. Environmental relationships of the structural types of Australian rain forest vegetation. Ecology 49:296–311.

Webb, J. L. 1977a. Ecological Considerations and Safeguards in the Modern Use of Tropical Lowland Rain Forests as a Source of Pulpwood: Example, The Madang Area of Papua New Guinea. Office of Environment and Conservation, Papua New Guinea.

Webb, J. L. 1977. The dynamics of tropical rainforests. Forestry Log 10:11–18.

Webb, J. L. 1978. A general classification of Australian rain forest. Aust. Plants 9(76):349–363.

Webb, J. L., and J. G. Tracey. 1978. Australian rainforests: Patterns and change. In A. Keast (ed.) Ecological Biogeographer of Australia, second ed. W. Junk, Amsterdam, Netherlands.

Westing, A. H. 1971. Forestry and the war in South Vietnam. J. Forestry 69(11):777–783.

Wetterberg, G. A., G. Padua, C. S. deCastro, and J. M. Carvalho de Vaseoncellos. 1976. An Analysis of Nature Conservation Priorities in the Amazon. UNDP/FAO/IBDF/BRA 545, Technical Series No. 8. Instituto Brasileiro de Desenvolvimento Florestal, Brasília, Brazil.

Wetterberg, G. B., and M. T. J. Padua. 1978. Preservção de Natureza na Amazônia Brasileira: Situação em 1978. Projeto de Desenvolvimento e Pesquisa Florestal PNUD/FAO/IBDF/BRA/76/027. Serie Técnica Numero 13. Instituto de Desenvolvimento Florestal, Brasília, Brazil.

Wharton, C. 1966. Man, fire and wild cattle in North Cambodia. Proc. Annu. Tall Timbers Fire Ecol. Conf. 5:23–65.

Wharton, C. 1968. Man, fire and wild cattle in Southeast Asia. Proc. Annu. Tall Timbers Fire Ecol. Conf. 8:107–167.

White, K. J. 1973. The forest resources of Papua New Guinea. Paper presented to the 12th Pacific Science Congress, August 18–September 3, 1971, Canberra, Australia.

White, K. J. 1976. Lowland Rainforest Regeneration in Papua New Guinea, with reference to the Vanimo Subprovince. PNG Forestry Department, Tropical Forest Research Note SR 32. Bamoko, Papua New Guinea. 9 pp., mimeo.

Whitmore, T. C. 1966. Guide to the Forests of the British Solomon Islands. Oxford University Press, Oxford, United Kingdom.

Whitmore, T. C. 1974. Plant Genetic Resource Survey in Dependent and Associated Territories. Ministry of Overseas Development, London, United Kingdom.

Whitmore, T. C. 1975. Tropical Rain Forests of the Far East. Clarendon Press, Oxford, United Kingdom.

Whitmore, T. C. 1976. Conservation Review of Tropical Rain Forests, General Considerations, and Asia. International Union for Conservation of Nature and Natural Resources, Morges, Switzerland. 116 pp., mimeo.

Whitmore, T. C. 1978. The forest ecosystems of Malaysia, Singapore and Brunei: Description, functioning, and research needs. Pp. 641–653 in Tropical Forest Ecosystems. Natural Resources Research XIV. UNESCO, Paris, France.

Williams, L. 1965. Vegetation of Southeast Asia: Studies of Forest Types: 1963–1965. Technical Report, Agricultural Research Service, U.S. Department of Agriculture, Washington, D.C.

Williams, J. T., C. H. Lamoreux, and N. Wulijarni-Soetjipto (eds.) 1975. South-East Asian Plant Genetic Resources. BIOTROP/Regional Center for Tropical Biology, Bogor, Indonesia.

Winslow, J. H. (ed.) 1977. The Melanesian Environment. Australian National University Press, Canberra, Australia.

Wint, S. M. 1978. Primitive economic formations and shifting cultivation in forest areas of Burma. Forest News 2(2):6–8.

Wirakuswerah, S. 1979. Diversified silvicultural and agrosilvicultural crops as aids to research, teaching and development. Pp. 124–127 in S. Adisaewarto and E. F. Brunig (eds.) Transactions of the Second International MAB-IURFO Workshop on Tropical Rain Forest Ecosystem Research. Special Report No. 2. Chair for World Forestry, Hamburg, West Germany.

Wiroatmodjo, P. 1978. Experiments in the use of remote sensing from satellite and aerial photography for forest inventory. Directorate of Forestry Planning, Bogor, Indonesia. 14 pp., mimeo.

Wittwer, S. H. 1978. Nitrogen fixation and agricultural productivity. (Editorial) BioScience 28(9):555.

Womersley, J. S., and J. B. McAdam. 1957. The Forests and Forest Conditions in the Territories of Papua and New Guinea. Government Printer, Port Moresby, New Guinea (now Papua New Guinea).

World Bank. 1975. Colombia, Caqueta Rural Settlement Project (Phase II). World Bank Office, Bogotá, Colombia.

World Bank. 1976. Appraisal of Forestry Projects in Burma. Report No. 374a-BA. The World Bank, Washington, D.C.

World Bank. 1978. World Bank Atlas, 1978. World Bank, Washington, D.C.

World Bank. 1978. Forestry: Sector Policy Paper. World Bank, Washington, D.C.

Yong Hoi-Sen. 1979. Natural habitats and distribution of Malaysian mammals. BIOTROP Special Publication 8:3–9. Regional Centre for Tropical Biology (BIOTROP), Bogor, Indonesia.

Appendix

PERSONS CONTACTED FOR INFORMATION ON CONVERSION RATES
OF TROPICAL MOIST FOREST

USA

DAVID M. BURNS, American Association for the Advancement of Science, N.W., Washington, D.C.

MICHAEL CALABRESE, Resource Observation Division, National Aeronautics and Space Administration, Washington, D.C.

RICHARD CARPENTER, East-West Environment and Policy Institute, Honolulu, Hawaii

ROBERT M. CHERVIN, Global Climate Modelling Group, National Center for Atmospheric Research, Boulder, Colorado

CHARLES F. COOPER, Center for Regional Environmental Studies, San Diego State University, San Diego, California

RALPH C. D'ARGE, College of Commerce and Industry, University of Wyoming, Laramie, Wyoming

WILLIAM M. DENEVAN, Department of Geography, University of Wisconsin, Madison, Wisconsin

CALWAY H. DODSON, Marie Selby Botanical Gardens, Sarasota, Florida

J. EWEL, Department of Botany, University of Florida, Gainesville, Florida

F. R. FOSBERG, Smithsonian Institution, Washington, D.C.

A. H. GENTRY, Missouri Botanical Gardens, St. Louis, Missouri

FRANK B. GOLLEY, Institute of Ecology, University of Georgia, Athens, Georgia

LAWRENCE S. HAMILTON, School of Forestry, Cornell University, Ithaca, New York

C. JORDAN, Institute of Ecology, University of Georgia, Athens, Georgia

W. W. KELLOGG, National Center for Atmospheric Research, Boulder, Colorado

S. KUNKLE, Office of International Forestry, U.S. Forest Service, Washington, D.C.

H. M. LACHOWSKI, Forest Inventory Specialist, Space Division, General Electric Company, Beltsville, Maryland

THOMAS E. LOVEJOY, World Wildlife Fund, Washington, D.C.

WILLEM MEIJER, School of Biological Sciences, University of Kentucky, Lexington, Kentucky

LEE D. MILLER, Remote Sensing Center, Texas A&M University, College Station, Texas

S. MORAIN, Director, Technology Applications Center, University of New Mexico, Albuquerque, New Mexico

A. G. NORMAN, Environmental Research Institute of Michigan, Ann Arbor, Michigan

W. E. PARHAM, Office of Technology Assessment, Congress of the United States, Washington, D.C.

Staff of the Population Reference Bureau, 1337 Connecticut Avenue, N.W., Washington, D.C.

G. T. PRANCE, New York Botanical Garden, Bronx, New York

WALTER ORR ROBERTS, Director, Project on Food, Climate and the World's Future, Aspen Institute for Humanistic Studies, 1919 Fourteenth Street—No. 811, Boulder, Colorado

D. RODRIGUEZ-BEJARNO, School of Natural Resources, University of Michigan, Ann Arbor, Michigan

JOHN W. TATUM, Engineering Experiment Station, Georgia Institute of Technology, Atlanta, Georgia

DARREL WILLIAMS, Goddard Space Flight Center, National Aeronautics and Space Administration, Greenbelt, Maryland

GEORGE W. WOODWELL, The Ecosystems Center, Marine Biological Laboratory, Woods Hole, Massachusetts

R. MICHAEL WRIGHT, The Nature Conservancy, Arlington, Virginia

AUSTRALIA

THE EXECUTIVE DIRECTOR, Division of Forestry Research, Commonwealth Scientific and Industrial Research Organization, Queensland

THE EXECUTIVE SECRETARY, Head Office, Commonwealth Scientific and Industrial Research Organization, Canberra

DAVID LAMB, Department of Botany, University of Queensland

J. G. TRACEY, Rain Forest Ecology Section, Commonwealth Scientific and Industrial Research Organization, Indooroopilly, Queensland

L. J. WEBB, Senior Principal Research Scientist, Rainforest Ecology Section, Commonwealth Scientific and Industrial Research Organization, Indooroopilly, Queensland

BANGLADESH

M. OMAR ALI, Director, Forest Research Institute, Chittagong

MD. SALAR KHAN, Bangladesh National Herbarium, Dacca

BOLIVIA

MANFRED SACHTLER, Manager of FAO Project on Inventory and Management of Forest Resources, Santa Cruz

BRAZIL

P. BERRUTTI, Director, Instituto Brasileiro de Desevolvimento Florestal, Brasília

J. C. DE M. CARVALHO, President, Brazilian Foundation for Conservation of Nature, Rio de Janeiro

SUSANNA HECHT, Department of Geography, University of California, Berkeley

W. E. KERR, Director (until February 1979), Instituto de Pesquisas da Amazonia, Manaus

R. A. NOVAES, Chief, Division of Research and Development, Remote Sensing Department, Instituto de Pesquisas Espaciais, São Jose dos Campos

C. PANDOLFO, Director of Department of Natural Resources, Superintendency for Development of Amazonia, Belem

J. M. PIRES, Museu Goeldi, Belem

M. REIS, Director, Forest Research Department, Instituto Brasileiro de Desenvolvimento Florestal, Brasília

A. L. SAMPAIO DE ALMEIDA, Executive Secretary, Project RADAMBRASIL, Salvador, Bahia

N. J. SMITH, Instituto Nacional de Pesquisas da Amazonia, Manaus

C. R. SONNENBURG, Head of Remote Sensing Department, Instituto de Pesquisas Espaciais, São Jose dos Campos

CANADA

JAMES B. HARRINGTON, Forest Fire Research Institute, Canadian Forestry Service, Ottawa

COLOMBIA

P. BRICENO, Director General, Instituto Nacional de Los Recursos Naturales Renovables y del Medio Ambiente, Bogotá
P. PLANTINGA, Proyecto Radargrametrico del Amazonas (PRORADAM), Bogota
W. M. PLANTINGA, Embajada de Holanda, Bogota

COSTA RICA

M. A. BOZA, Universidad Estatal a Distancia, San Jose
GARY HARTSHORN, Tropical Science Center, San Jose
L. R. HOLDRIDGE, Tropical Science Center, San Jose

ECUADOR

M. ACOSTA-SOLIS, President, Ecuadorian Institute for Natural Science, Quito
F. I. O. CRESPO, Director, Institute of Sciences, Pontificía Universidad Catolíca del Ecuador, Quito
ALLEN D. PUTNEY, FAO/UNDP, Quito

EUROPE

J. E. M. ARNOLD, Forestry Division, FAO, Rome, Italy
E. F. BRÜNIG, Ordinariat für Weltforstwirtschaft, Universität Hamburg, West Germany
R. H. KEMP, Forestry Advisory, Ministry of Overseas Development, London, England
J. P. LANLY, Forestry Department, FAO, Rome, Italy
FELIPE MATTOS, Program Officer for Latin America, International Union for the Conservation of Nature and Natural Resources, Morges, Switzerland
REIDAR PERSSON, National Board of Forestry/Skogsstyrelsen, Jönköping, Sweden

W. SCHULTE, Population Program Coordinator, Economic and Social Policy Division, FAO, Rome, Italy

G. SICCO SMIT, International Institute for Aerial Survey and Earth Sciences, Enschede, Netherlands

J. W. TREVETT, Hunting Technical Services Ltd., Boreham Wood, United Kingdom

GHANA

T. K. AMERKYE, Chief Conservator of Forests, Accra

GUYANA

C. A. DAVID, Conservator of Forests, Kingston, Georgetown

INDIA

K. R. RAO, Director, National Remote Sensing Agency, Secunderadad

R. D. H. ROWE, The World Bank, Resident Mission in India, New Delhi

INDONESIA

J. H. BLOWER, Department of Nature Conservation and Wildlife Management, Bogor

K. DARMOYUWONO, Deputy Chairman, National Coordination Agency for Survey and Mapping (BAKOSURTANAL), Jakarta

M. IRSYAM, Manager of Remote Sensing Project, Indonesian National Aeronautics and Space Institute, Jakarta

JEFF A. MCNEELY, Department of Nature Conservation and Wildlife Management, Bogor

MR. SOEDJATMOKO, National Development Planning Agency, Jakarta

P. WIROATMODJO, Directorate of Forestry, Jakarta

KENYA

ANTHONY DIAMOND, Department of Zoology, University of Nairobi at Chiromo, Nairobi

K. F. S. KING, Director, International Center for Research into Agro-Forestry, Nairobi

F. OWINO, Chairman of Forest Working Group, Faculty of Agriculture, University of Nairobi

LIBERIA

J. T. WOODS, Managing Director, Forestry Development Authority, Monrovia
F. A. CHENOWETH, Ministry of Agriculture, Monrovia

MALAYSIA

M. I. ALAM, Department of Geography, University of Malaya, Kuala Lumpur
D. CHAI, Senior Research Officer, Forest Research Center, Sandakan, Sabah
L. P. CHOONG, Economic Planning Unit, Prime Minister's Department, Kuala Lumpur
C. S. CHUNG, Department of Botany, University of Malaya, Kuala Lumpur
E. S. T. MOK, Directorate of Forestry, Kuala Lumpur
K. R. S. PROUD, Forest Department, Kuching, Sarawak
L. K. SIM, Department of Geography, University of Malaya, Kuala Lumpur

MEXICO

B. P. REYES-CASTILLO, Institute of Ecology, Museum of Natural History, Mexico City

NIGERIA

A. O. ADEOLA, Principal, School of Forestry, Forestry Research Institute of Nigeria, Ibadan
B. A. OLA-ADAMUS, Forestry Research Institute of Nigeria, Ibadan
G. E. PILZ, Department of Biology, Ibadan Polytechnic, Ibadan
D. M. WARD, Federal Department of Forestry, Ibadan

PAPUA NEW GUINEA

A. M. D. YAUIEB, Director, Department of Primary Industry, Office of Forests, Boroko

PERU

M. J. DOUROJEANNI, Former Director-General, Division of Forestry and Wildlife, Ministry of Agriculture, Lima

PHILIPPINES

R. C. BRUCE, Training Center for Applied Geodey and Photogrammetry, University of the Philippines, Manila

THE EXECUTIVE DIRECTOR AND HIS STAFF, Natural Resource Management Center, Ministry of Natural Resources, Quezon City

G. KERR, Paper Industries Corporation of the Philippines, Makati

B. F. NOBLE, Forest Research Institute, Baguio City

F. S. POLLISCO, Director, Forest Research Institute, College, Laguna

SIERRA LEONE

D. C. SCHWAAR, Project Manager, Land Resources Survey Project, Freetown

SRI LANKA

C. NANAYAKKARA, Deputy Surveyor-General, Surveyor-General's Office, Colombo

THAILAND

S. BOONKIARD, Forest Industry Organization, Bangkok

W. Y. BROCKELMAN, Department of Biology, Mahidol University, Bangkok

S. CHAIYAPECHIRA, Planning Division, Royal Forest Department, Bangkok

C. CHANDRASEKHARAN, Regional Forestry Office, Food and Agriculture Organization, Bangkok

B. KLANKAMSORN, Forest Management Division, Royal Forest Department, Bangkok

S. SABHASRI, Secretary-General, National Research Council, Bangkok

SOMSAK SUKWONG, Head of Department of Forest Biology, Kasetsart University, Bangkok

S. WACHARAKITTI, Director, School of Forestry, Kasetsart University, Bangkok

VENEZUELA

F. MATOS, Director, Foundation for Natural Sciences, Caracas

E. MEDINA, Centro de Ecologia, Instituto Venezelano de Investigaciones Cientificias, Caracas

J. A. STEYERMARK, Director of Herbarium, Botanical Institute, Caracas